T0319643

MAKING THE CUT

Making the Cut

Hiring Decisions, Bias, and the Consequences of Nonstandard, Mismatched, and Precarious Employment

David S. Pedulla

PRINCETON UNIVERSITY PRESS

PRINCETON AND OXFORD

Copyright © 2020 by Princeton University Press

Published by Princeton University Press
41 William Street, Princeton, New Jersey 08540
6 Oxford Street, Woodstock, Oxfordshire OX20 1TR

press.princeton.edu

All Rights Reserved

ISBN 978-0-691-17510-2
ISBN (e-book) 978-0-691-20007-1

British Library Cataloging-in-Publication Data is available

Editorial: Meagan Levinson and Jacqueline Delaney
Production Editorial: Jenny Wolkowicki
Jacket design: Chris Ferrante
Production: Erin Suydam
Publicity: Kate Hensley and Kathryn Stevens
Copyeditor: Joseph Dahm

This book has been composed in Adobe Text Pro and Gotham

Printed on acid-free paper. ∞

Printed in the United States of America

10 9 8 7 6 5 4 3 2 1

For Devah,
my academic inspiration
and
For Matt,
my inspiration in life

CONTENTS

Imagine that you have been tasked with hiring a new employee for your company. Hundreds of applications have started to pour in. You have a short cover letter and an equally short resume for each applicant. Your boss has made it clear that she wants to hire someone quickly. You have just a few seconds to scan each application. How do you decide who gets an interview?

You review the pile of materials. One applicant grabs your attention. She seems like a great fit. But then you realize that she has been unemployed for the past year. Do you throw out her application? Keep her in the yes pile? Scrutinize her record more closely? Another applicant looks good too. But he currently works part-time. Should this be a red flag? Why wasn't he working full-time? Should it matter? Would you be more or less concerned if it were a woman who had been working part-time?

Hiring is a challenging process. Applicants come from different social backgrounds and increasingly have complicated, nonstandard and mismatched experiences as part of their work histories. Employers need to make high-stakes, difficult decisions, under intense time pressure, and with limited information.

Under these conditions, who makes the cut?

This is the question that lies at the heart of the pages that follow.

ACKNOWLEDGMENTS

Making the Cut is the product of many hands and many hearts. I am grateful for the incredible community of family, friends, and colleagues who have offered their support and guidance over many years to make this book possible.

A decade of advice, critique, and love from Devah Pager were foundational to the research in this book. From my first day of graduate school until her death, Devah was my rock, my guide, my academic everything. Words cannot convey my gratitude to her for the millions of things—big and small—she did for me or my sadness that she is no longer here with us. Devah, you were simply the best.

My academic path has given me the opportunity to call three academic institutions "home." During my time at Princeton, when the roots of this book emerged as part of my dissertation, I received incredible advice and support from Viviana Zelizer, Paul DiMaggio, Sara McLanahan, Matt Salganik, Mitch Duneier, Martin Ruef, Delia Baldassarri, and Katherine Newman. I am also grateful to my graduate student colleagues and friends at Princeton who kept me going through the ups and downs of completing a PhD: Maria Abascal, Sarah Brayne, Liz Derickson, Rene Flores, Heba Gowayed, Angelina Grigoryeva, Tatiana Homonoff, Patrick Ishizuka, Karen Levy, Michelle Phelps, Meredith Sadin, Danny Schneider, Hana Shepherd, Naomi Sugie, and Sarah Thébaud.

I thank my colleagues at the University of Texas at Austin for making the start to my career as a faculty member both stimulating and supportive. For feedback on pieces this book and other aspects of academic life, I thank Becky Pettit, Harel Shapira, Ken-Hou Lin, Jennifer Glass, Daniel Fridman, Chandra Muller, Kelly Raley, Rob Crosnoe, Catherine Riegle-Crumb, April Sutton, and Christine Williams. At Stanford, I have found an incredible community of scholars. I am deeply grateful to Shelley Correll, Michelle Jackson, Aliya Saperstein, Florencia Torche, David Grusky, Jeremy Freese, Robb Willer, Cecilia Ridgeway, Michael Rosenfeld, Susan Olzak, Tomás Jiménez,

Mark Granovetter, Jackie Hwang, Forrest Stuart, Xueguang Zhou, Karen Cook, Andy Walder, Adina Sterling, Aruna Ranganathan, and Ashley Martin. Many thanks to my junior faculty colleagues and Stanford friends who have made the stresses of the tenure track a bit less stressful: Michaela Bronstein, Marci Kwon, David Riley, Angele Christin, Andrei Pesic, Chris Grobe, Rowan Dorin, Neir Eshel, Alia Crum, Erin Mordecai, Carly Walker, Alistair Boettiger, Barry Maguire, Meghan Maguire, Dustin Schroeder, and Devon Ryan. I am grateful as well to my undergraduate mentors, Crystal Feimster and Vanessa Rumble, who gave me the confidence to pursue this academic path.

I had the incredible opportunity to have my "dream team" of academics workshop an earlier version of this book. Thank you to Sandra Smith, Vicki Smith, Maria Charles, and KT Albiston for critical and constructive comments during the workshop that significantly improved the book. I am also grateful to the thoughtful insights provided by anonymous reviewers on the proposal for this book as well as the complete manuscript. For research assistance, feedback, and editing of various forms, I thank Luke Baker, Alan Ritari, John Muñoz, Katie Van Heest, T. Hoatson, Emily Paine, Anna Boch, Jacob Avery, Ryan Finnigan, Kate Weisshaar, Michael Gaddis, Cristobal Young, and Corey Fields. I could not have asked for better interviewers to work with me on the qualitative component of this project. Bethany Nichols and Jeff Sheng, you were all-stars at each stage of the interview process. Mike Bader and Alex Murphy read more drafts of this book and its various components than anyone else and consistently offered incredible and insightful feedback. Thank you.

I am also deeply indebted to the hiring professionals who took time out of their busy schedules to speak with me about the hiring process. Their thoughts and insights made me think in deeper and more complex ways about the recruitment and selection process. Their voices and perspectives made this book possible.

To the team at Princeton University Press, you have been amazing to work with. Meagan Levinson saw promise in the idea for this book and has made it better at every turn. I am so glad that Clayton Childress introduced us at ASA a few years back. Additionally, many thanks to Jackie Delaney, Joseph Dahm, Jenny Wolkowicki, and Theresa Liu for their assistance in moving the book into production.

Funding for various components of this project was provided by the National Science Foundation (SES 1203135); the UC-Davis Center for Poverty Research from the US Department of Health and Human Services (1H79AE000100-1); the Horowitz Foundation for Social Policy; the Employment Instability, Family Well-Being, and Social Policy Network at the University of Chicago; the Eunice Kennedy Shriver National Institute of Child

Health and Human Development (5 R24 HD042849); Princeton University's Department of Sociology, Fellowship of Woodrow Wilson Scholars, Center for African American Studies, and Center for the Study of Social Organization; and Stanford University's Department of Sociology and Clayman Institute for Gender Research. The Stanford Faculty Writer's Retreat provided the space and time to write and revise significant portions of this book.

Pieces of this book also benefitted from the comments provided during presentations at annual meetings of the American Sociological Association, the Eastern Sociological Society, and the Population Association of America as well as workshops and seminars at Stanford, MIT, Columbia, Harvard, Stockholm University, IZA, University of Chicago, University of Toronto, Boston College, Boston University, New York University, UT-Austin, Cornell, Brown, UW-Madison, UC-Irvine, UC-Davis, and UC-Berkeley.

To my chosen family that continually fills my life with love, excitement, and joy, I am deeply indebted to you: Jes Scannell, Zora Rooks, Rebecca McIlvain, MC Cooper, Paul Getsos, Gary Martyn, Carly Knight, Kristin Perkins, Trevor Baca, Julie Balasalle, Huriya Jabbar, Josh Roebke, Luke Elliott-Negri, Christine Elliott-Negri, Laura Tatum, Katy Mastman, Ben Davidson, Ana Muñoz, Peter Dahlberg, and Missy Dahlberg. Rourke O'Brien, I'm not sure where I would be without you. You have made this academic journey possible—even fun—and have held me together in the most challenging of moments.

To Debbie Brake, John Brake, Jessie Merritt, Thomas Merritt, and Marie Kincaid, I cannot thank you enough for welcoming me with open arms into your family. To Tara, my sister-in-law, I feel blessed every day that you are a part of my life. To Sachin and Wiley, my nephews, you bring so much love to my life. May you grow up to be compassionate, caring humans in our often troubled world. To Mark, my brother, thank you for walking through each day of nearly four decades with me and being a constant source of love, light, and inspiration. To my mother, Barbara, you have taught me what unconditional love and caring for me and the world looks like. To my father, Joseph, your support and love each stage of my life have been a source of great strength. Many thanks and much gratitude.

Finally, to Matthew, my husband and partner in life. You inspire me every day with your openness to the world, your drive to create a more just society, and your insistence that we can be better, individually and collectively. Your witty and dry sense of humor keep me smiling. Thank you for loving me in the darker times and celebrating with me in the lighter times. This book would not have been possible without you.

MAKING THE CUT

1

Hiring in the New Economy

Employment is central to the economic security and well-being of individuals and their families in the United States. Jobs provide wages and benefits. Jobs provide opportunities for skill development and growth. Jobs provide many of the building blocks necessary for other domains of one's life, such as health, housing, and family. At its core, this book is about the allocation of employment opportunities in the contemporary economy—an economy where millions of workers have experience in positions that are part-time, through temporary help agencies, and well below their skill level. In this environment, how do workers get jobs? How does the hiring process actually work? And, ultimately, who comes out ahead?

Accessing employment opportunities is a complex matching process between employers and workers.[1] Employers are looking for the right employees to execute the tasks needed by their companies. Workers are looking for the right jobs. Jobs that provide them with a set of material and subjective rewards, such as wages, benefits, and satisfaction. The underlying mechanics of how the matching of workers and employers actually happens, however, is far from straightforward.[2] There is no centralized system to assign workers and employers to one another. There is no single way that workers decide which employers they want to work for. And there is no single criterion on which employers evaluate job applicants.

Understanding how this matching of workers and employers takes place has been a central concern of social scientists for decades.[3] Scholars often conceptualize the labor market as a two-sided matching process. The supply side focuses on workers—their education, training, preferences, and behaviors. The demand side focuses on employers—their needs, desires, and evaluative criteria for hiring workers. While understanding both sides of the process is important, this book centers its attention on the demand side of the equation: employers and their decision making.[4] A large body of research concentrating on hiring finds that, more than simply prioritizing technical skills and credentials, employers and hiring professionals care about a broad array of other worker characteristics during the hiring process. They want workers who comply with "ideal worker" norms of commitment and competence.[5] They want workers with soft skills and the "right" personality.[6] They want workers who are a "fit" with the organization's culture, its workers, and its managers.[7]

The set of criteria that hiring professionals use to evaluate job applicants lies at the center of this book. Recognizing the changing nature of work and employment in the United States, *Making the Cut* asks whether the ways that employers evaluate potential employees have kept pace with this shifting economic landscape. As existing scholarship has demonstrated, the underlying organization of work in the United States does not look the same as it did in the middle of the twentieth century, a period when many of our current models of employment relations emerged.[8] There has been a decline in manufacturing employment and an increase in service sector employment.[9] The occupational structure has become more polarized, with both high- and low-wage job growth outpacing the growth of middle-wage jobs.[10] Technological advances, such as the increasing importance of computers and the internet, have reshaped the ways that work takes place.[11] Global economic integration has generated new forms of competition.[12] And employment relations have also changed. Internal labor markets—where companies promote workers through career ladders at the company—have declined.[13] Many organizations now rely on nonstandard and contingent labor too.[14] This set of shifts—as well as others—is part of the bundle of changes resulting in what scholars often refer to as the "new economy."[15]

Workers' experiences have been deeply altered by these realities. Feelings of economic insecurity are widespread.[16] Individuals and families feel pressed financially, uncertain of how they will survive and thrive.[17] And employment relationships—as well as the obligations between workers and employers—have shifted.[18] Millions of workers now labor through temporary help agencies, in part-time positions, at jobs below their skill level, and as independent contractors, freelancers, on-call workers, and day laborers.[19] At the same time, long-term unemployment and its associated challenges have become commonplace in the labor force, particularly during periods of recession and recovery.[20] While the growth in some of these types of alternative employment relationships may be overstated in the public imagination,[21] one thing is clear: millions of workers labor in nonstandard, mismatched, and precarious positions.[22]

Against this backdrop, *Making the Cut* inspects one key component of the insecurities faced by workers: nonstandard, mismatched, and precarious employment experiences. Specifically, I examine the consequences of part-time work, temporary agency employment, skills underutilization, and long-term unemployment for workers' employment opportunities. To date, scholars have examined how these positions affect a set of important worker outcomes: wages, benefits, autonomy and control, subjective well-being, job security, and health, to name a few.[23] Much less attention, however, has been directed to the consequences of these employment positions for workers' future opportunities in the labor market, specifically their ability to obtain a new job.

Have hiring professionals and employers updated the ways they evaluate job applicants to align with the current economic structure? If assumptions of an unrealistic and outdated economic landscape remain embedded in hiring professionals' criteria of evaluation, those assumptions might exacerbate or mitigate inequality during the hiring process. How would a hiring manager evaluate a college graduate with multiple years of managerial experience but who then ended up taking a retail job? What about an administrative assistant who spent a year working through a temporary help agency? How might a woman who moved in to a part-time sales position after many years of full-time sales jobs be perceived by recruiters and hiring managers?

Making the Cut takes on this set of issues. The pages that follow tackle the overarching question of whether employers systematically screen out job applicants with histories of nonstandard, mismatched, and precarious employment in favor of those who have remained in full-time, standard jobs at their skill level. If so, then workers with nonstandard, mismatched, or precarious employment experiences will be blocked from opportunities because they will be unable to move on to new jobs. In this case, these types of employment experiences may serve as an important driver of inequality in the new economy. But if the answer is no, then there may be an important role for these types of employment positions in serving as stepping stones to new employment opportunities for workers as they navigate the tumultuous labor market.

One can imagine, though, that the consequences of these employment experiences are not uniform or universal. Take the woman discussed above who moved from years of full-time sales experience in to a part-time sales position. What if she were a man? Would he be perceived differently? What if he were African American? While a significant body of scholarship indicates that women and racial minorities face discrimination during the hiring process, it is not clear how nonstandard, mismatched, and precarious employment histories may intersect and interact with these traditional axes of social inequality.[24] It is quite possible that employment experiences that deviate from common conceptions of a "good" job will reinforce existing inequalities by race and gender, further disadvantaging women and racial minorities. By contrast, there may be a complex interaction between social categories and employment histories such that those workers with more status and privilege in the labor market—such as white men—face particularly negative consequences of these types of nonstandard, mismatched, and precarious employment experiences. These contrasting possibilities hold important implications for understanding how inequalities in the labor market are produced and maintained in the new economy.

Making Hiring Decisions

Employers make hiring decisions behind closed doors. But as it turns out, we actually know quite a lot about how these decisions get made. One prominent line of research on hiring decisions focuses on discrimination.[25] While it is illegal to discriminate based on certain worker characteristics—such as race and gender—clear evidence shows that discrimination in hiring persists in the US labor market.[26] And scholarly interests in this area have focused on the underlying processes that may drive discriminatory behavior. While there are many theories as to why discrimination occurs, scholars often situate them in two broad groups: "statistical" and "preference-based" discrimination.[27] Statistical models of discrimination emphasize the ways that decision makers take attributions of group-level characteristics and then apply them to individual members of that group. For example, a hiring manager may take her perceived average productivity of older workers as a group and then assume that any individual worker who is older is as productive as that "average" older worker. By contrast, preference-based models of discrimination conceptualize discrimination as the result of biases and stereotypes about particular groups of workers. Discrimination against older workers may emerge, for example, due in part to employers' negative stereotypes of older workers as being less competent or motivated. While the precise mechanisms are distinct, under conditions of uncertainty and limited information—as are often the case when making initial decisions about job applications—these two broad perspectives on discrimination generally offer similar predictions about what groups will face discrimination during the hiring process.[28]

A second key line of scholarship on hiring decision making has focused on human capital, signaling, and credentialism explanations. These theories largely place education and skills at the center of employers' hiring decisions. While the precise driving force for decision making in each perspective is distinct, they all propose a key link between education and hiring outcomes.[29] In its most basic form, imagine a model of hiring decisions where employers are attempting to use information about job applicants' education and skills to match them appropriately to a position within their firm. Employers are aligning particular educational backgrounds with particular organizational tasks. The applicants who are the best matches—and therefore who are predicted to be most productive—are interviewed and then, ultimately, hired.

Yet scholars have complicated this stylized picture, highlighting additional factors that employers consider when making hiring decisions. Employers also care about soft skills and personality, compliance with ideal worker norms of commitment and competence, and fit.[30] Employers want to hire individuals who can interact well with customers and clients. They want individuals who are going to get along with other workers and with managers at their organization. They also want workers whose backgrounds and interests—particular types of music or sports[31]—align with the organizational culture. And—certainly in white-collar jobs—employers want workers who can exhibit complete dedication to their jobs, free from the competing demands that come with raising children or taking care of sick or elderly parents.[32] In other words, the worker who is likely to come out on top in the hiring process is not just the worker with the best education, technical skills, or knowledge for the position. To be hired, a worker needs to excel—or be perceived as excelling—on these other dimensions of evaluation as well.

Obtaining information about these deeper characteristics of job candidates early on in the hiring process, especially from just their resume and cover letter, is challenging. It is this moment in the hiring process—the point of initial applicant screening, where information and time are extremely limited—that is emphasized in much of *Making the Cut*. This moment is particularly important because it is where first impressions are formed and hiring professionals decide who moves forward in the hiring process and whose application is left in the pile. Yet it is difficult to get a sense of someone's personality and interaction style from a resume. Similarly, knowing whether someone will fit in well at an organization can be difficult if one has only a cover letter. Direct measures of commitment and dedication are also unlikely to appear in one's application materials. Yet this is information employers want to have. It matters to them.[33] Under these conditions of limited information, employers are likely to use whatever they can access in order to make inferences about these attributes of the job applicant.[34]

What information do employers actually have during the initial review of applicants? Because names appear on their resumes and cover letters, employers are often able to infer the gender—and sometimes the race— of applicants. This type of assumed demographic information has, indeed, been linked to discrimination in the hiring process.[35] Hiring professionals can also generally get a sense of the age of the applicants from their years of work experience as well as graduation dates from high school or college.[36] They will likely also know where applicants live and where they went to school.[37] Many resumes have information about volunteer and extracurricular activities as well.[38] Additionally, potential employers will have details about the applicants' employment history—the tasks they completed, the organizations they worked for, and their trajectory through different jobs. These pieces of information are likely used by hiring professionals, consciously or unconsciously, to make broader determinations about workers. They may lead to inferences about workers' soft skills, personality, fit, and likely compliance with ideal worker norms of commitment and competence.

Indeed, scholars have generated a large body of research documenting the ways that these observable signals—even the ones not directly related to productivity—are converted into decisions about which applicants to call back for an interview. Scholars have found that—holding all else equal—the following applicant attributes have a direct effect on callbacks: race, gender, prestige of one's undergraduate institution, parental status, sexual orientation, social class background, immigrant status, and religion.[39] Crucially, many of these observable signals—or inferred observable signals—are used as proxies for other, often unobservable, attributes during the hiring process and are commonly associated with deep sets of cultural beliefs or stereotypes.[40] In the case of race, for example, scholars have uncovered employers' stereotypes of African American workers as lazy and less skilled than their white counterparts, which may lead employers to make negative inferences about African American workers' expected productivity.[41] Here, an observable signal—race—ends up serving as a stand-in for a difficult-to-observe characteristic. From this example, we can see how stereotypes can bias the ways that job applicants are evaluated, resulting in durable inequalities between groups.[42] In another example that will be important later on, there is a gendered set of stereotypes that exist around parenthood: lower levels of perceived competence and commitment for mothers compared to fathers. These stereotypical beliefs can drive bias against mothers and women of childbearing age.[43] Indeed, stereotypes of this sort will play a central role in making sense of how gender intersects with certain types of employment experiences to influence hiring professionals' evaluations during the job applicant screening process.

The title of the book—*Making the Cut*—captures two important underlying currents that run throughout the following pages. First, it points to the key question of which workers are actually able to rise to the top of the application pool. What makes applicants good enough? What do they need to do to actually make the cut? Second, the title highlights the central decision-making moment examined in the book: hiring professionals deciding whom to interview for a job. What underlying processes lead employers to call back some applicants for interviews while excluding others? In other words, how do hiring professionals actually make the cut, separating the yes pile from the no pile?

———

Evaluating job applicants does not happen in a vacuum. The broader social and economic context matters. Next, we turn to the ways that work and employment have changed and developed in the United States. Understanding how the economic landscape has shifted in the previous decades will provide the necessary backdrop for thinking through the ways that hiring professionals make sense of nonstandard, mismatched, and precarious employment histories.

The Structure of Work and Employment in the New Economy

Many of us—including employers, hiring managers, and recruiters—hold on to largely mythical notions of what a job is, what a job should be. Or at least what a "good" job should be.[44] These ideas often suggest that a job should provide adequate wages and benefits as well as opportunities for advancement, should be full-time and have some sense of security surrounding ongoing employment as long as workers generally fulfill their workplace obligations, and should utilize workers' skills and training.[45] Of course some workers desire alternative types of arrangements, such as part-time employment or temporary work. Even as the work lives of an increasing number of Americans deviate from this ideal, there remains a powerful, common cultural understanding of a what work should look like.

While it is debatable whether this ideal type of job was ever the most common experience for workers in the United States,[46] it is clear that full-time, standard jobs at workers' skill levels are not a reality for many today.[47] Workers often find themselves in positions that deviate from core aspects of this paradigmatic "good" job. They may only have part-time employment, working for twenty instead of forty hours per week. They may be employed through an intermediary organization—a "temp agency"—and thus have limited security as to ongoing employment. They may have jobs that are well below their level of skill, experience, or education, which social scientists often refer to as skills underutilization. Or they may be unable to find employment at all, even though they are dedicated to searching, and therefore experience long-term unemployment. These four types of employment experiences are conceptually unified in that they all deviate from common conceptions of a "good" job.

As a somewhat crude proxy for having a "good" job, we could look at reported job satisfaction levels. Evidence from nationally representative survey data in the United States indicates a significant decline in workers' overall job satisfaction between 1977 and 2006.[48] And when workers are not able to obtain a "good" job, they often blame themselves and feel responsible for making things work and developing their own opportunities.[49] Indeed, in her in-depth account of how people search for jobs in the new economy, anthropologist Ilana Gershon highlights the ways that workers increasingly conceive of themselves as their own business. Workers see themselves as responsible for staying afloat, maintaining their skills, and pitching themselves to their customers, potential employers.[50]

Due to the prevalence of nonstandard and mismatched positions and the decline in internal labor markets—where individuals would advance in their careers within a given company—workers are more likely than in the past to have experiences in nonstandard, mismatched, and precarious positions when applying for new jobs. Yet while the structure of the new economy renders good jobs more difficult to attain for many workers, highly personalized and individualized perspectives on work and employment likely leave workers feeling as if they should be able to maintain full-time, standard, seamless employment trajectories. This raises the question of whether employers see things the same way. As employment experiences diverge from conceptions of the "good job" and the "ideal worker," have hiring professionals updated their evaluation criteria to align with changes in the structure and experience of the current economic landscape, or do they want workers who have consistently held "good" jobs?

This tension—between the changing economic structures that have made "good" jobs less available to many workers and employers' conceptualizations of what it means to be an ideal worker—drives this book. Throughout, I argue and present evidence that employers' hiring evaluation criteria have not developed to align with the structure of the new economy, resulting in a disjuncture between what employers want and the common experiences that workers have as they move through their careers. The result of this disjuncture is a complex set of inequalities that emerge in the contemporary labor market.

Building on these insights, I advance three primary arguments. First, I assert that hiring professionals extract meaning from workers' nonstandard, mismatched, and precarious employment experiences. That is, future employers infer from these types of employment histories information about workers' technical skills, their soft skills and personality, their competence and commitment, and to some extent their fit. At the same time, the meanings extracted from these employment experiences are not necessarily clear-cut or consistent across types of employment. And these experiences often end up raising questions and inducing uncertainty in hiring professionals about the quality of the worker. Second, I propose that the consequences of nonstandard, mismatched, and precarious employment experiences are not all equal. Some types of employment experiences are severely penalized by future employers, others are not. Yet it is difficult to separate the consequences of these employment experiences from the social characteristics of the workers who occupy these jobs. This leads to the third central argument of the book: identities matter. The race and gender of job applicants intersect in powerful ways with nonstandard, mismatched, and precarious employment histories to shape divergent outcomes for workers during the hiring process.

An overarching theme throughout the book—and supporting the three underlying arguments articulated above—is that hiring professionals express the need for a story, a narrative to make sense of workers' experiences with nonstandard, mismatched, and precarious work. Yet at the initial moment of applicant screening, workers are often unable to tell their story and employers are often left with questions. All the hiring professional has is an applicant's resume and cover letter. With this limited information and little time to evaluate job applicants, difficult decisions have to be made. Thus, hiring agents develop what I refer to as *stratified stories*. Using information about applicants not directly related to their employment trajectory, such as their race or gender, hiring professionals draw on group-based stereotypes to generate their own stories about workers' nonstandard, mismatched, or precarious employment experiences. The result is divergent gendered and racialized consequences of these different employment histories. While I develop and deploy the concept of stratified stories to understand the intersection of social identities and employment histories at the hiring interface, this concept likely translates beyond employment. Stratified stories may operate in other institutional domains and evaluative contexts, such as sentencing in the criminal justice system and diagnosing illness in the health care system.

Studying How Hiring Decisions Are Made

To examine how hiring works in the new economy and to understand the consequences of nonstandard, mismatched, and precarious work for hiring decisions, I draw on two complementary types of data throughout this book: (1) field-experimental data on actual hiring decisions and (2) in-depth interviews with hiring professionals. While the field-experimental data provide a direct lens into employers' behaviors—how they actually treat workers with different types of employment experiences—the interviews provide fine-grained insights into how employers think and talk about different types of workers and employment histories.

OBSERVING EMPLOYERS' BEHAVIORS: A FIELD EXPERIMENT

Two of the central questions addressed in this book are the following: (1) How do histories of nonstandard, mismatched, and precarious employment affect workers' hiring outcomes? and (2) Do these consequences vary by the race and gender of the worker? Answering these questions requires having data on hiring professionals' behaviors, rather than their attitudes, beliefs, and narratives. Obtaining data that directly capture how employers treat job applicants is a challenging task. Companies are often hesitant to share detailed information about their applicant pools and which of those aspiring employees receive interviews. And even if it is possible to gain access to that type of information, it can be challenging to isolate the direct effect of a given employment history or demographic characteristic on an applicant receiving an interview. There are many moving parts to an application that could drive employer decision making besides those two features.

To address these dual challenges—gaining a lens onto employers' behaviors and distilling the direct effects of employment histories as well as demographic characteristics—I conducted a field experiment where I sent fictitious job applications to apply for real job openings and then tracked employers' responses to each application.[51] For the experiment, I submitted 4,822 fictitious job applications to apply for 2,411 job openings in Atlanta, Boston, Chicago, Los Angeles, and New York between November 2012 and June 2013. The applications were sent to job openings in four broad occupational groups: administrative/clerical, sales, accounting/bookkeeping, and project management/management. Two very similar applications were submitted for each position. The main differences between the resumes in the experiment were (1) the type of employment the applicant had in the prior 12 months and (2) the names at the top of the resumes, which were used to signal the applicants' race and gender. Everything else was held constant, enabling me to isolate how these two applicant characteristics affect employers' decision making.

I signaled five different type of employment on the resumes that capture the key types of employment experiences that we are interested in understanding: (1) full-time, standard employment at the worker's skill level; (2) part-time work in the worker's occupation of choice; (3) temporary agency employment in the worker's occupation of choice; (4) skills underutilization, where the worker was employed in a job below their skill level; and (5) long-term unemployment. A diagram of how the employment histories were structured for the field experiment is presented in Figure 1.1.

Additionally, the applications for each job opening were randomly assigned to a demographic group, using the name at the top of the resume to signal race and gender.[52] Gender is relatively easy to signal with names; for example, putting Matthew or Emily on a job application makes it clear that the applicant is a man or a woman, respectively.[53] Signaling race is much more complicated. For this experiment, I utilized two sets of names. The first were likely perceived by employers as either white or not racialized: Jon, Matthew, Emily, and Katherine. These names may not actually prime employers to think in racialized ways, and therefore they may default to assumptions of whiteness. I also utilized a set of names that are racialized

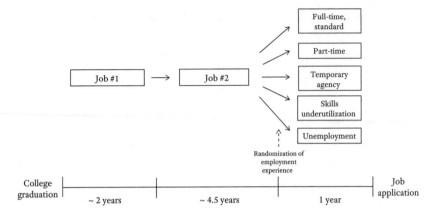

FIGURE 1.1. Employment History Structure for Field Experiment

as African American—Darnell, Tyrone, Kimora, and Kenya—and likely prime employers to perceive the applicant as African American.[54] I refer to applicants throughout the book as either "white/neutral" or "African American."[55] The distribution of applications submitted in the field experiment is presented in Table 1.1.

After submitting the applications, I waited to see whether an employer responded to each application via phone and email. All responses were coded. A request for an interview or an invitation to discuss the position in more depth was coded as a positive response from the employer, what researchers often refer to as a "callback." Given the design of the field experiment, I am thus able to estimate the direct, causal effect of each type of employment position on the likelihood of receiving a callback from an employer and how those consequences vary by the race and gender of the worker. In other words, the design of the field experiment provides direct evidence about the ways that nonstandard, mismatched, and precarious employment histories affect how employers treat workers. Additional details about the design and implementation of the field experiment are provided in the Methodological Appendix.

TALKING TO HIRING PROFESSIONALS:
IN-DEPTH INTERVIEWS

While the field experiment provides powerful traction regarding employers' behaviors, it leaves open questions about how hiring professionals actually think and talk about these different types of employment experiences. To

TABLE 1.1. Distribution of Applications Submitted in Field Experiment

	Frequency	Percentage
EMPLOYMENT HISTORY		
Full-time, standard	1,343	27.9
Part-time	707	14.7
Temporary agency	645	13.4
Skills underutilization	704	14.6
Unemployment	1,423	29.5
TOTAL	4,822	100.0
DEMOGRAPHIC GROUP		
White/neutral men	1,198	24.8
African American men	1,212	25.1
White/neutral women	1,222	25.3
African American women	1,190	24.7
TOTAL	4,822	100.0
LABOR MARKET		
Atlanta	598	12.4
Boston	952	19.7
Chicago	780	16.2
Los Angeles	1,010	21.0
New York City	1,482	30.7
TOTAL	4,822	100.0
OCCUPATION		
Accounting/bookkeeping	780	16.2
Administrative/clerical	848	17.6
Project management/management	1,642	34.1
Sales	1,552	32.2
TOTAL	4,822	100.0

Source: Field-experimental data.

unpack the processes and dynamics behind hiring in the new economy, *Making the Cut* also draws on data from fifty-three in-depth interviews conducted between late 2016 and early 2018 with a diverse set of hiring professionals in the United States. Hiring professionals are key gatekeepers.[56] They determine which workers obtain access to employment. Understanding their thought processes, decision-making criteria, and preferences can therefore provide valuable insights into how inequality in the labor market is produced and reproduced. The interviews both shed light on the meanings hiring agents attribute to different types of employment experiences and assist in understanding the mechanisms underlying the effects that are found in the field experiment.

The individuals who were interviewed held titles such as human resources manager, talent acquisition specialist, and field recruiter. While their exact job responsibilities varied to some extent, all of them were intimately involved in the hiring process. Most of the interview subjects worked to recruit and hire employees for their own companies. Some of them worked at staffing agencies, though, brokering the matching process between their client companies and potential employees. Three respondents had become unemployed within a few months of the interview but were directly involved in the hiring process before their spell of unemployment.

Along with two research assistants, I recruited hiring professionals to the sample through multiple channels, including posting advertisements online about our study.[57] Additionally, we identified companies that were actively hiring through a major, national online job posting board and reached out to them to invite hiring professionals at those companies to participate in the study. We also recruited some participants through referral channels, asking the individuals we interviewed to refer their colleagues to participate in the study. Before our interviews, we asked for respondents' resumes or LinkedIn profiles to ensure that they were an appropriate match for our study—focusing on whether hiring new employees was a central part of their job.[58]

The individuals we interviewed were primarily based in the same five labor markets that are investigated with the field-experimental data in this book. A few of the respondents we spoke with, however, were located outside of these labor markets. In terms of demographic makeup, our sample skews more heavily toward women, in part due to the feminized nature of the human resources profession.[59] Additionally, most of our interview subjects had at least a bachelor's degree, making them quite educated compared to the general population. In terms of race and ethnicity, age, and job tenure, our interview participants are quite diverse. There is also a well-rounded cross-section of industries and company sizes represented among the hiring professionals in the study. However, it is important to note that the interview respondents represent a nonrandom sample of individuals involved in the hiring process and are not representative of hiring professionals in the United States. The characteristics of the individuals who were interviewed for this study and the companies where they work are presented in Table 1.2.

TABLE 1.2. Characteristics of Individuals in the Interview Sample

	Percentage/*M*	Frequency/*SD*
WOMEN	81.1	43
RACE/ETHNICITY		
White/Caucasian	60.4	32
Black/African American	18.9	10
Hispanic/Latino	15.1	8
Other/multiracial	5.7	3
AGE (YEARS; *M, SD*)	41	12
EDUCATION		
Less than bachelor's	11.3	6
Bachelor's	58.5	31
Master's	30.2	16
TENURE AT COMPANY (YEARS; *M, SD*)	3.36	4.85
COMPANY SIZE		
2 to 50 employees	17.3	9
51 to 500 employees	38.5	20
501 to 2,000 employees	26.9	14
More than 2,000 employees	17.3	9
INDUSTRY		
Accommodation and food service	9.4	5
Construction	1.9	1
Educational services	3.8	2
Finance and insurance	5.7	3
Health care and social assistance	15.1	8
Information	15.1	8
Manufacturing	5.7	3
Professional, scientific, and technical services	24.5	13
Public administration	7.6	4
Real estate and rental and leasing	3.8	2
Retail trade	7.6	4

Source: Interview data with hiring professionals.
Notes: Data come from interviews with 53 respondents. Company size is missing for one respondent.
Information about most recent employer used for unemployed respondents.

The interviews started with broad questions about the respondents' role at the company and the hiring process where they work. They were asked general questions about what they look for when they are hiring and evaluating job candidates. Then, more specific questions were asked about how they perceive and think about various types of nonstandard, mismatched, and precarious employment as well as how their evaluations of job applicants may be impacted by someone having previous experience in one of those types of positions. Hiring agents' responses to this line of questioning offer valuable insights into the meanings that are extracted from various employment histories. I also asked whether these evaluations might differ depending on the demographic characteristics of applicants, such as their gender or race.

Toward the end of the interviews, after having discussed their views on various aspects of hiring and employment histories, the hiring professionals were also asked to react to some of the key findings from the field experiment. Their reactions to these findings help to make sense of the field-experimental results and assist in understanding the underlying mechanisms at play in shaping the consequences of nonstandard, mismatched, and precarious employment histories. Overall, the interview data provide a compelling lens into the thoughts and frameworks from which employers operate and how they think and talk about evaluating job candidates. All interviews were audio-recorded, transcribed in full, and systematically coded and analyzed using qualitative data analysis software. Additional information about the interviews is available in the Methodological Appendix.

An important thing to keep in mind when engaging with data from interviews with hiring professionals is that what employers say in an interview does not necessarily map exactly onto how they behave when making hiring decisions.[60] They may not be aware of their own biases or how those biases play out. And even if they are aware of their biases, they may not be entirely comfortable discussing them. Interviews are social in nature, and the actors involved care about how they are perceived and how they come across. In the interviews, efforts were made to ensure that the interviewees were comfortable being honest and open, but issues around social desirability bias and other concerns—such as the legal issues surrounding race and gender discrimination—may shape the narratives that I was able to obtain through the interviews. That being said, the interviews help to illustrate the ways that employers conceptualize and attribute meanings to various types of employment experiences. Additionally, they provide powerful data about some of the potential sources that drive the outcomes seen in the field experiment with regard to the effects of nonstandard, mismatched, and precarious work.

This type of data, in-depth qualitative interviews with employers, is not new in the study of hiring processes. Indeed, an important body of existing scholarship has utilized similar methods to shed light on the hiring process. In particular, two existing books—Philip Moss and Chris Tilly's *Stories Employers Tell: Race, Skill, and Hiring in America* and Lauren Rivera's *Pedigree: How Elite Students Get Elite Jobs*—have laid detailed theoretical and empirical foundations for understanding how employers make hiring decisions. Moss and Tilly focus on the low-skilled urban labor market, while Rivera examines hiring for elite jobs, such as those at investment banks.[61] In the pages that follow, I build on the insights offered in these books about the hiring process. However, I pivot away from these accounts on two significant fronts. First, the hiring professionals in my sample generally hire for mid-tiered jobs, rather than low-skilled or elite positions. Second, the focus of the interviews in this book is on the interpretation and evaluation of different types of employment histories: long-term unemployment, part-time work, temporary agency employment, and skills underutilization.

Critically, the hiring professionals interviewed for this study and the individuals who made the hiring decisions in the field experiment are not the same people. Thus, there is not a one-to-one correspondence between the individual decision makers in the two data collection efforts. Yet both samples consist of diverse and heterogeneous groups of individuals who make hiring decisions. Ultimately, by examining both the experimental data and the data from the interviews with hiring professionals, this book provides a holistic picture of how employment histories intersect with demographic characteristics to shape hiring outcomes and highlights the key mechanisms implicated in this process.

Overview of the Book

With broad economic forces changing, many workers feel insecure, and individuals in many cases are kept from building a career and obtaining "good" jobs. But it is unclear whether the evaluation criteria used by employers during the hiring process have kept pace with these changes in the broader economic structure and the ways that workers experience the economy. This is the tension animating the rest of this book, and each of the chapters considers one important part of the equation.

What do we already know about the causes and consequences of non-standard, mismatched, and precarious work in the new economy? Chapter 2 tackles this question by considering exactly what these categories of employment entail and detailing the changing nature of the broader economy. Key findings from the existing literature—most of which is on the supply side of the labor market—tell us how nonstandard, mismatched, and precarious work experiences shape workers' social and economic lives.

With the necessary background about nonstandard, mismatched, and precarious work established, the balance of the book is organized around three key arguments: (1) employers make meaning—albeit in a complex way—from nonstandard, mismatched, and precarious employment histories; (2) the consequences of these employment histories are distinct from one another; and (3) identities matter: workers' race and gender are implicated in shaping the consequences of each type of employment history.

What meanings do hiring professionals attribute to nonstandard, mismatched, and precarious employment histories during the hiring process? Chapter 3 draws on the in-depth interviews to address this question by mapping the terrain of meanings attributed to different employment experiences. Some of the meanings that employers extract from these types of work experiences clearly violate ideal worker norms and lead to negative perceptions of job applicants' soft skills and personality. Alongside these meanings and signals, however, significant uncertainty is induced in hiring professionals when they encounter workers with these types of employment experiences. In reconciling this uncertainty, hiring professionals turn largely to individualized explanation, rather than structural ones, and make it clear that they "need a narrative" from job applicants that explains their employment experiences, a narrative that workers rarely have the opportunity to provide.

What employers say does not always align with what they do. In Chapter 4, I draw on the field-experiment data to directly examine how employers treat workers with histories of full-time work, part-time work, temporary agency employment, skills underutilization, and long-term unemployment. The evidence from the field experiment demonstrates that not all nonstandard, mismatched, and precarious employment experiences have the same consequences. Indeed, the effects are contingent. The interviews with hiring agents help unpack and explain the varied consequences of different types of work histories.

Workers' social identities—their race and gender—matter in shaping how employers respond to workers with nonstandard, mismatched, and precarious employment experiences. The remainder of the book highlights key cases that illuminate the complex interactions between race, gender, and employment experiences. Chapter 5 aims to understand why part-time work and gender interact with one another in the field experiment. Chapter 6 then turns to how the consequences of long-term unemployment vary with the race of the applicant. Conceptually unifying Chapters 5 and 6 are what I refer to as stratified stories. Building on group-based gender and race stereotypes, hiring professionals deploy narratives about workers' employment histories that produce divergent evaluations of the same employment experience for workers from different social groups.

Stratified stories are also at play, albeit slightly differently, in shaping the ways that temporary help agency experience influences how African American men are treated during the hiring process. Chapter 7 tackles this set of issues. Together, the findings in Chapters 5, 6, and 7 expand our understanding of the ways that social categories—social group membership and experiences in the economy, for example—interact and intersect to produce divergent outcomes for workers.

Where does this all leave us? The concluding chapter, Chapter 8, discusses the broader implications of the findings for theoretical and empirical scholarship on work and employment, social inequality in the workplace, evaluation processes, and the intersection of social categories. This final chapter also articulates key points of interest for policy makers interested in improving the outcomes of working individuals. The book concludes by discussing pathways forward for increasing our knowledge about how the nature of work and employment affect the opportunity structure for workers in the new economy.

———

Making the Cut is about the social and economic opportunity structure—the processes of inclusion and exclusion—for workers in the United States. Obstacles often outside the control of individuals can keep workers stuck in place. To address these challenges and ensure a more broadly distributed opportunity structure that enables workers to attain economic security for themselves and their families, we have to ask a fundamental question: what does it take to make the cut in the new economy?

2

Nonstandard, Mismatched, and Precarious Work

All jobs are not created equal. Some jobs provide high wages, health insurance, and retirement benefits. Others do not. Some jobs offer high levels of autonomy and control. Others do not. Some jobs provide adequate and predictable hours, offer job security, and ensure the full utilization of a worker's skills and experience. Others do not. There is a broad conception in the United States that "good jobs" are those that generally meet these criteria: livable wages, fringe benefits, predictable hours, and so forth.[1] "Bad jobs" are those that do not.

In recent years, the "gig economy" has taken center stage in public conversations about "good" and "bad" jobs.[2] Driving for Uber or Lyft, delivering food through DoorDash, performing odd jobs through TaskRabbit, and myriad other technologically mediated jobs of this sort have emerged. The consequences of these types of positions for workers are hotly debated. On the one hand, some argue that gig economy jobs are highly insecure and poorly compensated. Workers in these positions may be, it is suggested, more vulnerable to exploitation and experience weaker protection under the law.[3] Others point to the potentially positive side of laboring through online platforms: this type of work can potentially help workers to make ends meet between stints of full-time, standard employment or can offer scheduling flexibility and autonomy when workers need it.[4]

While certainly a topic worthy of scholarly and public interest, gig economy jobs make up a relatively small swath of the overall employment landscape in the United States. Recent estimates indicate that only about 0.5 to 1.0 percent of workers labor through an online intermediary.[5] In this book I concentrate on jobs that—like gig economy jobs—deviate from common conceptions of "good" jobs, but that make up a much larger proportion of the labor market in the United States: part-time work, temporary agency employment, and skills underutilization. Granted, as the gig economy develops, it will be important to consider how employers' evaluations of workers with different types of employment histories—a central theme of this book—translate to work experiences with online platforms. For example, how might employers evaluate a job applicant with a year of experience driving for Uber or Lyft or taking on odd jobs through TaskRabbit?

While not the focus of this book, the gig economy connects to a broader theme of *Making the Cut*: an emphasis on the institutional arrangements and changes that have resulted in economic strain and anxiety for many workers in the United States. Since the 1970s, changes in institutional forces as well as shifts in the composition of the labor force have produced a polarization in job quality—a bifurcation between so-called "good" and "bad" jobs.[6] And it is not just job quality that has witnessed this polarization: over the same period there was also a dramatic rise in income inequality.[7] In the early 1970s, the income share of the top decile of the distribution was between 31 and 32 percent. By 1998, it had risen to over 40 percent.[8]

Myriad forces have contributed to rising inequality in job quality and income. Technological innovation and the increasing centrality of computers in many occupations and workplaces may be implicated in shaping job quality and inequality in the distribution of earnings.[9] Corporations have certainly restructured in many ways over this period: complex subcontracting arrangements and downsizing have taken hold as important corporate strategies.[10] Workers have experienced layoffs with real consequences for their future job prospects. There has also been a dramatic decline in unionization—a key institutional force that affects both job quality and pay—since the early 1970s. While 34 percent of men in the private sector were in a union in 1973, only 8 percent were unionized in 2007. Among women, there was also a sizable decline over this period: from 16 to 6 percent.[11] Additionally, the relative size of the manufacturing sector—a sector often associated with paradigmatic "good" jobs—has declined sharply, while service sector jobs have increased.[12] And the occupational growth that occurred over the latter part of the twentieth century was largely bifurcated, with both high-wage and low-wage jobs growing, but jobs paying wages in the middle of the earnings distribution lagging behind.[13] Those middle-wage jobs have historically been the heart of the middle class.

Alongside these changes in the economy, workers in the United States have experienced profound uncertainty and anxiety about their economic lives.[14] And with good reason. Arne Kalleberg, a leading scholar of employment relations and inequality, identifies a set of key economic and social changes in the United States that provide evidence of increasing precarity and insecurity among workers: (1) declining attachment between workers and employers, (2) increasing long-term unemployment, (3) growing perceived job insecurity, (4) shifting risk from employers to employees, and (5) growing nonstandard work arrangements and contingent work—the centerpiece of this book.[15] Together, these dramatic changes—and likely others—have resulted in an economic environment filled with challenges for workers and families as they struggle to make ends meet and plan for the future.[16]

Of course, not all changes in the world of work in recent decades have been negative. Legal protections for women and workers of color have increased.[17] The passage of the Civil Rights Act in 1964 outlawed discrimination on the basis of race, color, religion, sex, and national origin.[18] Employment practices in many organizations have formalized and standardized, which can benefit workers who traditionally have faced obstacles to entry and advancement in the labor market.[19] Although the United States still lags behind the rest of the industrialized world when it comes to parental leave policies,[20] some progress has been made in the availability of policies and programs to support workers in balancing work and family life: parental leave, flexible scheduling options, and subsidized child care.[21]

As we move forward, keep in mind that these broad economic and policy changes have not impacted all workers in the same way. Scholars have shown, for example, that black women have been hurt the most by the decline in unionization. Estimates indicate that the black-white wage gap for women would be between 13 and 30 percent smaller if higher rates of unionization had persisted.[22] In terms of workers' connections to employers over time, white men in the private sector—who had been heavily represented in "good" jobs in the middle of the twentieth century—have experienced the most intense declines in job tenure.[23] Among women, by contrast, married mothers have actually experienced increases in job tenure, while never-married women have seen declining job tenure.[24] And corporate downsizing has been shown to have differential consequences across sociodemographic groups, ultimately resulting in less gender and racial diversity in managerial positions.[25]

Alongside these changes, social exclusion by race and gender is pronounced in the US economy. Women continue to earn significantly less than men, even after accounting for occupational sex segregation.[26] At the same time, women are underrepresented in positions of business leadership, making up less than a quarter of all seats on the boards of *Fortune* 100 companies.[27] Disparities along racial and ethnic lines are also conspicuous. While the statistics have improved to some extent over time, black men and women continue to earn significantly less than their same-gender white counterparts.[28] And, in 2016, racial and ethnic minorities made up under 18 percent of the board seats at *Fortune* 100 companies, with women of color holding just 5 percent of these board seats.[29] Given the differential consequences of the changing economic landscape for women and racial and ethnic minorities as well as the continued social exclusion experienced by these workers in the contemporary economy, we must pay close attention to race and gender variation as we investigate decision making in hiring.

One key component of these broader changes to the economy—as Kalleberg notes—is the type of employment relationships in which people work.[30] Millions of workers in the contemporary US labor in part-time positions, work through temporary help agencies, or are in jobs below their skill levels. These types of positions deviate from common conceptions of the "good" job and often—although not always—result in precarious social and economic experiences for workers. Scholars have found that these types of jobs, on average, tend to have lower wages and lack fringe benefits, such as employer-sponsored health and retirement plans.[31] And, of course, when many people are facing long spells of unemployment, that is a deep and powerful sign of labor market precarity, with far-reaching social and economic consequences.[32]

Before delving in to the ways that these nonstandard, mismatched, and precarious employment experiences are evaluated by employers during the hiring process, this chapter provides basic definitions and background information about these types of employment experiences and how they overlap with race and gender divisions in the labor market. I then examine the existing scholarship on changes over time in these positions and how they impact the lives of workers, their families, and the organizations where they labor. This terminology and these studies set the stage for the chapters that follow.

Nonstandard, Mismatched, and Precarious Work: Definitions and Background

What exactly do we mean by nonstandard, mismatched, and precarious employment? While employment arrangements and experiences each have their own nuances, a key commonality among these positions is that they deviate from common conceptions of "good" jobs in which workers are assumed to be employed full-time, on secure bases, with expectations of ongoing work, and in positions commensurate with their skills and experience.[33]

Below, I introduce the contours of each type of employment experience that will be investigated in this book—part-time, temporary agency, skills underutilization, and long-term unemployment—and how these more specific employment arrangements map onto the broader categories discussed above: nonstandard, mismatched, and precarious work.

NONSTANDARD EMPLOYMENT: PART-TIME AND TEMPORARY AGENCY EMPLOYMENT

Nonstandard employment is generally characterized by what it is not. Work that is not full-time, not expected to continue indefinitely, or not performed at the legal employer's place of business or under the legal employer's direction is generally considered nonstandard.[34] Part-time work and employment through temporary help agencies clearly meet these criteria and are often classified as nonstandard employment relationships.

Part-time employment is defined in the United States as working fewer than thirty-five hours per week and is the most prevalent form of nonstandard work.[35] Approximately one in six workers in the United States is employed part-time.[36] And roughly a quarter of part-time workers—around 4 percent of the US workforce—would prefer full-time jobs.[37] This phenomenon is referred to as "involuntary" part-time work, since working fewer than thirty-five hours per week is not what the worker would ideally like. It is important to note that prime-age workers, individuals between twenty-five and fifty-four, are less likely than both younger and older workers to be in part-time positions.[38] Additionally, certain industries—for example, wholesale and retail trade as well as leisure and hospitality—have a higher representation of both voluntary and involuntary part-time workers.[39]

In the early and middle years of the twentieth century, up until 1970, the growth in part-time work in the United States was largely among so-called voluntary part-time workers: individuals wanting part-time jobs, such as young people still in school and individuals looking for reduced hours to balance work and family life, primarily women.[40] By contrast, scholarship suggests that after 1970 any increase in part-time work was due to rising "involuntary" part-time work.[41] Thus, the post-1970s changes in part-time work are largely due to changes on the demand side of the labor market: the ways that work and employment are structured. Some of this has to do with the growth of industries that are more likely to utilize part-time work.[42] Some evidence shows that rising incidences of involuntary part-time work are due in part to employers' drive to contain costs.[43] Part-time workers are often compensated at lower rates than full-time workers and are exempt from various legal and policy requirements that make them more attractive to employers.[44]

While part-time work is about the number of hours worked, temporary agency employment has more to do with the time horizon of the employment relationship. And in the case of temporary help agency (THA) employment, it also has to do with the identity of the legal employer. THA employment captures those workers who are on the payroll of one company (the "temp agency"), which is also their legal employer but who perform their tasks on a temporary basis at a separate company. Nearly half of all THA workers (46 percent) are in these nonstandard positions involuntarily, preferring a traditional job.[45] Like part-time workers, THA workers are not spread evenly throughout the economy. Estimates from 2017 indicate that THA workers are more likely to be found in manufacturing industries as well as production, transportation, and material moving occupations.[46]

Early on, THA employment was quite marginal to the overall economy. The THA industry had its origins in Chicago in the late 1920s, when the industry focused on provided calculating-machine operators on a temporary basis.[47] Even during the years following World War II, the THA industry was a relatively small, albeit growing, player in the broader economy. Despite its relatively small size, the THA industry played an important role in challenging the cultural and normative model of a "good job"—a job with strong wages and health benefits.[48] Indeed, both historically and in the contemporary economic landscape, temporary workers are paid less than standard employees, on average, and are less likely to receive fringe benefits, such as health insurance.[49]

In the middle of the twentieth century, the idea of a "temp" worker was at odds with standard conceptions of employment for many companies and the broader public. In the postwar period, the THA industry attempted to address this concern and actively worked to create a product—temp workers—who would be seen by companies as "good" workers.[50] They recast temps as effective, efficient, and committed workers.[51] This required significant effort, but was ultimately successful, and the THA industry began to rapidly expand in the 1980s and early 1990s.[52] One driving force behind employers' interest in having temp workers is that they provide companies with increased flexibility.[53] Companies can use temps to fill a vacancy while searching for a new standard employee or when someone is sick, on vacation, or on medical leave. Temp workers can also provide valuable assistance for companies when facing an unexpected increase in business or considerable seasonal variation in output.[54] And given that temporary workers are the legal employees of the temp agency, not the company where they perform their daily tasks, companies do not assume the full set of legal responsibilities for temps that come with hiring standard employees. It's no coincidence that THA employment tended to grow during the latter part of the twentieth century in the geographic areas where legal protections made it more difficult to fire workers,[55] suggesting employers use THA employment in part to avoid the liabilities that come along with hiring standard employees. Together, part-time work and temporary agency employment represent key forms of nonstandard employment, one through limited hours and one through limited time horizons.

MISMATCHED EMPLOYMENT: SKILLS UNDERUTILIZATION

Unlike nonstandard employment, mismatched employment occurs when individuals' skills or preferences do not fit the characteristics of their job.[56] Working in a job that is beneath a worker's level of skill, education, or experience—often referred to as skills underutilization or overqualification—is a classic example of mismatched employment, although other types of mismatches are certainly possible.[57] In general, less is known about skills underutilization than part-time or temporary agency work, in part due to the challenges with defining and measuring this type of employment with standard labor force survey data.[58] Yet there has been some important research in this area. For example, one recent report found that in 2014 fully 25 percent of workers with a college degree were overqualified for their jobs.[59]

The prevalence of overqualification and skills underutilization in the contemporary US landscape runs counter to common narratives about skill shortages. Popular media coverage often suggests either that our education system is failing to provide the next generation of workers with basic skills or that the specific job-related skills necessary, especially for technical jobs, are in undersupply in the US workforce.[60] Yet overqualification appears to be at least as significant of a challenge in the labor market as there being a skills gap or a skills shortage in the United States.[61]

Overqualification, or skills underutilization, has real consequences for workers' outcomes. A review of the literature on the earnings of workers who are overeducated for their jobs provides evidence that these workers generally earn less than workers with similar levels of education, most of whom are working in jobs that are good matches for their education levels.[62] And a recent report found that the earnings penalty for overqualification among college-educated workers has increased significantly over time, reaching 50 percent in 2014.[63] However, overeducated workers tend to earn more than the well-matched individuals in the same occupation.[64] This makes sense intuitively: if you have a master's degree in chemistry and are working as an administrative assistant, you may be able to perform better in that clerical role than someone with an associate's degree, given your background knowledge and general skill development. Thus, your compensation may be higher than other administrative assistants to reward that performance. But you are also probably going to be making less than someone who is fully utilizing the skills she gained through a chemistry master's program.

The two broad classifications of employment at issue—nonstandard employment and mismatched employment—can overlap. Under certain conditions, part-time work and temporary agency employment may also be mismatched employment. For example, when workers want a full-time, permanent job but are able to obtain only a part-time position or work through a THA, they would be in both a nonstandard as well as a mismatched employment relationship.[65] In other words, the boundaries between these different employment categories are often porous. For this book, though, I focus on part-time and temporary agency employment as nonstandard forms of work and skills underutilization as mismatched work.

PRECARIOUS WORK: LONG-TERM UNEMPLOYMENT

A final key category, precarious work, is aptly defined as "employment that is uncertain, unpredictable, and risky from the point of view of the worker."[66] This term captures workers who labor without the certainty of whether they will have a job the following day or the following week. Similarly, workers who toil at unsafe and unregulated workplaces could be classified as laboring in a precarious employment positions. For the purposes of this book, we explore precarious employment by examining long-term unemployment. As Kalleberg notes, "Not having a job at all is, of course, the ultimate form of work precarity."[67] Long-term unemployment can have particularly severe consequences for individuals' financial, social, and economic well-being.[68] And while the overall unemployment rate was 6.2 percent in 2014, roughly one-third of all unemployed people in that year—2.8 million people in total— were jobless for at least twenty-seven weeks.[69] The consequences of long-term unemployment, given its prevalence, are important for all of us to understand.

The discussion above makes one thing clear: nonstandard, mismatched, and precarious employment are central to the world of work in the contemporary United States. Millions of workers labor in these positions. They experience the challenges of not having enough hours, not having the security of ongoing employment, not utilizing their skills, or even not having a job at all.

An Unequal Distribution

While nonstandard, mismatched, and precarious types of work are widespread in the United States, affecting a notable swath of the workforce, they are also unevenly distributed across the population. Exposure to these employment positions varies by the race and gender of the worker. So in addition to exploring the consequences of histories of nonstandard, mismatched, and precarious employment for workers' labor market opportunities, this book also tackles whether these effects vary by the race and gender of workers. If these consequences do vary systematically by the demographic characteristics of workers, then nonstandard, mismatched, and precarious employment may have important implications for understanding not just economic inequality but also the ways that social inequality is reproduced.

UNEMPLOYMENT

Striking racial disparities exist in the experience of unemployment. The unemployment rate for African Americans consistently hovers at approximately double that for whites and has remained that way for decades.[70] Figure 2.1 presents the unemployment rate in the United States for the whole population as well as for white and black workers separately. The racial disparities are clear and consistent. Long-term unemployment—defined as looking for work for at least twenty-seven weeks—is also racially concentrated. In 2014, 39.6 percent of unemployed African Americans were long-term unemployed, compared to 31.5 percent of unemployed whites.[71]

Interestingly, there are limited gender differences in the experience of unemployment and long-term unemployment.[72] It is important to keep in mind, though, that unemployment captures only individuals who are not employed and who are looking for a job. Thus, individuals who are not currently working for pay or looking for work—such as people primarily taking care of children—are not included in unemployment numbers. Given the gendered division of household labor, therefore, women are more likely to be outside of the labor force altogether but are not counted in unemployment numbers.

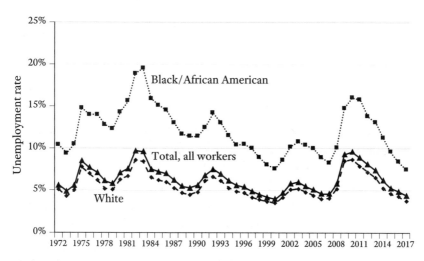

FIGURE 2.1. Unemployment Rate, by Race, 1972–2017
Source: Current Population Survey (CPS), Bureau of Labor Statistics.

PART-TIME WORK

While unemployment is heavily racialized, part-time work is heavily gendered. The gender gap in part-time employment has declined a bit over time, but significant differences remain in the likelihood of men and women working part-time. Currently, over 70 percent of part-time workers in the United States between the ages of twenty-five and fifty-four are women.[73] There are also some racial disparities in part-time work,[74] although part-time work does not necessarily take on a deeply racialized connotation. On average, both black men and black women are more likely to be working part-time for economic reasons than are white men and white women, respectively.[75] The black-white gap in involuntary part-time work among men was particularly pronounced in during the period after the Great Recession.[76]

TEMPORARY AGENCY EMPLOYMENT

The demographic composition of THA employment is slightly more complicated than it is for part-time employment. Historically, women dominated THA employment, as the sector developed after World War II.[77] However, there has been a significant narrowing in the gender gap in THA employment—with THA workers being roughly half men and half women in 2017.[78] There are important racial disparities in THA employment. Estimates from data collected in 2017 indicate that while African Americans make up

12.3 percent of workers with traditional employment arrangements, they con-stitute 25.9 percent of workers in temporary help agencies.[79] We are looking at a significant overconcentration of African Americans in THA employment.

SKILLS UNDERUTILIZATION

What do the demographics look like for skills underutilization? One key difference between skills underutilization and the other types of employment experiences under investigation is that there are less stark sociode-mographic differences in who labors in these positions. Women have not been historically overrepresented in this type of position.[80] Existing scholar-ship finds that between 1993 and 2002 approximately 20.3 percent of men and 19.8 percent of women were overqualified—that is, they had excessive education for their jobs.[81] However, nonwhites are slightly overrepresented in positions for which they are overqualified. Between 1993 and 2002, for example, 22.6 percent of nonwhites were overqualified for their jobs, com-pared to 19.4 percent of whites.[82]

Given the way certain types of employment positions map onto sociode-mographic groups, the consequences of these employment positions may also reinforce social inequality by race and gender. To date, however, little scholarship has investigated how race and gender intersect with nonstan-dard, mismatched, and precarious employment experiences to affect work-ers' future employment opportunities and, in particular, their ability to get a job. Not knowing this limits our understanding of the ways that social inequality emerges and is reproduced in the labor market.

On the Rise?

Public and media discussions give the impression that nonstandard, mis-matched, and precarious employment are on the rise. We likely all know people who have experienced these types of employment or have experi-enced them ourselves. Yet what do the data actually show about how the prevalence of part-time work, temporary agency employment, skills unde-rutilization, and long-term unemployment has changed over time?

Like the overall unemployment rate, long-term unemployment tends to move with the business cycle. During and after the Great Recession, long-term unemployment expanded, reaching a record high of 6.7 million work-ers (45.1 percent of the unemployed) in the second quarter of 2010.[83] Indeed, even in 2014—years after the Great Recession began—the proportion of the

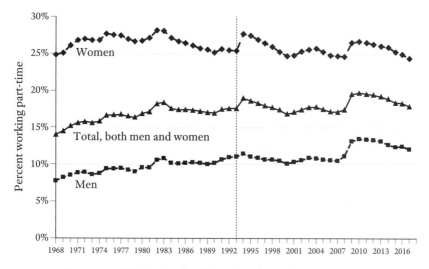

FIGURE 2.2. Percentage of Workers Employed Part-Time, by Gender, 1968–2017
Source: Current Population Survey (CPS), Bureau of Labor Statistics.
Notes: Part-time work is defined as working 1 to 34 hours per week. Data for 1993 and earlier
are not directly comparable to data for 1994 and later. This is due to changes to the CPS.

unemployed who were unemployed for fifty-two weeks or longer was over
20 percent, compared to just over 10 percent in 1995.[84] While these numbers
have continued to decline, researchers note that, by historical standards,
they have remained elevated.[85] Indeed, in 2017, 1.1 million workers had been
unemployed for at least a year, which is significantly higher than the one-year
unemployment level in 2007.[86]

The trend over time in part-time employment is a bit more complicated. Scholars suggest that much of the growth of part-time work in the
United States before 1970 was due to the growth of voluntary part-time
work. Since the 1970s, though, the increase in part-time work is largely
due to the growth of involuntary part-time work, among those who would
prefer to be employed full-time.[87] And there is clear evidence that the proportion of part-time workers rose significantly during the Great Recession.
Indeed, estimates indicate that involuntary part-time work grew by nearly
100 percent during and directly after the Great Recession.[88] Thus, the business cycle shapes rates of part-time work to some extent as well. Figure 2.2
shows the trend over time in part-time work, broken down by gender.[89] Over
the nearly fifty-year period displayed in the figure, women are consistently
much more likely than men to be working part-time. Indeed, the gender gap
in part-time employment is clear and persistent.

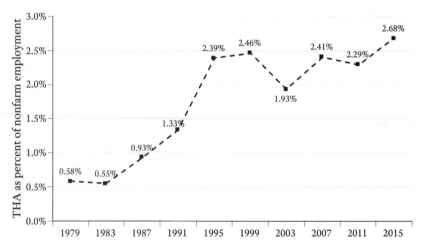

FIGURE 2.3. Temporary Help Services Industry Employment as a Percentage of Nonfarm Employment, 1979–2015
Source: County Business Patterns, US Census Bureau.
Notes: Estimates for 1979, 1983, and 1987 are drawn from Autor (2003). The remaining estimates are from the author's calculations.

More recent evidence also suggests that the increased prevalence of involuntary part-time work is not purely a result of the Great Recession and business cycle dynamics. Research by Robert Valletta, vice president in the Economic Research Department of the Federal Reserve Bank of San Francisco, and his colleagues indicates that changes in the industrial composition of jobs in the United States have contributed to underlying structural changes in the economy that partly account for the high levels of involuntary part-time work that have persisted since the Great Recession.[90] Valletta writes that their findings "imply that the level of [involuntary part-time work] is about 40% higher than would normally be expected at this point in the economic expansion."[91] These conclusions indicate that broader changes to the economy are important for understanding patterns of involuntary part-time work.

Employment through temporary help agencies rose dramatically between the late 1970s and mid-1990s. The THA sector grew at an annual rate of 11 percent between 1979 and 1995, more than five times the rate of growth of nonfarm employment in the United States.[92] Between 1995 and 2015, THA employment remained relatively stable at these higher levels.[93] Figure 2.3 presents data from the County Business Patterns database on the proportion of nonfarm employment in the United States that was on the payroll of temporary help services organizations in March of a given year.[94]

As can be seen, current rates of THA employment are markedly higher than they were in the late 1970s.

There is some indication that skills underutilization has also increased over time. One study finds that skills underutilization (defined as excessive education for one's job) increased significantly between 1972 and the early 2000s: the rate of overqualification (having at least one year of education more than is required for one's job) rose from approximately 30 percent to roughly 55 percent over this period.[95] Using a more stringent measure of overqualification—having at least three years of education more than is required for one's job—the rate of overqualification rose from roughly 10 percent to approximately 20 percent over the same period.[96] Indeed, writing about mismatched employment, Kalleberg explains, " . . . [T]he expansion of educational attainment has not necessarily been accompanied by an increase in the kinds of occupations that require people to make use of their high levels of education. Most white-collar jobs now require a college degree, but not because a college degree is required to perform these jobs. The requirement could also result from the surplus of college-educated workers."[97] It appears as though more workers labor in jobs for which they are overqualified now than did in the 1970s. This is likely particularly the case for workers with a college degree.[98]

As the summary of these time trends indicates, to what extent nonstandard, mismatched, and precarious work are on the rise is somewhat complicated. Insofar as there has been an increase in these positions, existing scholarship has offered multiple factors that may be implicated in their rise and prevalence,[99] including many of the same changes to the economy that were discussed earlier in this chapter. Global economic integration has increased competition for US firms, creating incentives for companies to outsource work to lower wage countries and implement "flexible," nonstandard employment relations for their US employees.[100] Legal changes have also paved the way for employers to alter the employment contract and increase the use of nonstandard employment relations, particularly THA workers.[101] Additionally, changes in key labor market institutions, such as the decline in the power of organized labor,[102] have likely enabled the emergence of nonstandard positions in the US labor market. Technological advances that improved communication and information systems also likely played a role in the increase of nonstandard employment relations by, for example, enabling employers to more easily coordinate their labor needs with temporary help agencies.[103] The changing education landscape and shifts in the occupational structure of the US economy are likely implicated in the rise of skills underutilization and overqualification.[104]

Importantly, though, there is still significant work to be done to understand the forces that give rise to nonstandard, mismatched, and precarious employment and to identify precisely how much change there has actually been over time in these types of positions. For example, sociologist Annette Bernhardt conducted a review of the evidence on changes over time in three types of nonstandard employment—temporary work, part-time work, and independent contracting. She concluded that it is difficult to identify a clear upward trajectory for the prevalence of these employment positions given the data sources that exist.[105]

Regardless of whether and to what extent nonstandard, mismatched, and precarious employment have risen over time, their current reach for US workers and employers is broad. The sheer volume of workers who labor in such positions means that it is important for us to understand their consequences. While much of this book focuses on the consequences of these positions for workers' employment outcomes, the impact of these employment arrangements extends beyond the economic realm.

Social Consequences

Nonstandard, mismatched, and precarious employment have consequences for other aspects of workers' lives and the organizations where they labor. Indeed, it is essential to understand the social consequences of these types of employment experiences if we want to more fully conceptualize how workers' experiences are shaped by these employment arrangements. Here, I briefly touch on a few of the consequences of these different employment positions for workers' health and family lives and for the organizations where they work.

HEALTH OUTCOMES

Social science research has long taken the relationship between employment and health seriously. Unemployment, for example, has been found to be negatively associated with individuals' mental and physical health.[106] In the case of subjective well-being, an indicator of mental health, there is compelling evidence that some of the effects of unemployment do not simply disappear upon reemployment, suggesting longer term, negative consequences of experiencing unemployment.[107] Researchers have started paying attention to how nonstandard and mismatched employment may impact workers' health. Summarizing findings from a review of related literatures, sociologists Sarah Burgard and Katherine Lin write, "While there has been relatively little assessment of its association with health, and associations seems to vary depending on the voluntariness and specific conditions of the arrangements, nonstandard working arrangements have been linked to greater psychological distress and, in some studies, poorer physical health."[108] In a comprehensive review of existing literature on the connection between temporary work and health outcomes, a group of scholars found that working as a temporary employee is associated with higher odds of psychological distress, although they also find that there is significant variation in the strength of this association.[109] While the link with psychological outcomes is clearer, there is less direct evidence about the association between temporary employment and physical health, although some preliminary evidence does suggest that temporary workers may be at increased risk for occupational injuries.[110]

Individuals in full-time employment have healthier eating habits, get more physical activity, and are less likely to smoke cigarettes, compared to part-time and unemployed individuals—or so found another group of scholars examining the health-related behaviors of individuals in New Haven, Connecticut. Additionally, the researchers found that stress and depressive symptoms assist in explaining these associations.[111] However, this study and many other studies in this line of research drew on cross-sectional data, which are data from a single point in time. With this type of data, it is difficult to disentangle cause from effect. It may be that individuals with worse psychological and physical health are more likely to end up in nonstandard, mismatched, or precarious employment, rather than the other way around.

As a step toward dealing with this issue related to causal ordering, some scholars have examined longitudinal data where the same individuals are tracked at multiple points in time, thus allowing them to examine the time ordering of events. Utilizing this type of data, researchers have found that adverse changes in individuals' employment are positively associated with depression at a later point in time. And this pattern holds even after accounting for individuals' prior psychological well-being.[112]

Together, the findings about employment relations and health outcomes are somewhat mixed, requiring additional scholarship to pin down the nuances of how these different types of employment experiences may be linked to workers' health.

FAMILY LIFE

The research goes beyond physical and mental health to connect various types of employment experiences with family life.[113] In the US context, recent studies provide evidence of an association between husbands' lack of full-time work and a higher risk of divorce.[114] Importantly, though, this association is limited to men; there is no association between women's lack of full-time work and divorce.[115] This finding highlights the importance of the gendered nature of employment statuses, a reality that is taken seriously throughout this book.

Outside the United States, scholars have found that, among partnered men and women in Australia, women who work part-time are actually more satisfied with their work hours than women working full-time, but the opposite is true for men.[116] However, they also examined the role of partners' hours in shaping life satisfaction. They found that women's life satisfaction is higher if their partners work full-time but that men's life satisfaction is not impacted by the number of hours worked by their partners.[117] Again, we see provocative gender variation in how employment shapes workers' outcomes, not just individually but in the home and for their families.

Much of the scholarship in this area emphasizes the role of nonstandard employment schedules—rather than the employment relations themselves—on family life.[118] Examining the role of work schedules in the retail food sector in the United States in shaping men's and women's perceptions of marital quality, scholars have found that when men work in the evenings or at nights, both they and their female partners report lower levels of marital quality.[119] However, women's varied employment schedules are not associated with either their own or their partners' perceptions of marital quality. In the Canadian context, researchers have compared the self-reports of family functioning among families where parents worked nonstandard schedules with those families where parents worked standard weekday times. They found that parents with nonstandard schedules reported worse family function as well as less effective parenting.[120]

While additional work is needed in this area, there are some findings that suggest nonstandard, mismatched, and precarious work can be associated with challenges in terms of family life and that these patterns often differ for men and women.

RELATIONSHIPS WITHIN ORGANIZATIONS

Workplace organizations and the dynamics within them are themselves shaped by the use of nonstandard and mismatched employment relations. When organizations utilize workers who are on nonstandard employment contracts, these workers often labor side by side with standard employees. This raises important questions about whether there are consequences for the outcomes of standard employees of working alongside workers who are in other types of positions.

Much of the work in this area has focused on temporary workers, and in general scholars have found negative associations between employers' use of temporary workers and various outcomes for the standard employees within that organization, such as workplace attachment, trust, and commitment as well as relationships with managers and coworkers.[121] Indeed, standard employees who work alongside temporary workers also express lower levels of perceived job security.[122] Thus, there appears to be something destabilizing about the presence of nonstandard workers within organizations, not just for the temporary workers themselves, but also for the standard employees they work with.

———

The scene has now been set. Job quality and earnings have become more polarized in the United States, coinciding with broader changes in the economic landscape. And nonstandard, mismatched, and precarious work are central components of the new economy. To date, scholars have documented the experiences of workers in these positions and the consequences of these positions for workers' subjective and material well-being. Yet only limited research has examined how employers evaluate workers who have moved through these employment positions. What signals are sent by these employment histories, and how do employers make sense of these types of work experiences? Have employers' conceptions of the ideal worker and the ideal job candidate kept pace with this broader set of economic changes? Or do workers with these employment histories get screened out during the job application process? How might the race and gender of the worker influence this process?

3

Making Meaning of Employment Histories

SIGNALS, UNCERTAINTY, AND THE NEED FOR A NARRATIVE

Hiring decisions are difficult to make. Employers are often faced with dozens, or even hundreds, of applications at a time. "I'd say I look through anywhere from five hundred to one thousand resumes a day," Carol, a human resources manager in commercial real estate, reports. "Don't spend more than like three to five seconds on a resume. We kind of just very, very quickly look through them, just glance at them." Bombarded with resumes from job applicants, five hundred to a thousand per day in Carol's case, hiring professionals have to sort through this information quickly—three to five seconds per resume—as they attempt to hire the best talent for their companies.

Time is limited, information is scarce, and the stakes are high. Under these conditions, hiring professionals draw on observable signals—such as educational credentials—from resumes and cover letters to make inferences about the underlying, unobservable quality—such as the potential productivity, work ethic, or fit—of job candidates.[1] Employment histories, particularly experiences that do not align with conceptions of "good" jobs or "good" careers, are likely highly salient in this process. But what meanings do employers attribute to the fact that an applicant has had these experiences in the labor market? And how might those meanings impact the evaluations of workers with nonstandard, mismatched, and precarious employment histories during the hiring process?

Drawing on the interviews with hiring professionals, this chapter develops an answer to these questions. To lay the groundwork, I first present one common set of steps by which companies hire new employees—from posting a job opening to extending an offer. Then I discuss the meanings employers ascribe to applicants with employment histories containing part-time work, temporary agency employment, skills underutilization, and long-term unemployment. I argue that hiring managers extract meaning from these experiences along key evaluative dimensions: technical skills, "soft skills" and personality, compliance with ideal worker norms of competence and commitment, and to some extent "fit." Importantly, however, these nonstandard, mismatched, and precarious employment experiences also induce in hiring professionals high levels of uncertainty about the job applicant. Hiring professionals want to know why a worker was employed part-time or working through a temp agency. And, specifically, they want the worker to provide a narrative allaying their concerns. When those worker-provided narratives are not available, hiring professionals often turn to individualized explanations, placing responsibility on workers themselves rather than focusing on broad structural and economic changes that may have resulted in workers laboring in a particular employment position. Applicants' social group membership—their race and gender—and its associated stereotypes are also used to make sense of nonstandard, mismatched, and precarious employment histories, resulting in a complex set of inequalities.

The Hiring Process: From Job Opening to Job Offer

Hiring happens in many ways. The typical hiring process, though, often follows a series of events that many of us are familiar with. John—a supervisor for talent acquisition at a large health care company—provides a useful overview of the hiring process at his organization, which is similar to what other hiring professionals described, particularly those who worked at midsized to large companies. Below, I trace the hiring process at John's company, as he described it.

A STYLIZED HIRING PROCESS

The first step in the hiring process, as might be expected, is that the company or organization has a job opening. Openings can arise either because someone left the organization (sometimes referred to as a "backfill" position) or because a new position was created, possibly because the organization is expanding or new work needs to be completed. As John states,

SALES REPRESENTATIVE

Job Purpose: Serve customers by selling key products; meeting the needs of customers and clients.

Job Duties:
- Sells to and services accounts within a B-to-B sales model.
- Identifies and establishes new accounts.
- Keeps management informed of progress. Submits activity and results reports to management, including call reports, weekly work plans, and annual territory reviews.
- Monitors competition through obtaining information about current marketplace information on pricing, products, delivery schedules, and merchandising techniques.
- Resolves customer complaints by investigating problems; developing solutions; preparing reports; making recommendations to management.
- Contributes to team effort by accomplishing related results as needed.

Required Skills/Qualifications:
- Motivation for sales, customer service, meeting sales goals, closing skills, territory management, prospecting skills, presentation skills.
- 3 to 5 years of outside sales experience.
- Functional skills with MS Office.

Benefits:
- Salary consistent with industry standards, commensurate with experience.
- Competitive benefits package.

FIGURE 3.1. Job Posting Example
Note: This job ad was adapted from an actual job posting.

"The first step is really, is this a backfill or is this a newly created position? If it's a backfill, somebody left the organization. What's going to happen first is the hiring manager will notify HR, as a whole, that somebody is leaving. We'll connect with that hiring manager and ask if they want us to back fill the position based on the existing job description or if they want to make any edits." An early step in the hiring process is to write the job description. These documents are powerful in that they outline the details of the position and define what the organization is looking for. A job posting's language can signal information about the company and the type of organization it is—its priorities, values, and culture—which in turn influence the types of applicants who apply.[2] Social scientists have found that the ways that job advertisements are written can perpetuate inequality, particularly along gender lines.[3] So getting the language of the job posting right is an important step in the hiring process. An example of a job posting for a sales representative position is presented in Figure 3.1, which provides a sense of what is mentioned and discussed in these postings.

After the job posting has been completed and agreed upon by the relevant stakeholders, it is time to get the posting out into the world for people to see. John describes this next step in the process: "[Then] we post it to various job boards and, from there, the recruiter will do a couple different things. First, they will start scouring our internal database, a database of former applicants to see if anybody could be a fit from that perspective. Then they'll start perusing various job boards to see if there's any candidates that maybe have posted a resume out for consideration but maybe haven't quite yet applied for our role." Some of the job boards that came up repeatedly in my interviews were Indeed.com, Monster.com, and CareerBuilder.com. These boards are highly trafficked by both job seekers and employers seeking to find the right match. Indeed.com, for example, receives two hundred million unique visitors per month.[4] After the posting is out there in the world, companies and recruiters are far from passive entities. According to John, they actively search databases and job boards to see if they are able to identify the right candidate for the job. John indicated that in cases where a position is likely to be difficult to fill, someone at his company actually takes additional steps to identify potential employees:

> This individual [the sourcer] doesn't go to job boards for people who are looking for jobs, but they identify people by industry, by skill set, who probably aren't looking for jobs but would be willing to listen to why [our company] is such a great organization and maybe an opportunity to advance their career. . . . She's looking at our competitors, looking at people who might be in a similar capacity to what we're looking for. She's identifying them, connecting with them, pitching this opportunity.

This step of the hiring process demonstrates that the company itself has a hand in constructing the pool of potential candidates, especially for more difficult to fill positions. The company may engage candidates who are not even looking for work—passive job seekers—in order to increase the quality of the candidate pool.

Once the pool of candidates has been generated, it is time to get down to business and start determining who could potentially join the organization. This decision point is particularly important for our purposes because it is the moment of concern for this book and is the point of the hiring process that we will be able to examine with data from the field experiment. Discussing this evaluative moment of deciding whom to interview, John notes,

> At some point we're going to have a pool of candidates that fit the criteria that we seek. Our department will forward those to the recruiting manager and get their input in regards to whether or not they feel that they are a good fit. We're going to solicit feedback on all those that don't fit so

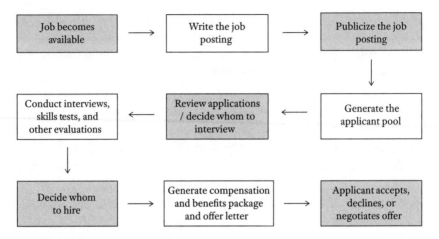

FIGURE 3.2. The Stylized Hiring Process

that we can recalibrate our recruiting efforts. Of course, they might say I need a little bit more this, or a little bit more of that, whatever the case is, then we go back and we look for that. At some point they're going to say, yes, I'm interested and bring in this person.

At this stage, some applicants are starting to get weeded out. Others are getting moved along in the process. Once the pool of candidates John's team has come up with is approved by the recruiting manager, those individuals are then invited to interview with the company. During the interview process, the applicants often meet with both the recruiting team and members of the unit where they would actually work, answering myriad questions about themselves and their experiences. This is also the time in the process when individuals are often given skills tests, personality tests, and other types of evaluations. Once a candidate is agreed upon as the person to hire, the human resources office puts together a compensation package for her and an offer is extended to the candidate. The candidate then accepts, declines, or negotiates the details of the offer. Figure 3.2 represents this stylized hiring process graphically.

ADDITIONAL COMPONENTS OF THE HIRING PROCESS

In reality, the hiring process outlined above is often complicated by additional components that can shape and alter the dynamics of applicant screening. Referrals through social networks, technology, and the policies and practices of the company itself all come into play. The data utilized throughout the book provide limited empirical traction on these issues, but it is important to keep them in mind when considering the broader context within which hiring occurs.

Referrals. While many job openings are heard about and applied for through company websites or through online job posting boards, such as Indeed.com or Monster.com, there are alternative channels through which individuals can learn about and apply for jobs. Referrals via social networks are one such pathway. In this case, current employees—or others in the know—will recommend that the company consider a family member, friend, or acquaintance of theirs for a position.[5] These referrals shape the pool of potential candidates in important ways and influence employers' decisions about whom to hire.[6] For example, referrers can provide information to the employer about the quality of a job applicant, assuaging any concerns or hesitations that an employer may have. Indeed, many companies have formal programs and offer financial incentives to encourage their current employees to refer people in their social networks for open positions at the company.[7]

Technology. There are also technologies that fundamentally affect the hiring process, such as applicant tracking systems (ATSs).[8] Many companies will use an ATS to organize the applicant screening process, and the ATS technologies may use algorithms to screen the resumes that are received for a given opening. At some companies, an algorithm even takes the first pass through the resumes that have been received, screening out certain candidates and indicating that other candidates should be given further consideration. The size of the industry generating and selling these types of technologies indicates that there is significant hope among employers that "big data," algorithms, and new tools for hiring have the potential to improve the quality of matches between workers and firms and thus increase productivity and profit.[9] A survey conducted by the Society for Human Resource Management (SHRM)—a professional organization for HR professionals—estimates that 22 percent of organizations used automated prescreening to review resumes from job applicants in 2016.[10] The proportion has likely increased since then. Yet there are also skeptics who raise questions about whether this technological intervention in the job screening process is working, asking whether the machine-learning approaches used in these contexts are able to adequately identify the best employees.[11] Others have raised concerns that algorithmic approaches to screening and evaluating potential employees can perpetuate social exclusion for racial minorities, women, and other groups of workers, further exacerbating inequalities in the labor market.[12]

Even those whose job it is to hire workers have complex feelings about the use of these algorithmic screening technologies. Marie, a recruitment manager at a production company, discussed the implementation of an ATS where she works: "I think technology is great. And tracking systems. We're in the process of implementing one, but I think you still have to have a human touch and get that eye open and your ear open and have an open mind." Technology can be important in assisting with the hiring process, but she and other interviewees emphasized that a "human touch" is still necessary to make things go as well as possible. The importance of social interaction and human decision making in order to overcome some of the limitations of technology is also echoed by those on the other side of the process: job seekers. Indeed, Ilana Gershon's fascinating study of job seeking reveals how job seekers try to use their social networks and connections to avoid their resumes being screened out by new technologies and algorithms.[13] Given their rise and prevalence, continued attention to technological interventions into the hiring process will be important for understanding the complex matching of workers to companies.[14]

Organizational Context. Hiring does not happen in a vacuum.[15] Individuals making hiring decisions are often embedded in business organizations. Organizations with rules, regulations, policies, and procedures. Organizations that are subject to a set of local, state, and federal laws. In the latter part of the twentieth century—partially in response to the Civil Rights Act of 1964—companies developed bureaucratic structures and organizational policies aimed at increasing diversity and inclusion within the workplace.[16] For example, between 1971 and 2002, private firms with more than one hundred employees became increasingly likely to have affirmative action plans, diversity trainings, and grievance procedures, among other policies.[17]

Contextual features of organizations are implicated in the dynamics of racial and gender inequality as well as segregation processes within workplaces.[18] Some interventions—particularly those that establish organizational responsibility for diversity, such as affirmative action plans and diversity committees—are most successful in increasing the representation of white women and African Americans in managerial positions.[19] Yet organizational reforms that aim to control managerial discretion—such as job tests and performance ratings—can actually have adverse effects on the representation of women and workers of color in management.[20] While these sets of organizational reforms have been well documented and linked in compelling ways to the representation of women and racial and ethnic minorities in managerial positions, less is known about how they shape the decision making of hiring professionals when they are screening job applications from the external labor market. Yet it is likely that the organizational and institutional contexts within which hiring agents work influence whom they decide to call back for jobs and ultimately whom they decide to hire.[21]

———

As we saw in John's account of the hiring process, many components of the application screening process impact who ends up being selected for an opening. One key moment—where a large number of applicants are cut from the process—is when a pool of job candidates is in front of an individual hiring professional and she decides whom to interview and whom not to. Much of the book focuses on this moment. Depicted by the central box in Figure 3.2, this is a juncture in the hiring process where signals are extracted from various aspects of workers' application materials—their race, gender, educational background, and employment history. And as the next section will show, this is also where we can see—perhaps more clearly than in other moments during the hiring process—how recruiters, hiring managers, and employers imbue nonstandard, mismatched, and precarious employment histories with meaning.

The Meanings of Nonstandard, Mismatched, and Precarious Work

Of the hundreds of resumes hiring professionals scan for a position, some applicants will undoubtedly have recent experiences in nonstandard, mismatched, or precarious work. How do hiring professionals interpret these types of employment experiences? To address this question, I draw on the interviews with recruiters, hiring managers, and others involved in the hiring process. After a general discussion of how the hiring process works at their company and the types of things that they look for when screening job applicants, I asked respondents how they think about workers with experiences in each of the four employment categories of interest: long-term unemployment, part-time work, temporary agency employment, and skills underutilization. Their responses provide a map of the terrain of the meanings and signals that employers attribute to and extract from these types of employment experiences. Below I outline the connections between each type of employment experience and four key evaluative domains that have been shown to be central to hiring decision making: technical skills, soft skills and personality, ideal worker norms of commitment and competence, and fit.

TECHNICAL SKILLS

As might be expected, employers care about whether a job applicant has the technical skills and training necessary to carry out the tasks required for a given position. Early on in the interviews, I asked hiring professionals what they generally looked for when evaluating job applicants. Responding to this question, John, whom we met earlier in this chapter and who works in the health care sector, responded, "It's going to be relevant skills, industry experience, appropriate education, job stability/gaps in employment." Echoing this sentiment, Louis—who works in HR in the education sector—responded, "Experience . . . it doesn't have to be direct experience, but it could be transferrable skills. For example, someone that may work in customer service, or someone that may have worked in a day care." Indeed, meeting the skill, education, and technical requirements for the job was key for many respondents. Yet there was also much discussion that skills and experience were not enough. Respondents often mentioned other characteristics, such as soft skills or personality, as important complements to technical skills. These nontechnical aspects of evaluation will be our focus later in this chapter.

In the interviews, employers made inferences about applicants' technical skills when discussing nonstandard, mismatched, and precarious employment experiences. Often, although not universally, the meanings attributed to these types of employment experiences related to concerns regarding skill atrophy and skill decay. These concerns were particularly salient in the interviews when hiring professionals were talking about long-term unemployment and skills underutilization. When asked a general question about her thoughts on unemployment, for example, Amy—who works in the staffing industry—said, "Yeah. Well, my worry's I want to make sure that candidates have updated their skills. Like they haven't just been doing nothing." Reiterating that thought process, Lauren, who focuses on hiring at her midsized health care technology company, reported the following when asked about her thoughts on unemployment:

> I think it goes back to finding out, even though they haven't been working, are they staying current with the industry, are they staying current

with what's the newest regulation, are they reading scientific journals of whatever function it is? What are they doing to stay current? . . . How are they staying current in that particular function or industry so that the learning curve is smaller and the time to hit the ground running is shorter?

Compared to workers who are employed full-time at their skill level, employers may worry that those who are not working may not be developing skills and their skills may even be deteriorating since they are not being used on a regular basis. Additionally, employers' concerns may even increase as the duration of unemployment experienced by a worker continues.[22]

These concerns about technical skills were also common when hiring professionals discussed how they make sense of workers who have moved into jobs below their skill level, but who are now applying for a job at their previous level of skill attainment. Laura, who hires for a professional services firm, responded when she was asked what comes to mind when thinking about someone working in a position below their level of skill or education:

> They probably wanted to pay bills, that's probably a sensible reason, but I'd want to know what they've done to stay updated on job requirements. Like, if, say you went from working in an office to working in a retail store and want to come back to an office, I want to—say if you were like a bank teller and went to a retail store as a cashier after being laid off or just not being able to find a job, you know. . . . I'd want to know what skills you gained, what you've done in between.

We can see in Laura's comment, though, that in addition to the concern about staying up to date on one's skills, there is also uncertainty about why someone was in a position below his skill level. She offers explanations that "probably" explain what was going on for the worker, but she is far from certain that her explanation is correct. Uncertainty becomes a major theme in candidate evaluation, which we will explore later. Reflecting on evaluating applicants who are in positions underutilizing their skills, Amber, an HR manager in the finance sector, echoed Laura's concern about human capital and skill maintenance: "To me, I am hesitant, because depending on the amount of time you've been out of your field, there's probably a ton of stuff that your peers have advanced in that you haven't. So, it's like if you were a nuclear physicist in 1990, that might not mean the same thing as a nuclear physicist in 2017." She then went on to say, "If you haven't done any sort of continuing education to, like, keep those skills intact then it makes you wonder if they're still able to achieve their job." Fields change.

Job requirements change. Even if the applicant is clearly competent, that is not enough.

Not all types of employment histories, however, led to such deep concerns about technical skills and skill atrophy. A number of hiring professionals indicated that they would take a history of temporary agency employment as a signal that a worker was keeping her skills up to date. Discussing how she thinks about workers with experience through temp agencies, Judy, who works as a contract staffing consultant, said, "Not a negative. I mean, it's a really, really—if anything, it can be a really good way to stay employed while you're looking for the next big thing, and get new skills. And, oftentimes, those temp jobs turn into full-time jobs, so it's a really good way to get your foot in the door." As Judy makes clear, "temping" can have some positive effects. Given the importance of "hard" and technical skills in the eyes of potential future employers, the skill maintenance offered by temporary agency employment may be useful. However, as we will see next, working through a temp agency can raise a separate set of concerns.

SOFT SKILLS AND PERSONALITY

While issues of technical or "hard" skills were clearly important to the hiring professionals who were interviewed, soft skills and personality mattered as well. Charles currently works at a staffing company but has significant experience in the insurance sector as well. He had this to say about what is most important to him when evaluating job applicants:

> What's most important to me is, and I think most of our recruiters here, it's the attitude, it's the energy of this person who's willing to take a position that they're qualified for to step into and to start their new position or their new career. . . . You know, there's a "can do" and there's a "will do," and I look for more of the "will do" what it takes, and that's from attitude and that's from what you bring from excitement and from passion.

Personality and attitude are central for Charles's evaluations of potential job candidates. He wants excitement and passion. The role of soft skills and personality in the hiring process is not new. In their large-scale study of the low-skilled labor market, economists Philip Moss and Chris Tilly found similar themes about the importance of these nontechnical skills.[23] As is clear from Charles's statement, some employers want soft skills and a good attitude because it will lead to a higher output of work—a "will do" attitude. And for some positions—such as sales—these types of personality dimensions may be directly related to the ability of potential employees to do their job, given the importance of interacting with customers and clients.[24] In some cases, employers' desires for applicants with a particular personality may also have a darker side. Some research finds that employers in the low-skilled labor market look for applicants with personality attributes that will make them more pliable and less likely to speak up in the context of poor treatment.[25]

In interviews with hiring professionals, their concerns about soft skills and personality were most salient when discussing unemployment and temporary agency employment. With respect to long-term unemployment, nearly half of the hiring professionals I interviewed mentioned concerns about soft skills or personality. One personality concern that arose about unemployed workers was laziness. Bruce, who works in the restaurant and hospitality industry, reported, "If they're unemployed currently, you know, sometimes that, you know, I hate to say it, but it does, it raises some red flags. It raises some red flags. Why, why don't you have a job right now, you know?" Then, when asked about why unemployment raises a red flag, he said, "The first thing that really kind of comes to mind is, you know, if this person is a bad employee, if they're lazy. If they just don't, you know, care enough—to go find another job?" Concern about an unemployed worker's lack of motivation and work ethic was a common theme in the interviews.

Beyond simply their work ethic and motivation, the underlying character of unemployed individuals came up as a question. After reporting that long-term unemployment worried her when evaluating job candidates, Evelyn—who works in the staffing industry—was asked why that was the case:

> The responsibility part of it, are they going to get up and get to work on time, are they going to prepare themselves not to go overboard, or days when they're hungover? These little things for me, as far as internally for the operations position, I expect more from someone working—my right hand person. . . . First we have to be an example, second of all if this person isn't there, I have to cover for them and I don't want someone to make my job harder. I'm looking for someone to make my job easier.

Evelyn's comments point to concerns that the unemployed are just not responsible. This underlying belief may have severe consequences for unemployed workers' likelihood of obtaining a new job, raising concerns about how they will contribute to the workplace, potentially even creating more work for their managers and coworkers.

This line of thinking that arose from the interviews with hiring professionals aligns closely with the existing body of research on the stereotypes, and related stigma,[26] associated with unemployment that may drive negative outcomes for unemployed workers. Previous research has found that unemployed workers may be deemed less competent, less ambitious, lacking skills and motivation, or having something that is "not quite right" about them.[27] These stereotypes about unemployed workers are powerful and contain information that overlaps with many of the attributes that employers seek in future employees. My interviews with employers and hiring managers point to this similar set of concerns.

Unemployment was not the only type of employment experience that primed concerns about "soft skills" and personality. In many interviews, hiring professionals attributed negative soft skill and personality meanings to workers with THA employment histories. Discussing what she hears her colleagues say about temp workers, Danielle—who is involved with hiring in the retail sector—reported, "Like I think for them it kind of signals like if somebody can't find a job on their own then it's like that—like there's something wrong with them as far as like their work ethic or, you know, being on time." Andrea, who hires workers in the retail sector, echoed the sentiments expressed by Danielle: "My coworker says temps are temps for a reason. They're not—sometimes, not all the times, but many times, more often than the permanent employees, they're not as reliable sometimes. They don't show up to work at all and they don't—they tend to be the ones who most likely don't show up to work and they don't call or they just don't really seem to care about their work." As with the unemployed, there are clearly concerns about temps as lacking certain levels of work ethic, reliability, and responsibility. This set of concerns was particularly salient when a worker had been in temporary positions for an extended period and those positions did not convert into permanent positions, suggesting that the person was passed over for a permanent position even after interacting with people at the company. While less salient in the context of skills underutilization and part-time work, concerns about "soft skills" and personality were also mentioned by employers for these employment histories.

Importantly, not all "soft skill" and personality signals were negative in the context of evaluating these divergent employment histories. Discussing part-time work, Marie, a recruitment manager at a production company, whom we heard from earlier, reported,

> If someone is working part-time for something they're overqualified for, it might show initiative. Some folks work part-time just to stay marketable and not have that gap on their resume. . . . I think it's a smart thing to

do because at the end of the day a lot of the employees or potential candidates, they're really not netting out very much by the time you factor their time, their transportation, if they have to get their clothes cleaned to go to work. They'd probably make as much on unemployment, but they're motivated. Sometimes besides that, too, it can show motivation because some people just can't sit home.

From Marie's point of view, then, part-time work is sometimes a sign that someone is motivated to work in lieu of remaining unemployed. From this perspective, it is evident that some employers perceive part-time work as a stopgap measure when other opportunities—such as a full-time job—are not available and they want to avoid unemployment. And the motivation and initiative to stay employed—even if not in a full-time position—can mean something positive in the eyes of future employers. Patterns of part-time employment, however, come with a particular set of concerns, as we will see next.

Overall, the interviews indicate that hiring professionals often—although not always—make negative assumptions about job applicants' personality and "soft skills" because they have a history of nonstandard, mismatched, or precarious work. The concerns tend to focus on issues of work ethic, responsibility, or just having something "wrong" with them and are most salient when discussing unemployment and temporary agency employment.

IDEAL WORKER NORMS: COMMITMENT AND COMPETENCE

Scholars of work, particularly of gender inequality in the employment domain, often highlight the ways in which organizations have an ideal worker norm, a standard against which real workers are compared.[28] Violations of, or noncompliance with, these ideal worker norms can result in penalties, such as exclusion from hiring and promotion opportunities.[29] Two primary dimensions of the ideal worker norm have been identified: competence and commitment. Competence clearly relates to one's ability to do the job. But competence also taps deeper beliefs about the underlying, innate ability of a worker. Existing research shows that competence is a key dimension of social perception and has important consequences for how workers are evaluated.[30] Of course, though, employers care about more than just a worker's level of competence. Perceived commitment—the expected effort and dedication that a worker is perceived to put forth—is also central to the ideal worker norm and to the evaluation of workers.[31] These commitment issues and concerns are also closely related to personality issues of motivation and passion for the job, which were noted above.

Ideal worker norms were salient in the interviews with hiring professionals. Responding to a question about what she looks for in job applicants, Alexis, who hires people for a home remodeling company, said, "So the basic skill sets of the position and then I'm looking the second thing is kind of what have they done in the past and how long have they stayed. If I got a resume of someone who's been in fifteen jobs in four years, and each job was six months to a year, I'm really wondering about their commitment to a job or why—why do they keep getting bounced from position to position?" The basic technical skills are noted first by Alexis, but then the issue of commitment—staying at company for an extended period—becomes important. Too much movement between employers raises concerns about commitment to a job and potentially about overall competence—why isn't the applicant able to keep a job? Issues of commitment and competence were commonly prioritized evaluative criteria in the interviews.[32]

Commitment. Nonstandard, mismatched, and precarious employment experiences raise concerns for hiring professionals about ideal work norm violations, including commitment. Questions of commitment were highly salient in thinking about part-time work, which is often associated with enabling workers to balance competing demands of work and family life. When asked about how they think about part-time employment, fully forty of the fifty-three hiring professionals I interviewed discussed ways that part-time employment is often used to deal with various nonwork obligations. On this topic, Ashley, a recruiter at a medical device company, discussed what comes to mind for her when she thinks of part-time workers:

> I would say they probably have small children, would be my guess. That's pretty normal, I would say. Or maybe, again, maybe they're in school. Typically, if they're working part-time, I would think there's a—it's like a means to an end, maybe, if you're getting additional education, if you're taking care of your children, maybe, again, taking care of a sick family member, but you're still working as much as you're able, but you have other obligations that are keeping you from working full-time would be my assumption.

While hiring professionals most frequently cited parenthood as the reason that people work part-time, the other explanations mentioned by Ashley were quite common too. Central to the meanings employers attribute to part-time experience is that individuals have something other than work—children, caretaking responsibilities, or school—that is demanding their time and attention.

The underlying threat of competing obligations runs directly counter to the ideal worker norms of commitment and dedication. Hiring professionals like Evelyn, who works in the staffing industry at a company where there are expectations for working many hours, highlighted the link between part-time work and commitment concerns:

> [A part-time work history] would be a concern for me because we do work sixty hours a week. So part-time to sixty hours is a huge difference. You're basically now married to the company and you don't have a life. That to me, in that type of position, would be a concern. It's not forty hours it's twenty more hours on top of the forty and you're not getting overtime because you're salary. For me that would be a huge concern. If it was a regular forty-hour position, receptionist, payroll clerk, data entry, customer service, janitorial, anything like that, it would not be a concern.

Many companies and job types require workers to extend their hours beyond forty per week. Referred to as "overwork" in academic research, these increasing demands on workers' time—a common feature of high-paying jobs in the new economy—appear to raise concerns that someone with part-time experience would not have the space or time to put in these long hours.[33] Compounding this is the concern that a worker may then leave the company after realizing that the time commitment expectations are too high, resulting in significant costs in terms of training time for hiring managers and other company employees.

Hiring professionals also relayed similar commitment concerns about temping. For Cheryl, an HR generalist in the information sector, individuals with temping experience were people who lacked a commitment to work: "Temping, I think, affords you the luxury of not really being committed, and you're going to different jobs if you're temping every few weeks and you're getting a chance to explore and see which industries or which types of environment or which type of work you enjoy." Respondents regularly discussed the how temp work can signal that someone is not committed to a given career, to a company, or to work in general. While commitment concerns were occasionally mentioned regarding skills underutilization and long-term unemployment, they were far less prevalent for these two types of employment experiences.

Competence. While competence concerns were not highlighted as much by hiring professionals when discussing part-time work, these concerns were relevant for the other three types of employment experiences: skills under-utilization, unemployment, and temporary agency employment. As Alexis, an HR manager at a home remodeling company, explained, if a person's skills were being underutilized at a previous job, that might be a signal that she is not very competent: "The other thing that sometimes makes you wonder is: were they not good at what they were doing before? So they have the skill set but they weren't very good at it and found that they couldn't be successful in it. And there's really no way to tell that except just to ask the right questions on the phone screen and on the interview."

Skills underutilization can raise concerns that the applicant is really not cut out for the more demanding work that requires a higher level of skill and more technical competencies. Along with this set of concerns, hiring professionals often discussed the ways that skills underutilization may have resulted from a worker being fired and then unable to find a new job at her skill level, an indicator that she may lack competence. Thus, workers' competence—a key component of the ideal worker norm—can be questioned when an applicant has experience in a job below her skill level.

Judy, who works as a contract staffing consultant identifying talent for particular companies and then shepherding workers through the applica-tion process, relayed how she thinks about unemployment as a potential "red flag" indicating that candidates are not "any good": "So, for me, if they have been unemployed for two years, that's a little bit of a red flag. If they are recently coming out of something and are, you know, taking a little sabbatical and looking to go into something else, that's not so much a red flag. Some of my clients won't even look at anyone who's unemployed, the assumption being that, you know, if they were any good, they'd be employed." While not a core issue for Judy herself, unemployment can be a deal breaker for some of her clients. "Good" workers—competent workers—are employed workers. This presents a real challenge for individuals who are not employed but trying to find new jobs.

Competence and employability were also significant concerns for some hiring professionals when discussing temp work. Rachel, a director of human resources in the information sector, remarked,

If I see that someone has temp work on their resume and they were never hired or they have like multiple temp agencies, I pretty much discard them. I don't think that shows—like if none of those places wanted to hire them, it's not a good sign that they're someone who's employable. . . . I just think that they may not be a high-quality candidate. It just shows maybe not being able to follow through on something and be committed.

Rachel's remark clearly shows the competence concerns that can arise from a history of temporary agency employment. But she also shows the how competence and commitment concerns—the two wings of ideal worker norm expectations—go together. Overall, the interviews with hiring professionals point to the ways that ideal worker norm violations are meaningful signals sent by certain types of employment experiences.

FIT: CULTURAL AND OTHERWISE

Employers often talk about how they are looking for employees who are a good fit. In recent years, fit as an evaluative criterion has received significant attention from scholars interested in the hiring process. Employers often discuss how important it is for potential applicants to mesh well on interactional and cultural dimensions of the workplace.[34] Time and again in the interviews with hiring professionals, issues of fit came up organically in conversations about what they were looking for during the applicant screening process. When asked generally about what she looks for in applicants during the hiring process, Lauren, who works in talent acquisition at a health care company, noted that technical skills were not enough in and of themselves:

Yes, we want the best technical person, but if they don't demonstrate our core values, or if they don't have the soft skills to manage appropriately, or if it's a position where they have to interact with people and they don't have the soft skills to interact with people, it doesn't matter how technically perfect or technically ideal they are for the position. If they don't possess the soft skills as well, then they're not going to be a cultural fit for our organization.

Lauren links soft skills and cultural fit. Technical skills are not enough. Although defined and discussed in many different ways, fit really matters. But when hiring professionals were asked to make sense of nonstandard, mismatched, and precarious employment experiences, issues of fit were not as central to employers' concerns as the other three evaluative criteria:

technical skills, soft skills and personality, and compliance with ideal workers norms.

That being said, issues of fit did arise occasionally when discussing different types of employment experiences. In the context of discussing THA employment, Amber, an HR manager at a wealth management company, reported, "I would say 60 to 70 percent of the time most of the temp workers we get are not good cultural fits. Like, they are really just strange. Like, they—strange is a bad word. They don't interact well. Like, they have bad interpersonal skills." She then went on to relay the following story about a temp worker who liked to work with the lights off in order to illustrate what she meant:

> We had one temp, he shared an office with two other people, so there were three people in the office. He would come in and turn the lights off, because he didn't like the lights. And, so, they—the two other people that he shared an office with—they were just really creeped out. Like, why do you keep turning off the lights, and he got really upset when they asked him. He's, like, I don't like lights. And he wanted the door closed all the time, and so no one knew if they were, like, in that office. Like, I would walk in just to check on them to make sure they were okay. Like, it was just really odd.

Amber's discussion of her experience with temp workers highlights that hiring managers may also have concerns about the ways that someone with temp agency experience would fit in with the current employees and culture of the organization. However, as a dimension of evaluation for workers with nonstandard, mismatched, and precarious employment histories, fit was less salient overall than the other common dimensions of evaluation discussed earlier in this chapter.

———

Hiring agents extract powerful meanings from employment histories. Yet the meanings they attribute to different employment experiences are highly varied. Concerns about technical skills map most clearly onto applicants with long-term unemployment and skills underutilization experiences. Soft skill and personality concerns were common when evaluating workers with temporary agency employment and long-term unemployment experiences. In terms of violating ideal worker norms, part-time work experience was closely linked to concerns about commitment, whereas competence concerns loomed large for skills underutilization, long-term unemployment, and temp agency employment histories. Together, these findings indicate that there are often—although not universally—negative meanings attributed to each type of employment experience under investigation, meanings that may lead hiring agents to penalize workers at the hiring interface compared to workers who maintained full-time, standard employment.

Inducing Uncertainty and Ambiguity: The "Why" Question

Hiring professionals clearly attribute meanings to histories of part-time work, temporary agency employment, skills underutilization, and long-term unemployment. And these meanings map onto key evaluative criteria that scholars have shown matter in the hiring process—technical skills, soft skills and personality, compliance with ideal worker norms, and, to a lesser extent, fit. While on the one hand hiring professionals were actively imputing meaning to nonstandard, mismatched, and precarious employment histories, those work histories also induced significant uncertainty about the applicant.

In the interviews, hiring professionals were asked about each of the four types of nonstandard, mismatched, and precarious employment experiences focused on in this book. Separately for each type of employment they were asked to describe what comes to mind when they hear that someone is working in one of the different employment arrangements (e.g., part-time) and how that type of position might influence their evaluation of a candidate. Across interviews and types of employment experiences, hiring professionals commonly expressed sentiments along the lines of "I always want to know why."

When discussing unemployment, more than forty of the hiring professional I spoke with indicated that they would want to know why an applicant was unemployed. For other types of employment histories, this questioning of the underlying reason for the employment experience was also common. A similar number of interviewees expressed uncertainty of this kind when discussing skills underutilization, and in more than half of the interviews, this type of uncertainty was expressed when discussing both part-time work and temporary agency employment.

When asked about how she thinks about workers experiencing unemployment, Angela, who worked in manufacturing before recently becoming unemployed herself, indicated a desire to figure out whether the reasons for someone's unemployment were cause for concern: "Well I obviously want to know the reason. There's a lot of legitimate reasons. There's reasons that could be cause for concern and then there are reasons that are concerning." In a similar vein, Jane, who works in IT consulting, responded, "Again, I think you just always try to get at the why, because also, you know, again, there's these personal situations that come up that people have to deal with them, and some things can go on for a long time, like a family illness or child care or, you know, a financial situation or various things, a divorce, but sometimes, you know, long periods of unemployment or choppy backgrounds can indicate some level of personality disorder, right?" Here, we see the uncertainty and lack of clarity that come with a history of unemployment, particularly long-term unemployment. Is the reason legitimate or not? And we see Jane beginning to fill in the story for a long employment gap, even jumping to the possibility of a personality disorder.

Similar tropes emerged for skills underutilization. As voiced by Charles, who has hiring experience in the staffing and insurance sectors,

> It's got to be to ask why? Why is it below? There are so many things it could be. Is it, again, did they lose a position somewhere and they wanted to continue to work? Did they lose a position and they needed to continue to work? Are they aware of what they're capable of doing? . . . A good recruiter should not just disqualify people because they think, why are you working washing cars when you have a master's degree? It's find out the why and then decide from there.

In Charles's discussion we see uncertainty: "There are so many things it could be." We also see his clear statement that skills underutilization alone should not disqualify someone. But in order for skills underutilization not to disqualify someone, hiring professionals would have to dig deeper. They would likely need to actually reach out to candidates and actually speak with them. Given the high volume of applications that hiring professionals receive and their limited time, it is not clear how often these types of conversations occur.

When discussing workers with part-time experience, Julia, who works in the nonprofit sector, made the following remarks: "Why are you working a part-time job? And again, it's because, do you like part-time? Is there something else you're doing that maybe you're doing on the side you have another part-time job?" There is uncertainty here. As might be expected, there are questions about what else the candidates are doing, what other obligations they have in their lives. Hiring professionals discussed myriad reasons that a candidate might be working part-time: often caretaking, but also being in school or being unable to find a full-time position. More information is needed to reconcile this uncertainty—information that is often not readily available.

Thinking about temporary agency employment, Julie, who works at a media company, responded, "Well, I would wonder why they were working for a temp agency. Is it for the flexibility or is it because they can't find a job? . . . Or is that what they're looking for? And that's what I would ask them on the first call, the phone interview. I would wonder—I would ask them why they were working at the temp agency rather than getting a regular job." We see the bifurcation of the understanding of temporary agency employment—it could be to increase flexibility or a sign of some significant personal flaw—in Julie's statement.

Beyond the specific meanings attributed to each type of employment experience, significant uncertainty is induced in hiring professionals when they see a history of nonstandard, mismatched, or precarious work. This has to do, in no small part, with the highly heterogeneous reasons that workers end up in these various types of employment situations. The question then becomes, how do hiring professionals reconcile their uncertainty?

Hiring professionals largely turn to individualized—rather than structural—explanations to deal with the uncertainty and ambiguity that arises when evaluating candidates with complicated work histories. Indeed, they shift much of the onus for reconciling the questions they have onto the job seekers. They want job applicants to provide a clear narrative explaining their employment history. Yet, applicants are rarely afforded that opportunity. The consequences are twofold. In some cases hiring professionals gravitate to the often—although not universally—negative meanings associated with different types of employment histories—poor "soft skills," limited commitment, and atrophied technical skills—to evaluate workers. In other cases, I will show that employers turn to group-based stereotypes and beliefs—such as those grounded in race and gender—when they do not have clear narratives from the workers. Research shows that uncertainty and ambiguity can result in the increased use of stereotypes and various biases are more likely to emerge under these conditions,[35] which we will discuss later on. In these instances, the ways that nonstandard, mismatched, and precarious employment histories affect workers diverge across social groups.

Individualizing Employment Experiences

One way that hiring professionals could reconcile the uncertainty and ambiguity that comes from histories of nonstandard, mismatched, and precarious employment experiences would be to place the individual workers in their broader social and economic context. The US economy has changed substantially over recent decades. These changes are largely structural in nature: individual workers have little say in or control over how these shifts emerged or the consequences of these changes for their daily lives. Situating individual job applicants with a history of temporary agency employment, for example, in the trajectory of the US economy could reduce the uncertainty in hiring professionals' eyes with regard to individual job applicants, limiting the impact this type of employment history would have on workers' hiring outcomes.

Yet the broader social and economic context was not particularly salient in my discussions with hiring professionals about how they evaluated applicants. When anything about the context that applicants are embedded in was discussed, it was often about smaller-scale contextual forces, such as having a family, getting an education, or caring for a relative or small child. And when economic forces were discussed—and they certainly were—the consideration was generally limited to business cycle issues, the Great Recession, and the unemployment rate. The changing nature of the occupational and industrial structure and the polarizing of job quality received limited attention in the interviews.

This is not to say that hiring professionals are ignorant of the broader economic context that both they and workers are experiencing. For example, discussing how she thinks about unemployment, Amy, who works in the staffing industry in Boston—where the unemployment rate was very low when she was interviewed—reported a clear awareness of the larger market dynamics: "When the market's different I think my answer would be different, but right now the market is so strong in Boston, I mean, you have to wonder, you have to ask the tough questions like what have you been doing?" For Amy, when the unemployment rate is high, it is less concerning for an applicant to be unemployed—presumably because there would be a structural reason for the job applicant not to have a job. When the unemployment rate is low, however, hiring agents indicated deeper concerns about workers experiencing unemployment. Indeed, Amy is using the broader economic structure here to make someone's unemployment experience an individual problem. The economic context is favorable for workers—unemployment is low—and therefore the problem is the individual. Yet this view—which was how employers tended to talk about the economic context—ignores all of the other changes to the economy that are beyond the metric of the unemployment rate.

In a limited number of interviews, hiring agents did broach broader economic changes, such as outsourcing and technological change. These were occasionally put forward as reasons that workers may experience employment gaps, exhibit skills underutilization, or need to take part-time or temporary positions. Alexis, an HR manager at a home remodeling company, discussed the challenges that arise with technological change: "So look at like someone who worked forty years for Illinois Bell or what became AT&T as an operator and now they need to come back into the working world—there is no job like that anymore. . . . It's not here, for one thing, it's been kind of technologically—it's gone and anything that is close to that has been outsourced for the most part so they don't have anywhere to go." Andrea, who works in talent acquisition in the retail sector, also discussed a wider economic change, outsourcing in this case: "I'd say that I see that there's a gap in your resume and can you describe why you had that gap and sometimes they'll say they outsourced their job to a different country and they didn't want to move, or they outsourced their job to a different state so they were laid off." Here, we see two instances where broader structural forces—technological change and outsourcing—are noted by hiring professionals as ways that they and the workers they interview make sense of individual employment experiences. Additionally, in a few cases, when discussing temp work, hiring professionals involved with the technology sector mentioned that short-term contract jobs would not be a significant concern given their prevalence among technology workers.

Context was not entirely absent from the interviews, but contextualized narratives were not the norm. In general, hiring professionals tended to individualize particular types of employment trajectories and hold workers accountable for their work experiences. Carol, who works in HR in the real estate sector, provides an example of how individual workers are held accountable for their trajectory through the labor market:

> So we look how close you are to the position [geographically], and then we look at your job history. Because we're very corporate America, we look for people that are going to come in and be able to grow with us, stay long term. We want people that are going to make a career and be here for ten or twenty years. So we very, very are seriously take how long you stayed at your last position. Anyone that held a position for six months to a year, something like that, we just can't even consider them. If I turned in their resume and said I interviewed them to our COO, he would throw it back at me and say, rescind the offer letter. We're not taking them.

In Carol's mind, short-term employment and moving from job to job are not connected to larger economic patterns but are an indication of workers' underlying quality. Across interviews there was an emphasis on workers' having put in time at previous jobs and not being "job hoppers." Indeed, there was large-scale agreement across interviewees that short stints with an employer were a negative signal. Yet individual workers—as opposed to their employers or the broader economic structure—were deemed responsible for this type of employment trajectory. Certainly, hiring agents are often in a challenging position when it comes to making these decisions. Besides time and information being scarce, they are under pressure to hire the best workers. They are accountable for their decisions about which workers they call back. And they want their supervisors and organizations to look favorably on the applicants they advance through the hiring process. Hiring agents thus face a set of their own constraints that help explain why they may gravitate away from structural explanations for the economic challenges faced by individual workers.

In the eyes of hiring professionals, individual workers—not the changing nature of the economy—are responsible for their career trajectory and ensuring that they have the right set of job experiences. These individualized explanations from hiring professionals resonate with existing scholarship on workers' own experiences in the new economy. One recent study, for example, shows that the structure of the job search process in the United States leads workers to blame themselves, rather than the larger economic context, for their inability to find a job.[36] Another study finds that workers express high levels of dedication and commitment to their employers but expect and demand little in return. And when things go wrong at work, they channel those negative feelings in multiple directions, but not toward their employers or the broader economic system.[37] An additional set of findings about the knowledge economy indicates that the current framework within which workers conceptualize themselves is to treat the "self as business," rather than an earlier model of seeing the "self as property."[38] In this conceptualization, workers enter into a business-to-business relationship when they are hired. Rather than under earlier models, where workers would exchange their freedom (staying at company) for security (a "good" job), now workers are free to be mobile. While there are certainly benefits to this type of freedom and mobility, it comes with reduced security and stability.[39] In turn, there is more onus on individual workers for their economic well-being.

Together, the findings from these studies paint a picture of a largely individualized experience of the new economy, with workers generally taking on some of the freedoms and the risks that come with the changing economic landscape. The interviews that I conducted with hiring professionals document that workers are not alone. Hiring professionals also maintain these individualized understandings of careers and employment trajectories. In part, this may be because hiring professionals are also workers. Being a frontline human resources assistant or a talent acquisition specialist does not insulate someone from the challenges of the new economy.

The Need for a Narrative

Without drawing on the broader structural context—and focusing instead on individual-level explanations—how do employers address the uncertainty and ambiguity that come with nonstandard, mismatched, and precarious employment experience? Decision making under conditions of uncertainty and ambiguity has been a core theme in sociological and psychological research writ large, beyond studies of work and employment.[40] Much of the focus in this literature has been on the cognitive shortcuts or heuristics that individuals use to make decisions in these situations. As will be discussed later on, I find that one shortcut that hiring professionals turn to when evaluating different employment histories is to utilize stereotypes about race and gender in their decision-making processes. Employers also discuss attempting to reduce uncertainty by obtaining a story, a narrative, from job applicants that could alleviate their concerns about why they were unemployed, temping, working part-time, or in a job below their skill level.

Hiring agents' need for a narrative becomes clear in the following exchanges. When asked about how she thought about skills underutilization, Rose, who is involved with hiring at a large health care organization, said, "I have candidates where I wondered oh, well they have their master's and they have their PhD, why are they, you know—why are they applying for a housekeeping position? I'm like what's the story there? There must be a story." Christian, who has experience hiring in multiple sectors of the economy and was unemployed himself at the time of the interview, said the following about unemployment: "You'd want to hear their story on why they left and why things got so bad." Hiring agents want a story.

It is quite challenging, however, for workers to tell their story when the job application process requires them to submit their application through formal mechanisms, such as online portals or application websites. Initial job applications are often short—including not much more than a resume and cover letter—with limited room for explanation. Thus, weaving a narrative within one's application materials can be difficult.

Without clear narratives, hiring professionals likely gravitate toward the often-negative meanings attributed to different employment experiences.

Consider, for example, how Rachel, a human resources director at an advertising company, automatically interprets long periods of unemployment that are "not explained" as a reason not to hire someone:

> They have to explain it [unemployment]. They have to explain it in their cover letter so I see it right away. When I'm scrolling through on our ATS [Applicant Tracking System], it goes cover letter, resume, which I like. So I kind of get like a—I don't usually read their cover letter very well. I know some people do. I just like skim it really quick for anything and then I go to their resume. If someone has like a long period of unemployment and it's not explained, I would just discard them. If they have a long period of unemployment and it's explained, then I will talk to them and make sure.

Categorical exclusion can be the result of not providing a compelling narrative to hiring professionals early on in the process. Yet applicants may not want to discuss, or may not know to discuss, their employment experience in their cover letter. And as Rachel notes, she doesn't read cover letters very closely. So even if there is an explanation there, it might be missed during a quick scan through someone's application. Remember, many hiring professionals spend three to five seconds on a first pass through an application.

That being said, the interviews with hiring professionals also suggest that telling one's story and weaving a narrative can lead to hiring success. Jennifer, a call center operations supervisor, explained that an explanatory narrative had a major impact on her evaluation of one job applicant in particular. Importantly, the narrative that allayed Jennifer's concerns about this job applicant was gleaned through and actual conversation rather than the application materials:

> Yes. I know recently we hired somebody who I think was just like a cashier or a receptionist or something at like a car wash or something. But prior to that, that person had so much experience in call center work that it was kind of odd. She did that for about two years. I believe I remember asking her specifically like, oh, what made you move to this type of customer service? Her answer was that, you know, she was tired of the phone calls and customer complaints. And the position she had before was a little bit more IT than customer service. So that was kind of draining on her. So primarily her complaint—she said she loved working with customers. She said she really loved it. She enjoyed the interaction. But the IT part was kind of draining and she just didn't like that. She went into detail, but

long story short, I guess she moved into this position still dealing with customers, face-to-face customers, and she's been happy doing it, but she needed to go back to call center work. . . . She wanted to I guess go back into the office. But I went off of basically just the attitude towards it. She really seemed very excited about customer service. She knew all the information before. I think she had a lot of experience in this same type of field that we're in with consumer credit cards and that type of work. So it worked well.

Providing clear explanations for why one moved into a position of lower skill may play an important role in mitigating the concerns employers can have about skills underutilization or other types of nonstandard, mismatched, and precarious employment histories. Of course, there are also questions about the generalizability of these positive effects when applicants tell their stories. Some of the hiring professional I spoke with were highly skeptical of workers' narratives and explanations, doubting that applicants would present the truth behind their employment trajectories. And some recent evidence indicates that narratives for employment gaps related to caring for family actually result in applicants receiving severe negative treatment from future employers.[41]

Employers say that they want a narrative. They want to make sense of why someone had a history of nonstandard, mismatched, or precarious employment.[42] Yet it is difficult for workers to communicate that narrative on an application. And even if they do, hiring professionals may not see it or may question the validity of the claims that the applicant is making.

———

The interviews clearly demonstrate that part-time work, temporary agency employment, skills underutilization, and long-term unemployment are meaningful signals to hiring agents. Yet there is a fair amount of complexity in how these employment histories map onto key evaluative axes, such as ideal worker norm compliance and soft skill concerns. Certain types of employment experiences map onto certain evaluative axes more than others, and in some cases—particularly when compared to unemployment—nonstandard and mismatched employment can send positive signals about a worker.

A common theme arising throughout the interviews was the uncertainty and ambiguity about job applicants that is primed for hiring professionals when they have a history of nonstandard, mismatched, or precarious employment. While some hiring professionals have a sense that the broader economic structure influences individual workers' employment histories, they generally downplay the importance of these broader forces and ultimately place the responsibility for a seamless, continuous, full-time, standard employment trajectory at the worker's skill level on the worker himself or herself.

Hiring professionals then reconcile the uncertainty of different employment histories, in part, by indicating that workers need to tell their story. Job applicants need a narrative that can explain why their employment experiences do not comply with the "good" job conception of a career trajectory. In order to provide a compelling narrative, however, workers need a forum for doing so. They generally need to be called back for an interview or phone screen and to actually speak with the hiring manager or recruiter. In the next chapter, we turn to the field-experimental evidence to see whether workers are given this opportunity to provide a story for their employment experience or whether they are screened out before that is possible.

4

Inclusion and Exclusion in Hiring

THE VARIED EFFECTS OF NONSTANDARD, MISMATCHED, AND PRECARIOUS EMPLOYMENT HISTORIES

Hiring professionals extract meanings from job applicants' histories of non-standard, mismatched, and precarious employment. At the same time, these types of employment experiences induce uncertainty in hiring professionals. Recruiters and hiring manager want to know why: they want a narrative or story from a worker that explains his or her particular work experience and allays any concerns that a "deviant" employment trajectory is actually informative about a worker's atrophying skills, having soft skills or personality issues, or noncompliance with ideal worker norms.

A key moment in the hiring process when workers have the opportunity to provide hiring professionals with this narrative is during an initial interview or phone screen. But this raises questions: Do workers with histories of nonstandard, mismatched, or precarious employment actually get called back for jobs? Do they ever get the opportunity to tell their stories? The following pages tackle these questions. Evidence from the field experiment—where fictitious job applications that randomly varied workers' employment experiences were sent to apply for real job openings—indicates that the answer is complex. Some types of employment histories result in far fewer callbacks from employers, cutting workers off from the opportunity to tell their story. Other types of employment histories appear to have limited effects, opening the door for workers to provide their narrative, to make their case.

This chapter delves into the effects of each type of employment experience—part-time work, temporary agency employment, skills under-utilization, and long-term unemployment—compared to full-time, standard employment on applicants' likelihood of receiving a callback for a job. As we will see, the effects are largely contingent. First, they are contingent on the type of employment history. Each type of employment experience—part-time work versus temporary agency employment, for instance—does not result in the same treatment from hiring professionals. Second, the consequences of a particular employment experience are contingent on the race and gender of the worker. Indeed, it is difficult to isolate the effect of a given employment history from the way it is refracted through a worker's social group membership. While this chapter highlights how the different types of employment experiences produce different likelihoods of being called back—the first type of contingency—the following chapters will explicitly probe how race and gender add additional contingencies into this complex picture.

Who Gets a Callback? Evidence from the Field Experiment

The field-experimental data provide a distinct and direct lens onto the ways that histories of nonstandard, mismatched, and precarious employment impact workers' employment opportunities: their ability to get a callback for a job. Whereas the interviews I conducted with hiring professionals shed light on how these key gatekeepers think and talk about different employment histories, the field experiment provides evidence about the actual behaviors of recruiters, hiring managers, and human resources profession-als. Here we get to open up the black box of hiring and see the ways the job applicants are actually treated.

In this chapter I utilize the field-experimental data to probe the effects of each type of employment history on the likelihood that a job applicant receives a callback for an opening. I present the findings separately by race and gender to explore the effects within each demographic group in the experiment: white (or neutral) men, black men, white (or neutral) women, and black women.[1] I have included as Figures 4.1 to 4.5 examples of the resumes used in the field experiment with the five different employment histories: full-time and standard, part-time, temporary agency employment,

Katherine Murphy

1254 East Canton St., #12B
Boston, MA 02111
617-858-5245
katherine.murphy.271@gmail.com

PROFESSIONAL EXPERIENCE

Anonymous Technology – Boston, MA   March 2012 – Present
Office Manager & Executive Assistant
- Coordinate all office management tasks, which includes working with computer and phone system vendors, maintaining necessary levels of office supplies, and managing all office filing systems.
- Answer and screen incoming phone calls, coordinate travel arrangements, and draft memos and letters for executive staff.
- Plan and coordinate all aspects of meetings for executive staff and key stakeholders.

Anonymous LLP – Boston, MA   July 2007 – Feb. 2012
Administrative Assistant
- Provided administrative support to a partner at this leading Boston law firm.
- Managed partner's schedule and answered all incoming calls from both internal and external sources.
- Wrote and revised documents, memoranda, correspondence, time entries, and office forms.
- Prepared monthly client bills and processed all reimbursement forms.

Anonymous Properties – Boston, MA   July 2005 – June 2007
Office Assistant
- Maintained schedule for executive staff, answered and placed telephone calls, and wrote memos and other correspondence.
- Set up and maintained paper and electronic filing systems for records and correspondence.
- Carried out special projects on an as-needed basis.

EDUCATION & TRAINING

Midwestern University – City, State   June 2005
B.A. in English

Central High School – City, State   June 2001

LEADERSHIP EXPERIENCE

Midwestern University Student Government   Sept. 2003 – May 2005
Treasurer
- Served as member and then Treasurer of student government during junior and senior year.
- Streamlined financial reporting system and maintained budget for different projects.

COMPUTER SKILLS

- High level of proficiency with Microsoft Word, Excel, Access, PowerPoint, and Outlook.

FIGURE 4.1. Full-Time, Standard Resume Example

skills underutilization, and long-term unemployment. The example resumes are for a white/neutral female applicant applying to an administrative assistant job in Boston. While the example resumes are nearly identical to the resumes used in the field experiment, slight alterations were made. Specifically, I anonymized the company names used in workers' employment histories, the schools that the workers attended, and the club for their leadership

Katherine Murphy

1254 East Canton St., #12B
Boston, MA 02111
617-858-5245
katherine.murphy.271@gmail.com

PROFESSIONAL EXPERIENCE

Anonymous Technology – Boston, MA   March 2012 – Present
Office Manager & Executive Assistant (Part-Time)
- Coordinate all office management tasks, which includes working with computer and phone system vendors, maintaining necessary levels of office supplies, and managing all office filing systems.
- Answer and screen incoming phone calls, coordinate travel arrangements, and draft memos and letters for executive staff.
- Plan and coordinate all aspects of meetings for executive staff and key stakeholders.

Anonymous LLP – Boston, MA   July 2007 – Feb. 2012
Administrative Assistant
- Provided administrative support to a partner at this leading Boston law firm.
- Managed partner's schedule and answered all incoming calls from both internal and external sources.
- Wrote and revised documents, memoranda, correspondence, time entries, and office forms.
- Prepared monthly client bills and processed all reimbursement forms.

Anonymous Properties – Boston, MA   July 2005 – June 2007
Office Assistant
- Maintained schedule for executive staff, answered and placed telephone calls, and wrote memos and other correspondence.
- Set up and maintained paper and electronic filing systems for records and correspondence.
- Carried out special projects on an as-needed basis.

EDUCATION & TRAINING

Midwestern University – City, State   June 2005
B.A. in English

Central High School – City, State   June 2001

LEADERSHIP EXPERIENCE

Midwestern University Student Government   Sept. 2003 – May 2005
Treasurer
- Served as member and then Treasurer of student government during junior and senior year.
- Streamlined financial reporting system and maintained budget for different projects.

COMPUTER SKILLS

- High level of proficiency with Microsoft Word, Excel, Access, PowerPoint, and Outlook.

FIGURE 4.2. Part-Time Resume Example

experience. I also slightly altered the address, phone, and email information. Otherwise, the resume examples represent what was actually sent to apply for job openings. Hopefully, these resumes make the field experiment feel more concrete. The resumes—while fictitious—were perceived to be real. They were sent to apply for actual job openings and resulted in engagement from actual employers. As can be seen, the differences between the resumes

Katherine Murphy

1254 East Canton St., #12B
Boston, MA 02111
617-858-5245
katherine.murphy.271@gmail.com

PROFESSIONAL EXPERIENCE

Anonymous Temp Agency – Boston, MA   March 2012 – Present
Temporary Administrative Assistant
Serve as a temporary Administrative Assistant through Anonymous Temp Agency. Assignments at different
companies have included:

- Answering incoming phone calls, scheduling travel arrangements, and writing letters and other
  correspondence for executive staff.
- Coordinating conferences, meetings, and retreats for staff, managers, and clients.
- Developing and improving office coordination systems, such as ordering supplies and updating
  administrative technology.

Anonymous LLP – Boston, MA   July 2007 – Feb. 2012
Administrative Assistant

- Provided administrative support to a partner at this leading Boston law firm.
- Managed partner's schedule and answered all incoming calls from both internal and external sources.
- Wrote and revised documents, memoranda, correspondence, time entries, and office forms.
- Prepared monthly client bills and processed all reimbursement forms.

Anonymous Properties – Boston, MA   July 2005 – June 2007
Office Assistant

- Maintained schedule for executive staff, answered and placed telephone calls, and wrote memos and
  other correspondence.
- Set up and maintained paper and electronic filing systems for records and correspondence.
- Carried out special projects on an as-needed basis.

EDUCATION & TRAINING

Midwestern University – City, State   June 2005
B.A. in English

Central High School – City, State   June 2001

LEADERSHIP EXPERIENCE

Midwestern University Student Government   Sept. 2003 – May 2005
Treasurer

- Served as member and then Treasurer of student government during junior and senior year.
- Streamlined financial reporting system and maintained budget for different projects.

COMPUTER SKILLS

- High level of proficiency with Microsoft Word, Excel, Access, PowerPoint, and Outlook.

FIGURE 4.3. Temporary Agency Employment Resume Example

are very small in an attempt to signal the particular type of employment
experience while holding all else constant.

An important feature to keep in mind about the field experiment is that
workers did not provide any information to the employer in their application
materials about why they had experience in a nonstandard, mismatched,
or precarious position. We know from the previous chapter that hiring

Katherine Murphy

1254 East Canton St., #12B
Boston, MA 02111
617-858-5245
katherine.murphy.271@gmail.com

PROFESSIONAL EXPERIENCE

Anonymous Retailer – Boston, MA   March 2012 – Present
Sales Representative
- Provide high-quality customer assistance in merchandise selection and other service areas.
- Maintain high level of cleanliness and a welcoming environment on the retail floor.
- Build and strengthen relationships with repeat customers.

Anonymous LLP – Boston, MA   July 2007 – Feb. 2012
Administrative Assistant
- Provided administrative support to a partner at this leading Boston law firm.
- Managed partner's schedule and answered all incoming calls from both internal and external sources.
- Wrote and revised documents, memoranda, correspondence, time entries, and office forms.
- Prepared monthly client bills and processed all reimbursement forms.

Anonymous Properties – Boston, MA   July 2005 – June 2007
Office Assistant
- Maintained schedule for executive staff, answered and placed telephone calls, and wrote memos and other correspondence.
- Set up and maintained paper and electronic filing systems for records and correspondence.
- Carried out special projects on an as-needed basis.

EDUCATION & TRAINING

Midwestern University – City, State   June 2005
B.A. in English

Central High School – City, State   June 2001

LEADERSHIP EXPERIENCE

Midwestern University Student Government   Sept. 2003 – May 2005
Treasurer
- Served as member and then Treasurer of student government during junior and senior year.
- Streamlined financial reporting system and maintained budget for different projects.

COMPUTER SKILLS

- High level of proficiency with Microsoft Word, Excel, Access, PowerPoint, and Outlook.

FIGURE 4.4. Skills Underutilization Resume Example

professionals' narratives and expectations for workers are in many ways at odds with the changing economic landscape; this chapter probes whether that disjuncture translates into how hiring agents behave toward job applicants. Without an explanation, how do employers treat applicants whose employment histories deviate from common conceptions of a "good" job? Are they afforded an opportunity to tell their story? Or are they screened out before being able to share their narrative?

Katherine Murphy

1254 East Canton St., #12B
Boston, MA 02111
617-858-5245
katherine.murphy.271@gmail.com

PROFESSIONAL EXPERIENCE

Anonymous LLP – Boston, MA   July 2007 – Feb. 2012
Administrative Assistant
  - Provided administrative support to a partner at this leading Boston law firm.
  - Managed partner's schedule and answered all incoming calls from both internal and external sources.
  - Wrote and revised documents, memoranda, correspondence, time entries, and office forms.
  - Prepared monthly client bills and processed all reimbursement forms.

Anonymous Properties – Boston, MA   July 2005 – June 2007
Office Assistant
  - Maintained schedule for executive staff, answered and placed telephone calls, and wrote memos and other correspondence.
  - Set up and maintained paper and electronic filing systems for records and correspondence.
  - Carried out special projects on an as-needed basis.

Anonymous Bank – Boston, MA   Summer 2004
Summer Intern
  - Assisted with meeting and conference planning, scheduling, and answering phones.
  - Drafted memos and correspondence and participated in special projects on an as-needed basis.

EDUCATION & TRAINING

Midwestern University – City, State   June 2005
B.A. in English

Central High School – City, State   June 2001

LEADERSHIP EXPERIENCE

Midwestern University Student Government   Sept. 2003 – May 2005
Treasurer
  - Served as member and then Treasurer of student government during junior and senior year.
  - Streamlined financial reporting system and maintained budget for different projects.

COMPUTER SKILLS

  - High level of proficiency with Microsoft Word, Excel, Access, PowerPoint, and Outlook.

FIGURE 4.5. Unemployment Resume Example

FAR TO FALL: THE EFFECTS FOR WHITE MEN

White men face severe penalties when their employment history deviates from a seamless trajectory through "good" jobs. Figure 4.6 presents the callback rates for the white (or neutral) male job applicants. As might be expected, the highest callback rate is for white men with a full-time, standard employment trajectory at their skill level: 10.4 percent. When white

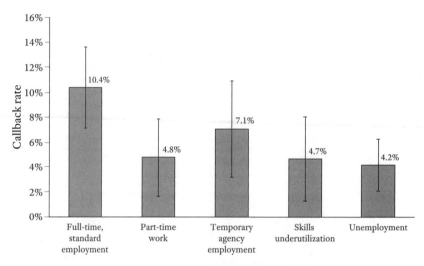

FIGURE 4.6. Callback Rates for White/Neutral Men, by Employment Status
Source: Field-experimental data.
Note: 95 percent confidence intervals presented.

men have part-time work experience, their callback rate is cut by more than half, falling to 4.8 percent. Similarly, skills underutilization results in strong negative effects, reducing the callback rate for white men to 4.7 percent. And white men with twelve months of unemployment are called back only 4.2 percent of the time, a finding that is consistent with some existing research in this area.[2] The only exception to these strong, negative, statistically significant effects is temporary agency employment.[3] While there is a dip in the callback rate for white men with temporary agency histories—to 7.1 percent—the difference compared to full-time, standard employment is not statistically significant. Additionally, there are no statistically significant differences between the callback rates for part-time work, temporary work, skills underutilization, and unemployment.[4] Essentially, part-time work and skills underutilization are as scarring for white men as a year of unemployment.

The picture that emerges for white men when it comes to nonstandard, mismatched, and precarious employment is one involving serious penalties. Yet extant research provides ample support for the idea that white men have high status, high power, and high privilege in the labor market as well as other institutional domains. On average, white men have higher wages and work in more prestigious and powerful jobs.[5] They are overrepresented as CEOs, on corporate boards, and in high-powered political offices.[6] Indeed, the very structure of the ideal worker norm is predicated on a conception of a white man with a wife at home to support his breadwinning status.[7]

How then do we make sense of the fact that white men face such severe penalties for employment trajectories that deviate from seamless movement through "good" jobs? High-status social positions can also be precarious social positions.[8] For example, studies show that men who deviate from a particular type of normative masculinity face significant stigmatization and exclusion.[9] Indeed, men are required to provide continual proof of their masculinity and manhood through social interactions and exhibiting particular types of behaviors.[10] In turn, when masculinity—but not femininity—is threatened, men tend to overcompensate and can even have physically aggressive thoughts activated.[11] Related findings emerge in scholarship on the intersection of gender and sexuality. A recent survey experiment asked participants to evaluate the sexuality of individuals in a vignette. The researchers found that men with a set of heterosexual sexual experiences who then engage in one same-sex sexual encounter are much more likely to have their heterosexuality questioned than are women who have the same sexual trajectory.[12]

Masculinity is precarious in nature. Against this backdrop, it becomes more understandable why white men face significant penalties for employment experiences that do not align with conceptions of the ideal worker and a career path through so-called "good" jobs. Status, power, and other benefits accrue to white men so long as they comply with normative expectations of a seamless, continuous trajectory through jobs that are full-time, standard, and at their skill levels. They need to demonstrate that they are the breadwinners, that is what is expected of them. Deviations from these expectations produce significant stigma and exclusion. When white men have histories of part-time work, skills underutilization, or long-term unemployment, they rarely get callbacks.

PERSISTENT DISCRIMINATION: THE EFFECTS FOR AFRICAN AMERICAN MEN

While white men face significant penalties for nonstandard, mismatched, and precarious employment histories; they also reap significant benefits in many aspects of the world of work. One such benefit is that they are not the targets of racial discrimination, a challenge for others in hiring that has been well documented in the social science literature.[13] A relatively low callback rate is expected even for black men who have maintained seamless, continuous

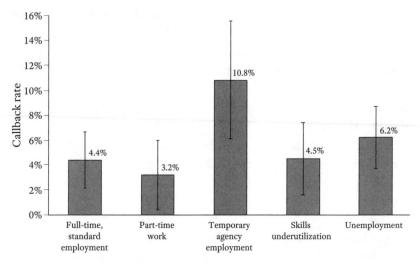

FIGURE 4.7. Callback Rates for African American Men, by Employment Status
Source: Field-experimental data.
Note: 95 percent confidence intervals presented.

employment in full-time, standard positions at their skill level. Indeed, this is precisely what we see in Figure 4.7, with black men in the full-time, standard condition receiving callbacks only 4.4 percent of the time. And nearly across the board, African American men receive low callback rates: 3.2 percent for part-time work, 4.5 percent for skills underutilization, and 6.2 percent for long-term unemployment.[14] Remember that for white men with full-time, standard employment histories, the callback rate was 10.4 percent.

For black men, a story emerges of deep racial discrimination and exclusion. Beyond those pervasive penalties, nonstandard, mismatched, and precarious employment histories have little additional negative consequence. One glaring exception exists: in the case of temporary agency employment, black men receive higher callback rates than they do in the full-time, standard employment condition. This finding will receive significant attention later on and be the central point of inquiry in Chapter 7, which aims to understand why this pattern may emerge.

CONCENTRATED DISADVANTAGE: THE EFFECTS FOR WHITE WOMEN

Gendered processes of exclusion loom large in the workplace and labor market. Women face myriad barriers to entry and upward mobility within occupations and organizations.[15] At the hiring interface, recent scholarship

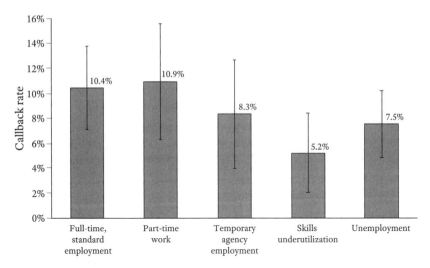

FIGURE 4.8. Callback Rates for White/Neutral Women, by Employment Status
Source: Field-experimental data.
Note: 95 percent confidence intervals presented.

has painted a complex picture of bias and discrimination. Gender interacts and intersects with other characteristics—such as parental status and social class background—to shape processes of inclusion and exclusion, leaving us with key questions about how nonstandard, mismatched, and precarious employment experiences will operate for women.[16]

The callback rates from the field experiment for white (or neutral) women are presented in Figure 4.8. Here, we see a callback rate for white women with full-time, standard employment of 10.4 percent. Interestingly, there is no penalty for white women with part-time work and small drop-offs in callback rates for temporary agency employment and long-term unemployment. It is important to note that none of these differences are statistically significant. The only type of employment history that results in statistically significant penalties for white women is skills underutilization, with a callback rate of 5.2 percent. When white women move into jobs below their skills level, they receive callbacks at only half the rate that they do when they have maintained full-time, standard employment at their skill level.

For white women, the field-experimental results indicate relatively limited consequences of employment experiences that diverge from normative conceptions of "good" jobs. However, the interpretation of this finding is important and a bit complicated, and Chapter 5 directly tackles the intriguing finding that the callback rate for white women with part-time employment experiences is nearly identical to that of white women with full-time, standard employment histories. We will see that what may seem like a benefit—no penalty for part-time work experience—appears to actually be rooted in deep-seated cultural beliefs about gender that effectively block women's opportunities for advancement in many other aspects of the labor market.

DISPERSED DISCRIMINATION: THE EFFECTS FOR AFRICAN AMERICAN WOMEN

Finally, we turn to the ways the employers treat African American women with histories of nonstandard, mismatched, and precarious employment. In Figure 4.9, we see that African American women receive callbacks 7.0 percent of the time when they have consistently been working in full-time, standard positions at their skill level. Interestingly, there is no statistically significant variation across the different types of employment histories for African American women. But the callback rates in all of the other conditions are lower than they are in the full-time, standard condition: 5.8 percent for part-time work, 4.6 percent for temporary agency employment, 3.7 percent for skills underutilization, and 5.5 percent for long-term unemployment. Thus, the data from the field experiment are not able to conclusively say whether the apparent lower callback rates for African American women with nonstandard employment experiences are due to chance or to them actually experiencing penalties for employment histories that deviate from full-time, standard work.

It is interesting to also note that the callback rates for each of the employment history conditions for black women are somewhat lower than they are for white women, reflecting the diffuse yet persistent nature of racial discrimination against African American women in the US labor market.[17] This finding is consistent with significant evidence that African American women face continued discrimination and bias in multiple domains of economic and social life. African American women encounter complicated bias due to belonging to two social groups—women and African Americans—that both often face discrimination.[18] The intersection of these two group memberships—which reduces an individual's alignment with the prototypical conceptions of a single group—can create a set of "binds" and "freedoms" that lead to forms of interactional and social experiences distinct from those of white women and African American men.[19] In some instances, this may limit the discrimination experienced by African American women compared

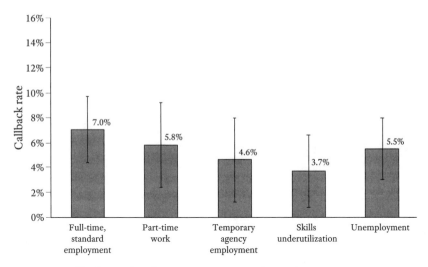

FIGURE 4.9. Callback Rates for African American Women, by Employment Status
Source: Field-experimental data.
Note: 95 percent confidence intervals presented.

to, for example, African American men. Other times, this intersectional identity may exacerbate discrimination for African American women compared to other social groups. How social location redounds on individual applicants varies, but certain types of employment experiences do appear to be particularly penalizing for some workers.

Down and Out: Skills Underutilization

> Your resume . . . says you were a senior director in the last five years and then you were an executive senior director in the last two years. And now you're like assistant manager, it's just not appealing anymore. Like, your value has been lost. It's like that product in the pharmacy that's been discontinued with like the yellow sticker and it's on clearance. And now I'm just . . . I'm just kind of like a little turned off.
>
> —JOYCE, HUMAN RESOURCES DIRECTOR

While the field-experimental findings demonstrate the varied and distinct effects of nonstandard, mismatched, and precarious employment, one overarching pattern is that skills underutilization is largely penalized.[20] It is also the only type of employment history under investigation that does not interact and intersect with race or gender in a statistically significant way.[21] That is, the field-experimental data indicate that the consequences of skills underutilization are not shaped by a worker's race or gender in a meaningful way.

This finding about skills underutilization means that it is quite rare for workers to have the opportunity to tell their story to potential future employers if they have been working in a position that is well below their level of skill and experience. And without the insights offered by a narrative for particular work experiences, employers appear to resolve the uncertainty regarding skills underutilization by attributing to job applicants the negative meanings of these types of positions outlined in the previous chapter: skill atrophy and competence concerns. These meanings appear not to be heavily shaped by the race and gender of the worker, potentially because, unlike the other types of employment investigated in this book such as part-time work, there is limited empirical evidence that women and racial minorities are overrepresented in these types of positions.[22] So there are likely limited ways that skills underutilization primes gendered or racialized stereotypes for hiring professionals. With its broad negative effects and limited intersection with race and gender, skills underutilization is unique among the types of employment experiences explored here.[23]

Further insight into the underlying mechanisms driving the negative effects of skills underutilization can be gleaned from the interviews with hiring professionals. Toward the end of the interviews, the hiring professionals I spoke with were presented with a key set of findings from the field experiment, including the negative effects of skills underutilization.[24] They were told that researchers had recently found that workers who were employed in positions below their skill level were less likely to get callbacks for jobs when they were applying for positions at their skill level. The hiring professionals were then asked to talk about whether or not that finding made sense to them and why that pattern may have emerged.

The negative consequences of skills underutilization aligned with the expectations of the hiring professionals I interviewed. When asked about applicants whose previous positions underutilized their skills, Isabel, an HR coordinator in the health care sector, dismissed the prospect: "This would be just a no. Like, I wouldn't call this person." Echoing Isabel's statement, John, who also works at a health care organization, explained,

> In an all things being equal type of situation, if you had a candidate who had continuous employment within the industry at that level, versus a candidate who had experience in that industry and then went to a much

lower level, I can see that. That does make sense to me. Would I expect that? Absolutely. I think that would be the way our organization would lean. Who wouldn't want somebody who has recent, relevant work experience in that capacity versus someone who maybe didn't?

The categorical exclusion of workers who have been in positions beneath their skill level made sense to many of the hiring professionals with whom I spoke.[25]

Amanda—a nonprofit human resources manager involved with hiring—offered insights into the devaluation of applicants with a history of skills underutilization: "It's probably that thing that I was saying about the perfect resume. So if you have a bunch of resumes and you have people who are at the level, they [the skills underutilization applicants] are going to be in the "B" pile. Does that make sense?" As can be seen in Amanda's comment, skills underutilization violates conceptions of what it means to be an ideal worker or have an employment trajectory of "good" jobs. The comparison point—whether real or imagined—is the "perfect" resume. And the "perfect" resume does not have employment beneath one's skill level. This is especially the case when there is competition for the position and a significant number of applications in the pool of candidates do not have this negative signal of skills underutilization. These workers end up in the "B" pile, excluded from interviews, unable to tell their stories.

Limited Penalties: Temporary Agency Employment

> If you're someone that's been with a temp
> agency for like five years and never been offered a
> full-time position or have a lot of temp work on your resume,
> we usually won't consider you for a permanent position.
> —CAROL, HR MANAGER

> When I evaluate them [temp agency workers] . . . I look at it as a
> positive. This was somebody who didn't stay unemployed, stay
> collecting unemployment, wanted to work, and continued
> to do something
> to stay in the work force, so it's a positive for me.
> —CHARLES, TALENT DEVELOPMENT MANAGER

In contrast to skills underutilization, which is generally penalizing for workers, temporary agency employment is the one type of employment experience in the field experiment where there were no statistically significant negative effects, relative to full-time, standard employment.[26] There are drop-offs in the callback rate for some sociodemographic groups when they experience temporary agency employment, but in no cases are those penalties able to be differentiated from noise. This lack of a finding may be somewhat surprising, given that the hiring professionals I interviewed certainly harbored some concerns about temporary agency employment, particularly with regard to commitment and personality or soft skills issues. Yet, as we recall from the discussion in the last chapter—as well as Charles's statement at the beginning of this section—some employers perceive temping as a good way to keep one's skills relevant and updated. It can even indicate that a given worker is motivated and driven. Thus, the negative meanings attributed to histories of temporary agency employment appear to be weaker than they are for other categories of nonstandard, mismatched, and precarious work.

A Comparative Approach to Understanding Temporary Agency Employment

In addition to asking the hiring professionals about their perceptions of temp workers generally, I also asked an interview question that stimulated conversations about comparing temporary agency employment to other types of nonstandard, mismatched, and precarious work. This question came after the hiring professionals were asked about each type of employment experience separately. Specifically, I asked people to imagine that a friend of theirs, someone who had recently lost their job, had come to them for advice. The friend asked them whether it would be best to take a part-time job, a temporary agency position, or a job below their skill level or to remain unemployed. The responses are quite revealing.

Among the forty-four hiring professionals I interviewed who provided a response that I was able to code as indicating a clear recommendation,[27] twenty-three of them—slightly more than half—said that they would recommend that someone take a temp position over a part-time job or a job below their skill level or remaining unemployed. Another five people indicated that they would recommend either a temp job or a part-time position with equal weight. The strong sense among the hiring professionals I spoke with was that taking a temp position would be the most beneficial response that someone could have to losing their job. It may not be surprising then that the penalties for temporary agency employment in the field experiment were more limited, almost nonexistent, compared to other types of nonstandard, mismatched, and precarious work.

Equally of note, not a single one of the interviewees said that they would be least likely to recommend someone take a temp position if they lost their job. All other types of employment—part-time work, skills underutilization, and long-term unemployment—were mentioned as the type of position they would least recommend by at least a few respondents.[28] From a comparative standpoint, temporary agency employment is seen quite favorably by this set of hiring professionals.

The reasons for recommending that a friend who experienced job loss should take a temporary agency position fell into a handful of categories. When asked about what type of position she would recommend a friend take, Martha, an HR manager in the manufacturing sector, told us,

> MARTHA: Probably through a temp company. . . . They have a lot more opportunities. . . . A lot more job availability and they could probably find a job tailored to what they're looking for. And, I mean, it won't look bad because they're through a temp company.
>
> INTERVIEWER: . . . So you don't consider a temp agency to be a negative at all?
>
> MARTHA: No.
>
> INTERVIEWER: Okay. Do you know if that's unique to what your industry is versus others or is that kind of a common way that people in hiring roles think of temp agencies?
>
> MARTHA: I think it's common. I mean, I've been in other industries where—yeah. And the temps are more mostly go-getters. They're willing to go out and run and, I mean, most of them are excited. They want a full-time position, so they know if they perform well, after ninety days, they'll have a full-time position.

Here we see that for Martha temp agencies are a good option because they have lots of available jobs, people can find the type of work they want, and it will look good, presumably to future employers. We also see her mention that her experience with temp workers is that they are motivated workers, "go-getters," which aligns with the earlier discussion of temp work signaling positive aspects about a worker's motivation.

Undergirding many of the respondents' rationale for recommending that recently unemployed people take a position with a THA was that doing so enables them to keep their skills up to date and gain new experiences that may be useful down the road. Diana, a director of human resources in the hospitality industry, responded, "I would say take a temp job. . . . If it was equivalent to their skill level and what they, you know, because it's a good way to learn different industries, it's a good way to figure out what your next move is. . . . And it's a great opportunity to be able to continue looking for something versus, you know, taking a job lower than, you know, what you're doing." Echoing this sentiment, Kathleen, who works in a marketing firm, said, "They're [temp workers are] staying current with it and temping to continue to show that you want to do this type of work." For workers who are able to temp in their occupation of choice, they can maintain and develop their skills, a key component of the evaluation process for obtaining future employment.

Charles, who works as a talent development manager, offered advice that was in line with the thinking about temp work as positive because of its utility in maintaining one's skills. However, he offered an additional rationale for temping as well: "First of all, an agency, I believe, is going to be a better fit for you because it's going to be full-time. It's, again, people looking out for you and people looking to utilize your skills. . . . Temp can turn into long-term temp, and long-term temp can turn into permanent. So I think that by far beats out anything else of the other options." Beyond the skill-maintenance benefits of temping, Charles concluded by discussing one direct benefit of temp agency work: it can lead to a permanent job at the same company. Amy, who works at a staffing agency, seconded this notion: "Ideally, if you can find a temp job in your area of expertise that's great. If not, you know, at least keep the money coming in it's a great way to get your foot in the door." Beyond the experience, there may be direct, positive employment consequences of working through a THA.[29]

The beneficial aspects of working through a THA—and its comparative advantage over other types of nonstandard, mismatched, and precarious work in the eyes of hiring professionals—align with the field-experimental findings. Employers' discussions of how they think about temping and how it compares to other types of employment histories help to make sense of the mechanisms that may be driving the limited penalties identified in the field experiment for job applicants who have histories of temporary agency employment.

———

The consequences of nonstandard, mismatched, and precarious employment are conditional. They are not all the same. Skills underutilization appears particularly penalizing, resulting in low callback rates for applicants. Unpacking these effects suggests that hiring professionals have deep concerns about workers' skills and competence when they move into jobs beneath their capabilities. Skills underutilization does not carry with it the same overlap with deep-seated racial and gender stereotypes that comes with other types of employment experiences. And as we saw in the field experiment, the consequences of skills underutilization do not vary systematically by race or gender.

THA employment, by contrast, is the only type of employment experience where there is no statistically significant negative effect across any of the four race and gender groups. While hiring professionals certainly do not have universally positive conceptions of temp work, there is enough positive sentiment about temporary employment that it appears to insulate workers from severe penalties. Temp work can provide positive signals, particularly in the evaluative areas of skill and motivation.

Additionally, the findings shed light on how race and gender operate in the labor market. Black workers continue to face severe discrimination even when they maintain seamless, continuous, full-time employment at their skill level. And white men, while positioned at the top of the economic and social hierarchy, face strong penalties nearly across the board when their employment experiences deviate from what it means to have a "good" job or comply with expectations about being an ideal worker.

The consequences of part-time work, temporary agency employment, and long-term unemployment are also contingent in a second way: they vary with the social group membership of the worker. Part-time work is not universally penalizing. The effects of unemployment are not consistently negative. Temporary agency employment can even have positive effects. The sociodemographic characteristics of the worker interact and intersect with these employment histories in particular ways to exacerbate and mitigate the varied effects of nonstandard, mismatched, and precarious work. The next three chapters draw on key cases where social identities and employment experiences intersect and unpack the underlying processes that give rise to these divergent effects.

5

"What Type of a Grown Man Doesn't Have a Full-Time Job?"

GENDER AND PART-TIME WORK

Millions of workers—roughly one in six in the United States—are employed part-time, working fewer than thirty-five hours per week. And approximately a quarter of part-time workers—roughly 4 percent of the labor force—are involuntarily in part-time positions, preferring a full-time job.[1] While many workers experience part-time employment in the United States, its consequences for workers' future labor market opportunities are not universal. As we saw in the field experiment in the previous chapter, there appear to be gender differences in the effects of part-time work on the likelihood that a worker will get a callback for a job, particularly among men and women applicants with names that either were perceived as white or conveyed limited racial information. Why would gender matter when it comes to how part-time work histories affect workers?

Concerns about the violation of ideal worker norms—particularly with regard to perceived levels of commitment—loom large for hiring professionals when they think and talk about part-time employment. The vast majority of the individuals I interviewed discussed how they thought of part-time work as a way for workers to balance nonwork demands—caregiving, parenthood, and school, among other obligations—with paid employment. The very nature of part-time employment is in direct opposition to key components of the ideal worker norm: constant availability and the prioritization of work above all else.[2] The ideal worker is a committed worker.[3] The ideal worker is a dedicated worker. And indeed one of the primary meanings that the hiring professionals read into part-time employment experience was divided commitment and dedication on the part of the worker.

The ideal worker norm is far from gender-neutral.[4] It takes on a masculine form, given the disproportionate demands that are placed on women for child care, other types of care work, and household labor.[5] The gendered construction of the ideal worker stems in part from the heavily masculine nature of the very structure, routines and procedures, and reward systems of workplace organizations.[6] Complete devotion to work. The ability to show up at the workplace on demand. In the abstract, the ideal worker is conceived of as the (male) worker who has no obligations outside the workplace, often supported by a (female) spouse who is able to take care of all domestic responsibilities.[7] The broader social patterning of caregiving and housework makes it difficult for many women to align with this image in the eyes of employers.

At the same time, men benefit heavily from employers aligning the ideal worker so closely with masculinity. Men are unlikely to be seen as having considerable caretaking responsibility outside of the workplace, so they enjoy notable privileges due to their gender. That being said, deviations from the expectations of the ideal worker norm can be problematic for men.[8] These normative pressures hold men accountable for breadwinning, insisting that they provide financial and material resources to the household.[9] In turn, men can face penalties for violating these expectations about presenting a particular form of masculinity or a particular way of supporting a family.[10]

While the ideal worker norm is highly masculine, part-time employment is heavily feminized. Over 70 percent of part-time workers in the United States between the ages of twenty-five and fifty-four are women.[11] In line with this broader pattern, and given expectations around caregiving, it may be deemed appropriate for women to work part-time. At the same time, gendered conceptions of family and work life may make it quite problematic for men to work part-time. Marie, a recruitment manager at a production company, stated, "What type of a grown man doesn't have a full-time job?"[12] Her language here is clear. Men—particularly men who are "grown," or who are real adults—need full-time jobs. A similar sentiment arose in other interviews. Jessica, a virtual recruitment coordinator who works on contract for a chemical company, used feminized language to discuss her thoughts about part-time work. When following up on this, she was asked what she would think about a man working part-time. She expressed surprise at this question, and while unpacking her surprise she said, "Most men, you know, usually will have the full-time jobs and, you know, they're the breadwinners. I guess I view it like that." Expectations are different for women, as will be discussed in more detail below. Part-time work is more common for women and also more socially acceptable.[13]

Early on in the interviews with hiring professionals, but after discussing their general perceptions of part-time employment, they were asked whether those thoughts differed by key sociodemographic distinctions, including gender. Revising a quick response that her thoughts about part-time work were not different for men and women, Andrea, a talent acquisition specialist in the retail sector, articulated the following:

> I would say that if a man was working part-time, it's my internal bias. I would definitely look at that a little bit differently. I think because in our society women tend to work part-time more often than men, especially women who have families. So if it's a man, I think I would definitely question that a little bit more before talking. . . . I think we're just taught that men bring home the bacon and the women take care of the homes, but that's not how it is anymore. I understand that I need to change that a little bit and not look at it as such a negative.

Andrea held clear negative conceptions of men working part-time. Yet, for women it is normal. These thoughts were echoed by other hiring professionals I interviewed. Indeed, they brought up caregiving when talking about part-time work much more than they did when discussing either temporary agency employment or skills underutilization.[14] And it was not just caregiving in general, but rather motherhood, that was highlighted most commonly. Fatherhood was less frequently brought up by the hiring agents in the context of part-time work. Part-time work is heavily gendered as feminine and intersects with caregiving expectations, particularly motherhood. In Andrea's words, a piece of this dynamic has to do with gender differences in the prevalence of part-time work: women are more likely to work part-time than men. But there is something deeper here as well. The way that gender is constructed means that we live in a world where men "should" be breadwinners and women "should" be caretakers. At the same time, we see in Andrea's statement the uncertainty and ambiguity that arises from part-time work for men: "I would definitely question that a little bit more before talking." Looking at men with part-time histories, hiring professionals are left with questions and concerns that may make it less likely that they will reach out to those applicants. In turn, these men are not able to tell their stories to allay employers' concerns. What then do hiring professionals do?

The masculine nature of the ideal worker norm and the feminized nature of part-time employment are central to understanding the gender-differentiated ways that hiring professionals treat workers with histories of part-time employment. During initial screening, employers likely do not have information about why a worker was in a part-time position, leaving them with significant uncertainty. Given a job applicant's narrative is unlikely to be available at this moment of initial screening, one way that employers make sense of part-time employment is by drawing on the stereotypes and cultural beliefs about the gender of the worker to weave a narrative about the applicant's part-time experience. In this way, hiring professionals develop stratified stories. After examining the field-experimental data more closely, we will return to this idea.

Gender and Part-Time Work: The Field Experiment

With the field-experimental data, it is possible to compare the callback rates for men and women job applicants with histories of part-time employment. We are also able to compare the callback rates for applicants with part-time work experience to the callback rates for applicants with both full-time, standard employment trajectories and experiences of long-term unemployment. As a reminder, here are a few key details about part-time work and the field experiment. To signal that applicants had a history of part-time employment, their resume included the words "part-time" in parentheses after their most recent job title.[15] This is consistent with how workers presented part-time employment experience on sample resumes that were reviewed when designing this experiment. Job applicants may include information about part-time employment this way on their resumes to ensure that employers do not feel deceived later on in the hiring process when they find out that a component of the worker's employment history was part-time. As Kathleen, a human resources generalist in marketing and advertising, discussed in her interview: "If it's [part-time work] something that someone tries to mask on their resume and kind of sneak by, again, it comes by as questionable and makes you think is this person being honest and truthful? And we wouldn't hire someone who doesn't really appear to be being honest and truthful." Other than the addition of that one term ("part-time"), the full-time and part-time resumes in the field experiment were the same.

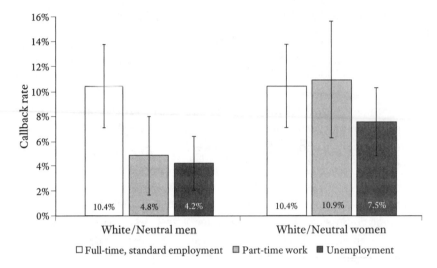

FIGURE 5.1. Callback Rates for White/Neutral Applicants, by Gender and Employment Status
Source: Field-experimental data.
Note: 95 percent confidence intervals presented.

Below I focus on the differences between the callback rates for men and women with white names or names that were unlikely to prime a particular race for employers. Given that there are complex intersections between race, gender, and employment histories—including severe discrimination against African American applicants with full-time, standard employment histories—the ways that part-time work differs by gender are most salient among white or race-neutral applicants. The callback rate for all women (including African American women) with part-time employment histories, however, is twice as high as the callback rate for all men (including African American men) with part-time employment histories.[16]

In Figure 5.1, the callback rates are presented for the men and women applicants with white or neutral names, broken down by full-time continuous employment, part-time employment, and long-term unemployment. As we saw in the previous chapter, these men and women received almost identical callback rates in the full-time, standard employment condition (both 10.4 percent after rounding). However, women fare slightly better than their male counterparts in the unemployment condition, with a callback rate of 4.2 percent for men and 7.5 percent for women, although this difference is only marginally statistically significant.[17]

But our primary interest here is part-time work.[18] The findings reveal that women with part-time employment histories look very similar to women with full-time, standard employment histories. By contrast, men with part-time work histories look very similar to men with histories of long-term unemployment. But is the difference in the callback rates for men and women with part-time employment histories statistically significant? Indeed it is.[19] This finding provides compelling evidence that part-time work histories are evaluated differently for male and female applicants at the hiring interface. While men face severe penalties for part-time work, there is no penalty for part-time work against female applicants, at least among white applicants or those applicants for whom a particular race is not primed.

The finding that part-time work results in worse outcomes for men than for women aligns with some of the existing research that has focused on the relationship between part-time work and wages. One study, for example, found weaker wage penalties for part-time work against women than against men in the United States.[20] Similarly, histories of involuntary part-time work have been shown to be associated with lower future earnings for both men and women, but the negative effects are stronger for men.[21] Even among older workers, the gendered effect of part-time work remains. Scholars have found that there are strong penalties in hourly wages for older men who move into positions with reduced hours.[22] However, they have found little evidence of this effect for women.[23] Thus, the evidence on the relationship between part-time employment and wages indicates that there are gender disparities, with men being penalized more heavily than women. The gendered nature of the findings from these earlier studies on a distinct labor market outcome—wages—is thus quite similar to what the field experiment reveals about the relationship between part-time work and getting a callback for a job.

The above findings examining callback rates for applicants combine all four occupations studied in the field experiment: accounting/bookkeeping, sales, administrative/clerical, and project management/management. Yet it is possible that the gendered effects of part-time work may be different in different occupations. In more male-dominated occupations, for example, part-time work may be less common, and thus its signaling power may be stronger, particularly for women. There is considerable variation in the gender composition of the occupations examined in the field experiment, providing a lens into this possibility. While roughly 40 percent of workers in management occupations are women, over 70 percent of workers in administrative and clerical occupations are women.[24]

It is also possible, though, that gender stereotypes and the gendered meanings attributed to part-time work are strong enough that they

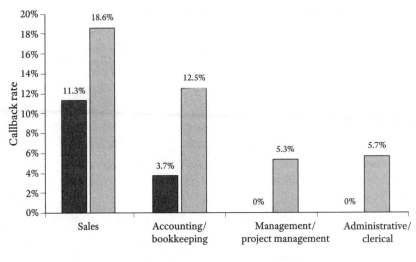

FIGURE 5.2. Callback Rates for Part-Time Employment Histories, by Gender and Occupation
Source: Field-experimental data.
Note: A similar figure appeared in Pedulla (2016).

transcend particular occupations. A woman with part-time experience may not trigger deep concerns, regardless of occupation. A man with part-time experience, by contrast, may always raise concerns for employers and hiring managers. Figure 5.2 presents the callback rates for men and women with white or neutral names in the part-time condition, broken down by the four occupations in the field experiment. The descriptive pattern that emerges is quite striking. In all four occupations, women with part-time experience receive a higher callback rate than men with part-time experience.[25] This finding suggests that the ways that hiring professionals make sense of gender and part-time work are not deeply influenced by the occupational context.

Making Sense of Gender and Part-Time Employment

The findings presented above are striking: part-time work penalizes men similar to long-term unemployment, but women are not penalized for part-time work, at least among those applicants with white or neutral names. And this pattern is consistent across four occupations that vary in their gender composition as well as other characteristics, such as the training and skill required for job.

Gender stereotypes and norms about what men and women should do help make sense of these findings.[26] Substantial existing research points to deep-seated gender stereotypes of women as communal and caring and men as agentic.[27] Strong normative expectations also hold that men will be the primary breadwinners for their families, providing economic security for their wives and children.[28] Together, these gendered beliefs frame the way that part-time work is evaluated and thus assist in accounting for the findings from the field experiment. Indeed, the idea that gender stereotypes shape the evaluations of individuals' other social category memberships or attributes is in line with insights from scholarship in social and cognitive psychology. Experimental research in this area, for example, has highlighted how gender stereotypes and beliefs intersect with evaluations of agentic qualities and leadership attributes to produce divergent effects for men and women.[29]

The interviews with hiring managers illuminate the role of gender stereotypes in shaping the disparate consequences of part-time work for men and women. In some instances, the gendered meaning making of part-time work emerged early in the interviews when broadly discussing part-time work. Additionally, toward the end of each interview the hiring professionals I spoke with were also presented with key findings from the field experiment. For example, I asked hiring professionals their thoughts regarding why men were penalized for part-time work during the hiring process but women were not penalized for this same type of employment.[30] No racialized information was provided to the hiring professionals when they were asked this question; it was posed purely in gendered terms. Hiring professionals' reactions to this finding are revealing.

There was a high level of consistency across interviews in how hiring professionals reacted to this finding from the field experiment. Rachel, the director of human resources at an advertising company, offered the following explanation: "Yes. That makes sense because there's an expectation that women are going to care for children and men aren't." Hiring agents' responses to the field-experimental findings also aligned with the ways that many of them discussed part-time work earlier in the interview. Remember Andrea's remark in response to a question toward the beginning of the interview, before the experimental findings were discussed: "I think we're just taught that men bring home the bacon and the women take care of the homes."

These unsurprised reactions to the field experiment are unlikely to be due to the hiring professionals simply agreeing with a set of academic research findings. As we'll see later, when discussing other findings from the field experiment, respondents were open and honest that they were not sure what was going on or indicated that they were not sure what would be driving the research findings. Yet the pattern in the field experiment about the intersection of gender and part-time work resonated with respondents in a particularly deep way. There was a high level of consensus that this finding made sense.

JUSTIFYING WOMEN'S PART-TIME WORK: CAREGIVER STEREOTYPES

Stereotypes about women as caregivers—and the associated stereotypes about motherhood—played an important role in how employers understood women's part-time employment histories. Early in the interview, when asked what comes to mind when she sees that someone has been working part-time, Kelly—who had recently become unemployed after three years working in talent acquisition at a technology company—responded, "Part-time could also look like a mother or, you know, somebody being—taking care of a child and then, you know, that child being ready to kind of be on their own." Of particular interest, though, is that it is not just any type of caretaking or parenting. It is motherhood—an image of women as parents—that is most closely linked to part-time work for employers. While Kelly then stepped back and made her comments less gendered, her clear instinct was to think of the individual working part-time for caregiving reasons as a woman.

The link between motherhood and part-time work is not neutral in its consequences. Later in the interview, for example, when presented with the finding from the field experiment that women are not penalized for working part-time compared to those women working full-time, Kelly noted, "I think it—I sort of understand it because if the woman, you know—I—I always go back to, you know, the woman could have been a mother or could have been a caregiver, so it's understandable that they had part-time work." Kelly was not alone in her thinking. Rose—a senior HR coordinator in the health care industry—echoed these thoughts: "I think people in general, women, tend to because, you know, of being a mother and a wife. Part-time is more acceptable, unfortunately, with women than it is for males still." We see here that there is a clear way for an employer to weave a narrative about why a woman was working part-time. They have a story they can tell.

Given that women have consistently been expected to do the lion's share of child care and housework, employers have a ready conceptual framework to draw on for understanding part-time work for women. As Judy, who works as a contract staffing consultant, responded,

Women can take time out to deal with family issues, because that's what women traditionally do. They're traditionally the caretaker of the family. Whereas, men who do that, they're looked at kind of funny. How come? . . . I think it's because it's a traditional—the traditional child rearing role is for women. . . . I think it's just, you know, it's—that's our perception of the way the world should be, or our upbringing or whatever. I don't know that people consciously know it, but I think they unconsciously think that.

We see here that the stereotypes about women—and the roles that they play at home and in the labor market—appear to give more space to working part-time without raising additional concerns for employers and hiring managers. In Judy's response we also see a number of references to what is "traditional" in terms of gender norms. This implies that things may be changing to some degree. Yet our beliefs about what men and women should be doing in terms of housework and child care have not necessarily kept pace with reality.[31] The use of the term "should" here is important because it points to the ways the gender stereotypes can be prescriptive, rather than just descriptive.[32] In other words, women should be particular ways and men should be other ways. Judy pointed to something crucial when she articulated that these beliefs about gender, caregiving, and part-time work are not necessarily conscious. They are subtle and hiring professionals may not even be fully aware of them. Yet they powerfully shape the ways that we interpret what is in front of us.

As demonstrated, employers can easily explain women's part-time employment. Part-time jobs are often viewed as part of the "mommy track"—an employment option for women attempting to balance the "competing devotions" of work and family life.[33] By providing a way for women—particularly mothers—to work in the paid labor force but keep their hours limited, part-time work, at least in theory, provides a form of work-family balance.[34] In this sense, part-time employment experience is highly congruent with stereotypes about women and mothers as workers, and thus part-time work experience appears to do little to negatively impact the hiring outcomes of women job applicants.

PROBLEMATIC EXPLANATIONS: STEREOTYPES OF MEN AS BREADWINNERS

While stereotypes of women as caregivers can be used by hiring professionals to make sense of part-time work in a way that minimizes its penalties during the hiring process, hiring professionals were also asked why men might experience significant negative treatment for part-time work histories.

In many cases, the underlying signal of part-time work remained consistent with what was seen when discussing women. Many hiring professionals interpreted part-time work for men as having to do with caregiving responsibilities. But that signal was then refracted through gender stereotypes— particularly the belief that men should be breadwinners—to result in negative evaluations of men with part-time experience. Here, the content of the meaning attached to part-time work—caregiving responsibilities—was not altered by the gender of the worker. Rather, the interpretation of that meaning differed for men and women.

To account for the finding that men are penalized for part-time employment, Janice, a field recruiter, said, "Because men are viewed as being the breadwinners and they should always be working. How can you have a part-time job when, you know, you should be working full-time? And—and that's just stereotypical because men are looked at as the breadwinners. So, yeah, that's the way I would probably look—see that. That's probably why that was a finding." This type of rationale was quite common among the hiring professionals with whom I spoke. Men with part-time employment experience are stigmatized in large part because the signal of caregiving that comes with part-time work experience violates gendered expectations about men as providers. These explanations are consistent with a long line of research documenting how stereotypes about masculinity hold men accountable for being breadwinners for their families.[35]

These findings align with those from existing research exploring how men and women are perceived for utilizing work-family policies, such as parental leave, family leave, or flexible scheduling options. While these policies are distinct from part-time work in some ways, they overlap with part-time work in that they are often perceived as ways of balancing work and family demands. Additionally, work-family policies and part-time employment are feminized in similar ways and violate aspects of ideal worker norms.[36] This parallel line of research demonstrates that men are often penalized for the use of these types of leave and flexibility policies, in part because the use of these policies is perceived as a violation of gender norms around masculinity.[37] The men who avail themselves of these types of policies are seen as more feminine, going against expectations regarding breadwinning and particular types of masculinity, and are therefore penalized. Working in a part-time position appears to produce similar effects for men.

There were two other primary ways that the hiring professionals I spoke with made sense of part-time work for men. Both of these resulted in negative evaluations of male job applicants with part-time employment experience. First, some hiring professionals perceived men with part-time employment histories as being lazy, uncommitted, and limited in their ambitions. In these cases, part-time work experience violated a key component of the ideal worker norm.[38] Judy, who works as a staffing consultant, articulated this point in her discussion of part-time work: "For men, [employers] don't assume [caregiving] for whatever reason, and the perception is maybe he's not ambitious enough. You know, maybe he will come here and join us and, you know, in a year will get tired of it and want to leave." We see here concerns about motivation level as well as the possibility that a man with part-time experience would not be dedicated to the work. For some hiring professionals, part-time work experience for men was worse than just lacking ambition. Amber, an HR manager at a wealth management company, responded to the findings from the field experiment this way: "Because if a man's working part-time, he's just lazy. If a woman is working part-time, she's just accommodating for something else." We see here the notion that part-time work signals that men are deficient in some way—lacking ambition or commitment or simply being lazy.

Gender also influenced hiring professionals' perceptions in that sometimes they did not assign meaning to part-time employment experience for men. As we saw in Chapter 3, nonstandard employment histories in general can produce significant uncertainty for hiring professionals. In the case of part-time work, gender stereotypes can resolve this uncertainty for women by attributing their part-time work experience to caregiving. But for men, hiring professionals may not be able to attribute a particular meaning to part-time work, leaving significant questions and uncertainty for them. In these cases, hiring professionals were left grasping for a rationale explaining men's part-time work. When it comes to hiring, this type of uncertainty about an applicant often leads to their exclusion.

Lauren, who is involved with talent acquisition at a health care company, discussed the ways that breadwinner stereotypes for men can leave hiring professionals uncertain about why a man was working part-time. Here, she responded to the findings from the field experiment: "I think people just assume it's more common for women to be in a part-time position because they're the caregiver, they're the homemaker, they're the child raiser versus men who are in a part-time position. I could see there being some bias or stereotypical things people may think." When asked to expand on what biases or stereotypes she was thinking about, Lauren continued, "Well, I mean, I think men still struggle with this, right. They're supposed to be the provider. They're supposed to be the breadwinner." Here, we see the ways

that masculinity stereotypes around breadwinning and femininity stereotypes around caregiving can provide explanations for women's part-time
work experience while leaving questions, uncertainty, and ambiguity about
men's experiences with part-time employment.

Lauren then went on to say, "If you have a male interviewing a female
or a man that are both part-time, why is this guy working part time, what's
going on? I understand why the woman's working part-time because she
probably has valid reasons. I could see that stereotype." Here, Lauren is
suggesting that the gender of the evaluator may matter in this process and
she was not the only hiring professional I spoke with who mentioned this
possibility. Debra, a director of human resources at a food manufacturing
and distribution company, remarked, "Men expect other men to work full-
time. And they would feel more strongly against a man working part-time.
They would be less accepting perhaps of a man taking on family care or
something like that then a woman would be." This is an interesting possibility.[39] In the interviews that I conducted, however, I did not see systematic
differences in the ways that the men and women I spoke with talked about
gender and part-time work. Yet the sociodemographic characteristics of hiring professionals—not just their gender, but also their race, age, and other
characteristics—could certainly be important in shaping their perceptions
about and treatment of workers and job applicants.

A DOUBLE-EDGED SWORD?

The field-experimental evidence demonstrates that men face penalties for
part-time work experience during the hiring process, but women do not.
The interview data indicate that gendered stereotypes and normative expectations are likely implicated in shaping the pattern in the field experiment.
While the set of stereotypes about women as caregivers may make part-time
employment less penalizing for women than men during the hiring process, these same beliefs about caregiving and motherhood can disadvantage
women in other ways at different points throughout the employment process. First, employers may perceive women who have worked part-time
as being willing to accept lower pay. As Debra, whom we just heard from,
noted,

> I think it's more acceptable for a woman to work part-time. You know in
> the attitudes of the people. Certainly plenty of women work full-time and
> plenty of people in really challenging positions work full-time but if you

were to see a resume, I mean I still work with people who I think of as being fairly open minded who still say things like well why don't we just get one of those part-time people who wants mothers' hours. You know? Do you know what that means? We don't have to pay them as much.

Debra led off by indicating the acceptability of part-time work for women. But she then pivoted to discussing how women will accept lower wages for a part-time job. It is a short jump to seeing how a history of part-time work may lead employers to think that they can underpay a woman, regardless of what type of position she is in.

Having a clear explanation for a woman's part-time employment due to child care responsibilities primes employers' thoughts about women as mothers. Existing research has documented strong motherhood penalties in terms of both hiring and pay.[40] Thus, even though part-time work may not negatively affect the likelihood of a woman getting a callback for a job, it may produce other negative effects because it reifies women's status as mothers in the labor force—a status that is often devalued by employers.

This small step from part-time work to motherhood came out in the interviews. In the midst of discussing the gendered consequences of part-time work, Andrea, who works in the retail sector, slipped into discussing how motherhood can lead to concerns during the hiring process. Pointing out how some hiring managers have concerns about hiring mothers, Andrea noted,

> That they're not going to be able to put in their hours as much or stay late when needed. They just assume that they're their child's primary caregiver so they're like: "Oh, she might have to leave early if her kid gets sick or she may have to leave exactly at five p.m. which is not possible every day." But my manager personally just tries to make it so that everyone gets a fair chance and that we actually ask them in the process what your hours will be. Not if you have kids or anything, but like what do you expect your hours to be? Is there anything else that you have to do outside of work or any obligations that would get in the way or would you be able to stay late if necessary? They tend to say "yes." And we can't really ask them if they have kids or a family but a lot of other hiring managers in other departments do because they don't really know the rules and the laws.

Part-time work may therefore be conflated with motherhood, producing concerns that manifest themselves in the broader evaluations of workers and job applicants. This conflation can have consequences for key labor market outcomes, such as wages and promotions.

More broadly, gendered stereotypes about women's nonwork responsibilities—which can more easily justify part-time work experience—can have pernicious effects on how women are perceived. Joyce, an HR director in the retail sector, discussed the finding from the field experiment this way: "A woman probably has an excuse and we expect her to come like, full of baggage. Whereas a man we expect minimal baggage so like, what is he doing with his free time?" The idea that women are expected to be "full of baggage" is powerful. It is this very idea that leads employers' conceptions of the ideal worker—the worker who is fully dedicated to his employer with no responsibilities outside of work—to exclude women.[41]

On the one hand, gendered caregiving and parenthood expectations serve as a way for employers to tell a story about women's part-time work, a story that limits the penalties women face during the hiring process. On the other hand, this same set of expectations may prime stereotypes about caregiving and motherhood that can disadvantage women in other ways, putting them at odds with conceptions of ideal worker norms. Employers may offer them lower pay, fewer opportunities for advancement, or less status within the organization.

The Stratified Stories Employers Tell

As we have seen above, hiring professionals rely on gender stereotypes and normative expectations about men and women to make sense of part-time work histories. These stereotypical ways of making sense of part-time work result in what I refer to as stratified stories. Hiring professional utilize group-based stereotypes and norms to weave stories and narratives about job applicants with part-time work histories. The stories they tell then diverge based on key axes of social stratification, such as gender. In turn, as we can see in the field experiment, disparate treatment of workers by their gender emerges.

As scholarship by cultural sociologists has demonstrated, narratives and storytelling are important in evaluation processes. From college and graduate school admissions to academic review panels, employment, and beyond, sociologists and social scientists have examined the ways that stories and narratives are deployed during the process of making decisions.[42] Philip Moss and Chris Tilly even title their book about hiring in the low-skilled labor market *Stories Employers Tell*.

In recent scholarship, sociologist Barbara Kiviat draws out the importance of storytelling in a distinct, but relevant, case: the ways that employers utilize credit reports in the hiring process. She identifies a key challenge for employers. They need to determine whether a bad credit report is worthy of concern about a job applicant or whether it is excusable. This is an evaluative challenge not dissimilar from deciding whether a history of part-time work or some other nonstandard, mismatched, or precarious employment experience is disqualifying for a job candidate. Drawing on in-depth interviews with hiring professionals, Kiviat develops the concept of moral storytelling to understand how employers navigate this moment, this decision. In an effort to address the challenge articulated above—whether a bad credit report is disqualifying—Kiviat writes, "Hiring professional turned to storytelling. They did this in two ways. First they inferred stories about a person's life from their credit report. Second, they contacted job candidates to see if they could tell a story about their financial problems in a redeeming way."[43]

My interviews with hiring professionals also demonstrate the importance of stories and narratives in the context of employers making sense of nonstandard, mismatched, and precarious employment histories. Employers want to understand why a worker was employed in a particular type of position, and the answer to that question assists in determining whether an applicant's employment experience would be disqualifying. Indeed, similar to Kiviat, I find that employers tell stories to make sense of workers' employment histories. But the stories that emerge in the process of developing evaluations of workers are deeply intertwined with group-based stereotypes and normative expectations.

In the case of part-time work, gender stereotypes were utilized to produce stratified stories. The following chapters turn from gender stereotypes to racial stereotypes and examine the ways that a similar process of stereotype-based evaluations of employment histories plays out in two other cases: first, for race and long-term unemployment and then, second, for how THA employment influences the ways that African American men are treated. While the precise ways that stratified stories operate differ to some extent in each of these cases, they offer a unified way to understand the different empirical patterns that emerge in the field experiment.

———

The consequences of part-time employment for workers' future labor market opportunities are not universal; they are contingent on the sociodemographic characteristics of the worker. As we have seen in this chapter, identities matter. The data presented above provide evidence that stratified stories emerge as the result of gender stereotypes and normative expectations to make sense of men's and women's part-time employment experiences. The highly varied meanings and potential concerns that hiring professional attribute to part-time work are refracted through gender stereotypes to produce divergent outcomes for male and female job applicants. Gendered stereotypes of men as breadwinners and women as caregivers—as well as the heavily gendered nature of part-time employment—enable employers to draw on readily accessible narratives about part-time work for women.

For men, by contrast, part-time work is profoundly mismatched with gendered ideas of men as the primary breadwinners and providers for their families. Additionally, the ideal worker norm violations that come with part-time work lead to explanations rife with concerns about commitment and dedication. And in other cases, hiring professionals are unable to tell a compelling narrative about men's part-time employment experience, leaving significant uncertainty and ambiguity about the applicant. These stories appear to be key drivers of the gender-differentiated effects of part-time work histories. In this way, gender fundamentally frames the interpretation of what it means for a worker to be employed in a part-time position.

In this particular case—the effects of gender and part-time work during the hiring process—ingrained gender stereotypes about breadwinning and caregiving produce stronger negative penalties for men than they do for women. Yet it is important to keep in mind that these same stereotypes and beliefs produce significant obstacles for women in the labor market, often resulting in lower wages, fewer opportunities for advancement, and myriad other negative outcomes relative to men.[44] Stereotypes and beliefs about gender—which are in many ways outdated and inaccurate—can fundamentally shape evaluations of others, with broad consequences for inequality in the structure of opportunity.

6

"Maybe It's More Natural for Them to Have Been Out of Work for a Little While"

RACE AND UNEMPLOYMENT

Being unemployed is often a difficult, challenging, demoralizing experience and can have severe negative consequences for workers' economic standing. Sometimes referred to as unemployment "scarring," scholars generally find that there are negative consequences of long-term unemployment for workers' future labor market outcomes—including their earnings and employment status.[1] This suggests that unemployment may beget more unemployment. Yet, as we saw earlier, the effects of unemployment are not universally negative. The results from the field experiment indicate that while certain groups of workers are severely penalized for a year of unemployment, others are not. This chapter probes those differences and develops our understanding of how and why race and experiences of unemployment interact in the ways that they do.

The Intersection of Race and Unemployment

The direct effect of unemployment on getting called back for a job has been examined by a few prior research efforts.[2] To date, however, we know little about the ways that unemployment intersects with race to produce evaluations of workers.[3] Two of the prior field-experimental studies in the United

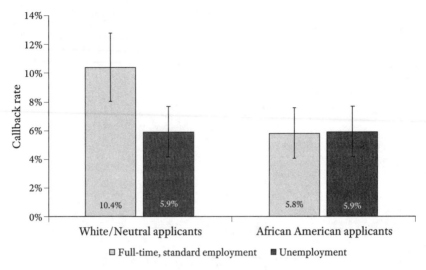

FIGURE 6.1. Callback Rates, by Race and Unemployment Experience
Source: Field-experimental data.
Notes: 95 percent confidence intervals presented. A similar figure appeared in Pedulla (2018).

States on the effects of unemployment, for example, utilized names for their fictitious job applicants that were "minimally informative about the race of the applicant."[4] In other words, these two studies did not systematically vary the race of the applicant. Yet there are many reasons why it is important to understand how race and unemployment intersect in the production of employment opportunities: among the most central is that the unemployment rate for black workers consistently hovers at approximately twice the unemployment rate for white workers.[5]

When the field-experimental results were discussed earlier, they were presented separately for each demographic group. Here, in Figure 6.1, I display the effects of unemployment and race in the same figure, pooled by the gender of the applicant. Comparing the callback rates for white and black applicants with full-time, standard, seamless employment demonstrates that racial discrimination persists in the United States. Whites with seamless employment histories receive callbacks at nearly twice the rate of blacks with identical employment histories (10.4 percent vs. 5.8 percent).[6] Additionally, the results clearly demonstrate that white applicants see severe negative penalties for unemployment. Whites with continuous employment histories receive callbacks 10.4 percent of the time, compared to 5.9 percent of the time for white applicants with spells of unemployment.[7]

Yet the callback rate for black applicants with continuous employment histories is almost identical to the callback rates for both white applicants with twelve months of unemployment and black applicants with twelve months of unemployment. These differences are neither substantively nor statistically significant, indicating that black applicants who maintain full-time, continuous employment fare no better than unemployed white or black workers. I also examined whether the effects of unemployment differed in a statistically significantly way for white and black applicants. The results from this statistical test provide compelling evidence that this is indeed the case.[8] While racial discrimination is strong and persistent, and long-term unemployment has negative effects for white job applicants, there is little additional negative effect of unemployment for black applicants.

Stratified Stories: The Case of Race and Long-Term Unemployment

Much of the existing literature on how negatively stereotyped social categories—such as being African American or being unemployed—will combine with one another offers two primary predictions. One line of thought suggests that these characteristics will be treated as independent social categories and will therefore combine in a straightforward, additive manner.[9] In this model, one would expect unemployment to negatively impact white and black workers' labor market opportunities in a similar manner. A second line of thought emphasizes that belonging to multiple negatively stereotyped social groups might have multiplicative effects.[10] In that model, the negative stereotypes associated with being African American and being unemployed may reinforce one another, leading to deeper penalties of unemployment for African Americans than for whites.[11]

Neither of those patterns emerge in the field-experimental data. What might be going on? Scholarship in social psychology offers important insights about how information about multiple category memberships will be aggregated in the evaluation process.[12] In a review of scholarship on expectations states theory—one strand of social psychology—sociologists Shelley Correll and Cecilia Ridgeway write about this set of issues: "The attenuation effect assumes that additional consistent information is subject to a declining marginal impact. If we already know that a person is a Harvard trained lawyer, learning that he is also a white man will have only a slight positive effect."[13] In line with this view are additional insights from social psychological research on impression formation.[14] Individuals often want to spend as few cognitive resources as possible when evaluating others, and this can particularly be the case when time is scarce, as is often the case when screening job applicants. Group-based stereotypes are used toward the beginning of the impression formation process as a way to classify others quickly and easily. Beyond that preliminary act of categorization, additional information is processed and deployed in different ways. As psychologists Susan Fiske and Steven Neuberg write in early work on this topic, "If the additional information is interpreted to be either consistent with or adaptable to the initially determined category label, then the perceiver's affects, cognitions, and behavioral tendencies are likely to be based on the initial category."[15] Together, these lines of research offer the key insight that additional group-based information that is in line with the initial stereotypes about a target's group membership will not shift the evaluator's initial impression, or will have a limited effect on shifting that initial evaluation.

Stereotypes about African Americans and the unemployed overlap greatly. A large body of extant research finds that employers hold strong negative stereotypes about both groups. Many of those stereotypes have to do with having lower levels of ability and competence as well as poor work ethics and limited motivation.[16] Thus, the stereotypes about unemployed individuals are highly congruent with the stereotypes of African Americans, with both centering on issues of motivation and competence. I argue that, given these highly overlapping stereotypes, employers develop stratified stories whereby long-term unemployment is interpreted as disqualifying for white applicants but does not have the same disqualifying effect for African Americans. In this respect, the case of race and unemployment is similar in certain respects to the case of gender and part-time work.

Toward the beginning of the interviews, each hiring professional was asked their general thoughts about different types of employment experiences—including unemployment. As a follow-up question, they were asked whether their thoughts about unemployment would differ by the race, gender, or age or the worker. A large number of respondents said something along the lines of "No, they would not." And when respondents did offer a detailed answer, it was most often about age. Yet in a few cases respondents mentioned race. Lori was one such respondent. From her experience with hiring for the food and beverage industry, she said, "In the case of unemployment, I think if somebody older, with more education, who is white, I would judge more harshly for that. Yeah . . . I think I would." When asked why, Lori responded, "I would just—I would have a hard time not associating them with all of those 'trustafarians' that I've know who are just kind of, like, freeloading. And I would try to get over that, but that is something that I would probably—I think—I think that that is true. I think that I probably would judge them more harshly for that." Lori's comment emblematized the storytelling that occurs around unemployment experiences. For those with privilege—such as white workers—unemployment may be judged more harshly.

There were too few comments about how race might intersect with unemployment from the early components of the interviews to draw firm conclusions. However, toward the end of my conversations with hiring professionals—after discussing many topics with them and attempting to gather information from them without shaping their responses—each respondent was presented with a set of the key findings from the field experiment. One of the findings concerned the intersection of race and unemployment: while white workers faced penalties for unemployment and African American workers faced racial discrimination, there were limited additional effects of unemployment for African American applicants. Hiring agents were then asked to discuss their thinking about the finding.

It is important to note that a sizeable subset of hiring professionals responded that this finding did not resonate with them. Indeed, throughout the interviews, there was a hesitancy among many respondents to discuss race. And even with this finding, where it was clear that I was not asking them about their own racial attitudes or preferences, many were still hesitant. Thus, one set of interview responses to the finding about the intersection of race and unemployment was not informative about the underlying mechanism that might be driving the interactive effects of race and unemployment in the field experiment.

The hesitancy or lack of response about the intersection of race and unemployment, however, was by no means universal. Indeed, a subset of hiring professionals pointed to stereotypes and group-based perceptions as likely to be driving the field-experimental findings. Elizabeth, an HR generalist in the food and beverage industry, interpreted the findings this way: "So it's expected of African Americans to be more unemployed more often, and it's like, okay a little bit that, more than for white people." Also regarding the finding about race and unemployment in the field experiment, Bruce, who hires in the restaurant and hospitality sector, said,

I mean, is there a kind of skewing over to, you know, is there a sense of, you know, somebody who is African American is probably, you know, maybe there's a certain stigma, you know attached to that. Well, maybe it's more natural for them to have been out of work for a little while than someone who's white and so I don't mind if they kind of come in. Because if they've been unemployed for a little while, you know, but again I think that's kind of a crappy, you know.

Bruce's language points to the perception that some may hold that unemployment is more "natural" among African American workers. He noted that this is about stigma and that it is "crappy," but it nonetheless exists. Of note in the case of both Elizabeth and Bruce is that they are not changing the content of what it means to be unemployed. Rather, racial stereotypes shape whether or not unemployment is a disqualifying experience for the worker.

Responding to the same findings from the field experiment, Joyce, who hires workers in the retail sector, reported,

Interesting. I—I never thought about that. Um, if I had to say that we have a preconceived expectation of an African American male just continuously having gaps in their employment, and like that's what we expect, then it's on par with their reputation and then we're not disappointed. Like, that's what we see at face value. We expect them to be a certain way. They didn't disappoint. Um, whereas a white male, I think our expectations might be higher. The standard is higher and, I could see that.

This language of "expectedness" came up in multiple interviews. This particular term is important because it aligns with the ways that cultural beliefs and stereotypes often operate. They can lead us to have expectations about the individuals that are being evaluated and influence how we think about, perceive, and treat others.[17] And while nothing about gender was mentioned in the question she was asked, Joyce made her response about men. That she highlighted how these processes are likely to play out for men, rather than women, is telling. We will turn back to this insight later in the chapter when we revisit the field-experimental data.

Employers produce different stories to make sense of workers' unemployment experience, depending on the race of the worker.[18] While some employers were hesitant to offer their insights about the intersection of race and unemployment, other hiring professionals pointed to the overlapping nature of the stereotypes about being a black worker and what it means to be unemployed. These two categories—and their associated stereotypes—go together. There is little new information about African American workers when the employer finds out they are unemployed—their story can remain similar to their initial story, imbued with negative racial stereotypes likely having to do with issues of motivation and work ethic. By contrast, for white applicants (or applicants where there are limited racial cues), the experience of unemployment is more striking and less expected and in turn induces more uncertainty. For white applicants, the stories about unemployment may be harsher, producing negative outcomes for this group.[19]

Additional Evidence from the Field Experiment

GENDER-DIFFERENTIATED RACIAL STEREOTYPES

Is there any evidence from the field-experimental data that employers utilized group-based stereotypes and stratified stories to make sense of workers' experiences with long-term unemployment? Unemployment may mean something different in the eyes of employers, depending not only on the race but also on the gender of the worker. Indeed, racial stereotypes about workers are strong, but they also vary in important ways by the gender of the worker. Thus, whether a job applicant is a man or a woman may influence the ways that race and unemployment interact with one another in the eyes of employer. I therefore examine in the field experiment additional variation in the effect of race and unemployment by the gender of the applicant.

Joyce's response to the findings in the field experiment—noted above—highlights the ways that racialized and gendered perceptions enter into hiring decisions. When employers were presented with the findings about race and unemployment in the field experiment, nothing was mentioned about gender. But Joyce highlighted that the perception of African Americans as having gaps in their employment is specifically about black men. This gendered nature of racial stereotypes came up in other interviews as well. Janice, who is a recruiter in the information sector, reported, "I would say that I think they probably treat African American males a lot different than African American females and white males and females. I think the African American male gets treated worst." Black men are often negatively stereotyped as unmotivated, unintelligent, and having poor work histories,[20] stereotypes that overlap closely with those of the unemployed. Stereotypes of black women, by contrast, tend to emphasize single motherhood, domineering personalities, abrasiveness, or a lack of self-control.[21] Importantly, though, these stereotypes about black women tend to be less directly aligned with those of unemployment than are the stereotypes about black men.[22]

Employers generally have more positive conceptions of black women's competence and motivation than black men's. Drawing on data from their interviews with employers, Moss and Tilly write, "Respondents described

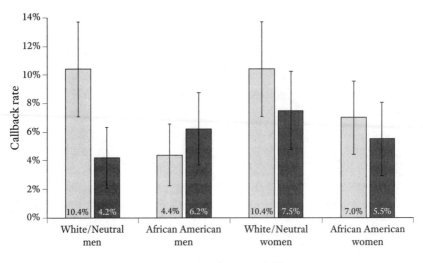

FIGURE 6.2. Callback Rates, by Race, Gender, and Unemployment Experience
Source: Field-experimental data.
Notes: 95 percent confidence intervals presented. A similar figure appeared in Pedulla (2018).

black women as having 'better communication skills, better work skills in everything,' and being 'a hell of a lot sharper' and 'very impressive' com-pared to black men, who 'tended to be less skilled, less educated.'"[23] The strength of the overlapping stereotype content between race and unemploy-ment is therefore likely weaker for black women than for black men. If this is the case, then the negative stories employers tell about unemployment may be weaker for African American men than white men (as it is for the full set of applicants). For women, however, this pattern may not hold, as the stereo-types between unemployment and race are less pronounced for women.[24]

Evidence from the field experiment, disaggregated by the gender of the job applicant, is presented in Figure 6.2. Gender differences do appear to exist. Among male applicants, there are strong penalties of unemployment for whites and discrimination against African American men who remain employed full-time, but there are no additional penalties of unemployment for African American men. Among women applicants, the pattern is distinct: each additional lower status position seems to generate additional disadvan-tage. Overall, the intersection of unemployment and race seems to operate differently for men and women. These findings about gender differences provide additional support for the idea that overlapping stereotypes—and the related narratives employer tell—about race and unemployment contribute to the divergent effects observed in the field experiment.[25]

THE LANGUAGE IN JOB POSTINGS

Another way to use the data from the field experiment to examine whether stereotypes and their associated stratified stories may be at play is to draw on data from the content of the job postings to which applications were submitted.[26] Job postings provide a wealth of information about the types of workers that a given employer seeks. Each job posting to which applications were submitted was coded for a range of topics, including whether the posting emphasized a desire for highly motivated workers or workers with strong work ethics.[27] Lower levels of motivation and work ethic are among the key stereotypes that are highly overlapping for both unemployed and African American job applicants, so whether these attributes are highlighted in the job posting may influence the interactive effects of race and unemployment.

To determine whether a job posting prized motivation, each listing was coded for whether it mentioned: work ethic, enthusiasm, being energetic, being motivated or a self-starter, being passionate, or being reliable or dependable.[28] If one of these terms was mentioned, the posting was coded as emphasizing motivation. If none were indicated, it was coded as not emphasizing motivation. If overlapping stereotypes about motivation are involved in driving the ways that race and unemployment intersect, then we would expect different patterns to emerge among job postings that do and do not emphasize these types of applicant characteristics. In the cases where these attributes were emphasized, they were likely to be salient during the applicant evaluation process, heightening the role of race- and unemployment-based stereotypes along these dimensions. In cases where these attributes were not mentioned, stereotypes about motivation and work ethic were likely to be less salient.

If indeed hiring professionals utilize stratified stories in the ways outlined above, we would expect the differential effects of unemployment by race and gender to exist primarily among the job postings where these applicant attributes—motivation and work ethic—are articulated. This is precisely what the data show. Among the job openings whose postings emphasized work ethic and motivation, unemployment was less penalizing for African American men job applicants than white men job applicants. However, that was not the case among job postings where motivation and work ethic were not highlighted. Nor was this the case for women job applicants, regardless of the content of the job posting.[29] Thus, the field-experimental data are in line with the idea that stereotypes—and the stratified stories they produce—are likely a mechanism that explains the ways that race and unemployment interact with one another.

———

Taken together, the evidence presented in this chapter aligns with the idea that hiring professionals develop stratified stories when considering job applicants that vary in terms of race and unemployment experience. When faced with uncertainty and ambiguity, employers are likely to draw on stereotypes and group-based perceptions to make sense of what they are seeing and arrive at evaluations of individual job applicants. In the case of long-term unemployment, hiring professionals draw on different narratives depending on the race of the applicant. The deep-seated cultural beliefs and stereotypes about African Americans lacking a strong work ethic, being unmotivated, and even having "spotty" employment histories are very similar to those held about unemployed workers. The result is divergent interpretations of whether unemployment is disqualifying depending on the race of the job applicant.

The type of stratified story that employers utilize with race and unemployment is similar to one of the patterns that emerged in the case of gender and part-time work discussed in the previous chapter. The meaning of the employment experience remains similar for each of the two social groups, but how that content influences the ultimate evaluation is shaped by group-based stereotypes. The underlying process—where there is limited additional effect of a second category membership that is highly consistent with stereotypes about the first group-based stereotypes—is also similar to what would be expected on the basis of some social psychological scholarship on how social categories may combine with one another.[30]

Thus far, we have seen how stratified stories operate when hiring professionals evaluate gender and part-time employment and then also race and long-term unemployment. In the following chapter, I turn to the ways that experience with a THA shapes the employment outcomes of African American men. While the process is slightly different in the case of THA employment and the treatment of African American men, the idea of stratified stories is again useful for understanding the aggregation of these different social and economic positions.

7

"They Do a Pretty Thorough Background Check"

THA EMPLOYMENT AND AFRICAN AMERICAN MEN

Millions of workers now labor through temporary help agencies, with consequences that are somewhat unique for future labor market opportunities. Among the types of employment histories examined in this book, THA employment experience was not meaningfully penalizing for any of the sociodemographic groups in the field experiment when compared to full-time, standard employment experience. In some cases, there was a dip in the callback rate for THA work, but none of these penalties reached statistical significance.[1] Why might THA employment occupy this unique position?

Hiring professionals' interviews pointed to a few key reasons that THA employment may be different from part-time work, skills underutilization, and long-term unemployment. While temp work can come with limited hours, it is frequently full-time work, just with a concrete time horizon at which point the work will stop. And individuals often work through THAs at jobs that are in their field of choice. This means that there may be fewer concerns about skill atrophy for temp workers since they may be working the same number of hours as full-time workers and in a relevant occupation.

There may even be some human capital benefits of temping because the THA sends temp workers to perform their job at different companies on a short-term basis. Temp workers' mobility between different companies may enable some knowledge gains about how work is performed differently across organizations, providing THA workers with unique insights about how different organizations and people approach similar types of work. This movement among companies may also increase the size of a worker's social network, an important resource for finding out about new jobs.[2] In turn, these new contacts may play a key role in increasing the likelihood of hearing about new job prospects. Some temp jobs even carry the possibility of becoming secure and ongoing positions, making THA employment a possible stepping stone on the path to standard employment.

Compared to how other types of employment histories fare in relation to full-time, standard employment, THA employment appears to have more modest consequences. At the same time, the effects of THA employment were not universal. For one sociodemographic group—African American men—the effects of a history of THA employment were striking, surprising, and unique. This chapter examines the complex interaction of race, gender, and THA employment histories and attempts to understand the effect of temp work experience on the employment prospects of African American men.

Discrimination, African American Men, and Temp Work

In the field experiment, the consequences of THA employment varied for men of different racial backgrounds. As a reminder about the design of the field experiment, to signal that a job applicant had experience in a THA, each resume in the "temporary agency employment" condition included a most recent job—held for one year—that was through one of two major temp agencies.[3] The occupation associated with the work done in the temp agency condition was the same as it was in the full-time, standard employment condition. Additionally, the information provided about the applicant's work tasks and accomplishments was quite similar to the description of the work performed in the full-time, standard employment condition. This way, the THA experience manipulation in the field experiment attempted to hold everything constant between the applicants except that one applicant had maintained employment directly at a company where they performed their tasks and the other had been working most recently through the temp agency.

In Figure 7.1, I present the callback rates for the full-time, standard condition, the temporary agency employment condition, and the long-term unemployment condition for African American men on the left and for white (or race-neutral) men on the right. As we saw in the field-experimental

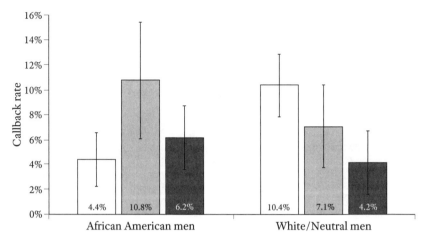

FIGURE 7.1. Callback Rates for Men, by Race and Employment Status
Source: Field-experimental data.
Note: 95 percent confidence intervals presented.

data in previous chapters, the callback rate for African American men with seamless employment histories is quite low (4.4 percent). However, as Figure 7.1 demonstrates, for black men with temporary employment histories, the callback rate jumps up to 10.8 percent, which is among the highest callback rates for any group in the field experiment. And the difference between full-time standard employment and THA employment is statistically significant (4.4 percent vs. 10.8 percent),[4] providing evidence that employers treat black men with THA employment histories more favorably than black men with full-time, standard employment histories. At the same time, black male workers with THA employment histories also fare better than black male workers with histories of unemployment (10.8 percent vs. 6.2 percent).[5]

By contrast, white men saw a slight decline in the callback rate for applications with THA employment. However, the difference between full-time, standard employment and THA employment is not statistically significant for this group. One additional test of interest is whether the effect of THA employment—compared to full-time, standard employment—is statistically significantly different for white and black men. A statistical test indicates that, indeed, the effects of THA employment are different for white and black men.[6]

This finding about the consequences of THA employment for African American men is a bit counterintuitive. While we might expect African

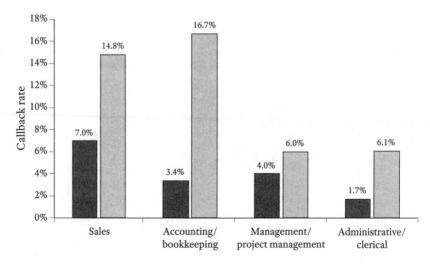

■ Full-time, standard employment   ▫ Temporary agency employment

FIGURE 7.2. Callback Rates for African American Men, by Occupation and Employment Status
Source: Field-experimental data.

American men to not face penalties for THA employment—which would be in line with the other sociodemographic groups of workers—it is surprising that it actually improved their outcomes over full-time, standard employment experience. I was therefore eager to tease apart this effect a bit more to see if it was concentrated in a particular place. Does this pattern hold across the four occupational groups in the field experiment: sales, accounting/bookkeeping, administrative/clerical, and project management/management? One could imagine that THA employment might operate in different ways for black men across occupations, and therefore a single occupation may be responsible for driving the overarching finding. However, when I examine the callback rates for black men across these different types of occupations, we see relatively consistent results. As Figure 7.2 reveals, across all four occupational groups black men with THA employment histories receive higher callback rates than their counterparts in full-time standard jobs.[7] The finding that African American men fare better when they have a history of THA employment is not driven by a single occupation but rather appears to be more general.

Another type of variation in the field experiment is the labor market where the applications were submitted. Thus, I can also examine the callback rates for African American men in full-time, standard employment and THA employment, broken down by city. The results from these analyses indicate that, with the exception of Chicago, African American men with THA employment experience received higher callback rates than African American men with full-time, standard employment histories across the different labor markets in the field experiment. The complex and surprising intersection of race, gender, and THA employment experience appears to be relatively consistent across the different types of contexts in the field experiment.

The Additional Meanings of THA Employment

Why might the consequences of THA employment be positive for African American men? This case is slightly different from the patterns that emerged for the intersection between gender and part-time work or race and unemployment, topics discussed in the previous chapters. Indeed, it is the only case in the field experiment where a nonstandard, mismatched, or precarious employment history actually improved a worker's callback rate over full-time, standard employment. Also, unlike the case of gender and part-time work or race and long-term unemployment, it is unclear whether there are strongly linked stereotypical beliefs about African American men and working through temporary help agencies, which was a key mechanism driving the findings with the other intersections. In the interviews with hiring managers and recruiters, few of them mentioned racialized conceptions of temporary agency employment on their own. Even when hiring agents were asked specifically about whether their thinking about temporary agency employment differed by the race of the worker—one of the questions asked early on in the interviews, before findings from the field experiment were presented—most respondents indicated that they did not have racially or ethnically distinct perceptions of or thoughts about temp work. In part, this may be a function of hiring professionals' general hesitancy to discuss race and racial stereotypes, as was the case throughout many of the interviews. But the lack of a finding here may also point to the possibility that there are not particularly strong perceptions linking African American men and temp work.

Yet some clues in existing scholarship do assist in explaining the finding about the consequences of THA employment for black men from the field experiment. In *The Good Temp*, sociologists Vicki Smith and Esther Neuwirth draw on historical documents and ethnographic data to understand the emergence and construction of the THA industry and its operation in the contemporary economic landscape.[8] Among their many insights are relevant ideas about why THA employment may produce distinct outcomes for black men. Citing early statements from the THA industry itself, they write, "Interestingly, as far back as the early 1970s [THA] industry lead-ers bragged that people of color could benefit by using agency services to overcome the barrier of racial discrimination in the labor market."[9] As part of this line of thought, it was argued that THA work could provide an entry point for minority workers to gain relevant skills that would help them attain standard employment. Insofar as African American men face particularly strong obstacles in the labor market for standard positions, such as racial discrimination, THAs may be a point of entry to gain skills and experience that can then be converted into a standard, secure position.

Beyond circumventing discrimination, other mechanisms may also be at play. In the same book, Smith and Neuwirth go on to write, "Other research-ers have noted that finding temporary jobs through agencies can be a boon to individuals who might, in the eyes of employers, appear to be high-risk hires. Temporary employment can offer people with difficult personal and workforce histories and opportunity to gain work experience and possibly reinvent themselves as workers with good employment records."[10] Thus, THA employment may provide an opportunity to gain job experience for those who may be deemed "high risk" in some way. We can imagine that high-risk workers could be those with spotty employment histories or other challenges in the labor market. There is reason to think that THA employ-ment may serve as a pathway for workers who face obstacles and challenges due to myriad social and economic forces.

These are compelling possibilities. There is something intriguing about the idea that THA employment may serve as a mobility-enhancing institu-tion for particular workers. Insofar as temp agencies are less discriminatory, African American workers may be more likely to get a foot in the door. Yet on this first mechanism—discrimination—it is unclear whether temporary agencies are actually less racially discriminatory in their hiring practices. An experimental audit study conducted in the early 2000s found evidence of preferences for white applicants compared to African American applicants among temp agencies in California. While relatively small, the study suggests that THA agencies may exhibit racial discrimination in a way not dissimilar from employers in the broader economy,[11] meaning THA employment may actually not serve as a stepping stone to standard employment if African American workers are blocked from accessing THA employment due to discrimination within the THA industry.

The second possible mechanism discussed above is that temp agencies may provide an opportunity for workers who are ostensibly more "high risk" to obtain experience and smooth out their employment trajectory.

The role of risk and mitigating risk may be central to understanding why THA employment enhances the employment outcomes of African American men. When the hiring professionals I spoke with discussed their general thoughts about THA employment—early on in the interviews—they pointed to the role of temp agencies as key screening entities. Discussing her general thoughts on THA employment, Alexandra, an HR and payroll manager at a business services organization, reported, "As far as I know, temp agencies are pretty detailed in the hiring process. They still do all the background checks and all of that, so . . . at least this is a somewhat qualified candidate that a temp agency provided to another company, because a temp agency's name is kind of on that hire." Alexandra's statement about the screening processes conducted by THAs was not unique; other hiring professionals brought this up as well. In turn, hiring managers and recruiters may be inclined toward hiring applicants with a history of temp agency employment because they assume that the temp agency has vetted them extensively. And as can be seen in Alexandra's comment, an additional positive signal of quality may emerge from the institutional "stamp" that a temp agency puts on its workers. If the temp agency is willing to associate a given worker with their brand, then the worker likely meets some minimal level of quality.[12] Thus, there may actually be positive signaling that comes from these two aspects of a THA history: prescreening and putting the temp agency's reputation on the line.

A Different Type of Stratified Story

The question remains, why do African American men with THA employment histories, in particular, benefit from that employment experience? While it is difficult to make strong conclusions about the processes driving this finding—particularly due to its unexpected nature—Alexandra's discussion of THA employment was echoed by other hiring professionals with regard to race and THA employment. As with other key findings from the field experiment, toward the end of the interviews—after asking respondents for their general thoughts about temporary employment and all of the other types of employment examined in this book—each hiring professional was asked to make sense of the finding from the field experiment that African American men with THA histories of employment were preferred to African American men with full-time, standard employment trajectories. Many respondents indicated that they were uncertain about why such a connection would have emerged, offering little to the understanding of the consequences of THA employment for black men.

Some respondents, however, had a hunch about what might be going on. When presented with the findings about the benefits of temporary agency employment for African American men, Ashley, who works as a recruiter at a medical device supply company, responded,

> The one thing about temp agencies is that they do a pretty thorough background check. They check references, they do the background screening. They're—typically temp agencies do want to send their higher caliber candidates to work, because it represents their agency, so maybe employers think, oh, if they were sending them out on jobs, then they're reliable, or they performed well, especially if they stayed with a temp agency, assignment after assignment. What that shows you is they did well on their first assignment, so the temp agency sent them on the next assignment, and then—so, if they're with the same agency and they have some tenure, that might speak well to their validity as a solid worker, so I don't know if that has something to do with it.

Ashley offers a comment in line with Alexandra's general perception of THA employment above: agencies offer high levels of screening and are putting their reputation on the line. We see in Ashley's comment, though, that these mechanisms may be particularly salient when evaluating African American male workers. Although many employers hold deep-seated, negative stereotypes about African Americans and particularly African American men, THA employment experience may enable employers to tell a different story about black male job applicants. Experience with a temp agency may therefore be counterstereotypical information for employers when evaluating black men and produce positive effects for black men.

Multiple respondents picked up on a line of thought similar to Ashley's, emphasizing two key explanations. First, temp agencies often conduct thorough screenings and checks on applicants before hiring them, including criminal background checks. Considerable research suggests that employers often hold ingrained stereotypes about African American workers— particularly African American men—as having poor work ethics and being aggressive, violent, and even criminal.[13] In turn, temp agency experience may serve a screening role in the labor market for black workers, particularly black male workers. Given that temp agencies often screen workers using personality tests, cognitive ability tests, and criminal background and drug tests, having worked at a temp agency may send a unique and positive signal about African American men to future employers.

Accordingly, Jennifer, who works as a call center operations supervisor, offered the following when asked about the finding from the field experiment regarding the benefits of temp agency work for black men: "I would say probably because you feel like if they've gone through a temp agency, they've got like their screenings and background checks, maybe computer tests. They've just gone through more rigorous testing. You know, a lot of those temp agencies make you do so many tests on the computer to make sure that your skill set really matches what you put on your resume." In a similar vein, Christina—who works in HR in the education sector—responded, "Probably because of the screening process for most of the agencies. It's pretty high. You have to get through a lot of testing so that would make sense." A history of temp work potentially signals to future employers that these workers have cleared the bar in terms of competence and work ethic, that they are drug free, and that they do not have a criminal record. Temp work may signal to future employers that the worker has been "prescreened" for quality, which could increase the likelihood of African American men being called back for a job.

Second, reputation matters. The temp agency's reputation is on the line when it sends its temp workers to a given employer. If a temp worker is able to maintain employment through a temp agency for a significant amount of time—remember that in the field experiment, workers had a year of experience with the temp agency—then it may signal that the worker is particularly reliable, dependable, and perceived by other employers as a high-quality worker. As Karen, who works at a health-care-related startup, said in her interview, "If you work in a temp agency, every time you go to a new company, that company's sort of giving feedback on you. So you have more of a range of screening would be my guess." Of course, some employers indicated that long periods of temp work would be a negative signal because it meant the worker was not converted to a permanent position. But it is also possible that temping for the same agency for an extended period indicates that the agency sees value in the worker. This positive signaling may be particularly strong for workers about whom potential future employers hold negative stereotypes and beliefs, such as African American men.

Challenging Stereotypes

African American men appear to benefit markedly from temporary agency work when applying for new jobs. Existing scholarship and the interviews with hiring professionals hint toward two potential mechanisms driving this finding. First, the screening, testing, and background checks completed by temp agencies may matter. And second, THAs putting their own reputations on the line when they send workers to client companies could be important. These positive signals provided by a history of temporary agency employment may enable hiring professionals to tell a different, more favorable type of story about African American men during the hiring process. The institutional stamp of the temp agency provides counterstereotypical information that appears to assist in mitigating employers' negative stereotypes of black men as aggressive, criminal, or unmotivated.[14] In turn, employers are then able to create a narrative about African American male job applicants that diverges from the entrenched cultural beliefs that they may hold about this group of workers.

With African American men and temp agency work, the stratified stories that employers develop operate a bit differently than in the previous chapters. Rather than particular types of employment experiences being interpreted through racial and gender stereotypes, here it appears as if the reverse is also possible. The stereotypes about a worker's social group membership can actually be shifted by the signals that come from a particular type of employment history.

There is a significant body of existing scholarship on the ways that counterstereotypical information can shape people's attitudes and behaviors.[15] One study, based in Germany, for example, used a method similar to the field experiment presented throughout this book. The researchers sent applications to apply for student internships and varied the ethnicity of the applicants by sending some applications with a Turkish-sounding name and some with a German-sounding name. Overall, the applicants with German-sounding names had approximately a 14 percent higher likelihood of receiving a callback. But for some applicants the researchers provided reference letters with positive information about the applicants' personality. Among the cases where these reference letters were provided, there was no discrimination against the candidates with Turkish-sounding names.[16] This finding aligns with the idea that providing information that counters the stereotypes employers hold—in this case, having a winning personality for Turkish applicants in Germany—can reduce discrimination.[17] It is possible that a history of THA employment in the US context plays a similar role for African American men, although of course there are some differences between our case and the study in Germany, where concrete positive information was provided about the candidate.

In other research on race and stereotypes, including some of my own, scholars have found similar patterns when examining how race and sexual orientation intersect for men.[18] In a survey, for example, I asked white individuals in the general US population to evaluate resumes and then provide salary recommendations for the candidate that they reviewed. The people who took the survey, however, were randomly assigned to review different applicant profiles: a white straight man, a black straight man, a white gay man, or a black gay man. I found that white gay men and black straight men received lower salary recommendations that white straight men. But gay black men were not penalized in terms of salary compared to straight white men. Indeed, gay black men received higher salary recommendations than straight black men. Additional evidence indicated that this positive effect for black gay men was driven by perceptions of how threatening the job applicants were: gay black men were perceived as being less threatening than straight black men. In this context, there is a way that counterstereotypical information—being gay and its associated stereotypes—can shift perceptions of African American men. The evidence presented in this chapter suggests that previous experience with THA employment can serve a similar role, counteracting negative stereotypes and improving the outcomes of African American men. Stereotypes can be challenged. Different stories can be told.

———

We again see stratified stories emerge in the case of THA employment histories and the employment opportunities of African American men. The findings from the field experiment indicate that employers' often negative stereotypes of black men can be counteracted by them having experience working through a THA. Employers' conceptions of the role of temporary help agencies in screening, testing, and "marking" workers as "good" employees appear to serve as counterstereotypical information, enabling them to produce new narratives about job applicants about whom they hold negative stereotypes. As was noted above, nothing in the job applicants' materials in the THA condition in the field experiment indicated that they had received particular skills or personality tests or that they had received a criminal background check or drug testing. Yet hiring professionals appear to extract from histories of temporary agency employment signals about job applicants that can offset deep-seated cultural beliefs and stereotypes about African American men. Thus, the hiring agents produce stratified stories, crafting new narratives about black male applicants that make them more desirable job applicants than black men with standard employment histories.

Given the counterintuitive nature of this finding, it will be important for future scholars to examine whether this effect is consistent across time and space and to more deeply probe the underlying mechanisms driving this relationship. But it is powerful that institutional markers—such as THA employment—may be able to combat negative stereotypes about African American men. Perhaps other types of institutional and organizational experiences may be able to play similar roles in reducing discrimination.

We see here—as we did in the previous two chapters—a key lesson: identities matter. They matter independent of nonstandard, mismatched, and precarious employment histories: African American workers with full-time, standard, seamless employment histories face persistent discrimination. However, they also play an important role in shaping the ways that employers make sense of distinct types of employment trajectories. Stereotypes about the racial and gender groups to which workers belong are utilized in combination with histories of long-term unemployment, part-time work, and temporary agency employment to evaluate job applicants. Employers draw on and develop stratified stories. And the divergent stories that employers tell have real consequences. Part-time work histories are severely penalizing for men with white or neutral names, but not for this group of women. While long-term unemployment is severely penalizing for white workers, it has limited additional negative consequences for African Americans, after accounting for racial discrimination. And temporary agency employment can actually improve the outcomes of African American men compared to African American men who have maintained full-time, standard employment histories. A complex picture emerges. Far from having universal consequences, social identities and nonstandard, mismatched, and precarious employment histories interact to produce complex inequalities for workers in the new economy.

8

Conclusion

"Good" jobs can be hard to come by. The underlying changes in the US economy have meant that workers often struggle with insecurity and economic anxiety. And millions of workers labor in nonstandard, mismatched, and precarious employment positions. They work part-time, through temporary help agencies, in positions below their skill level, or are unable to find work altogether. The pages of this book have focused on the experiences of these workers. Yet rather than study the day-to-day lives of nonstandard, mismatched, and precarious workers or track them through the labor market to capture their wages, benefits, and employment trajectories, I have examined how they are treated and perceived by key gatekeepers in the labor market: hiring professionals.

Individuals who make hiring decisions—recruiters, HR professionals, hiring managers, talent specialists, and the like—wield significant power in the labor market. They decide who gets interviewed and, ultimately, who gets hired. They manage the boundaries of the organization, deciding which workers get a foot in the door. The meanings that they extract from workers' job applications and then the ways that they mobilize those meanings to decide which applicants to interview have broad consequences for workers' opportunities and economic security in the so-called new economy.

As we have seen from the interviews with hiring professionals as well as through the field experiment capturing actual hiring decisions, the processes of inclusion and exclusion in the labor market are far from straightforward. While hiring professionals extract meanings from the nonstandard, mismatched, and precarious work histories on job applicants' resumes, they do so in a complex way. Different types of employment experiences signal different information about workers' technical skills, personality, and compliance with ideal worker norms, among other things. Yet hiring professionals are also left with significant uncertainty and ambiguity when it comes to evaluating applicants with nonstandard, mismatched, and precarious work experience. They are left wanting to know why—why was the worker in a position that deviates from common conceptions of a "good" job? We also saw the ways that the effects of these different types of nonstandard, mismatched, and precarious employment histories operate differently from one another when it comes to how they affect workers. While some types of experiences are nearly universally negative, others produce virtually no negative effect at all. And the consequences of different types of employment experiences are shaped in powerful ways by workers' social group memberships. Race and gender matter, not just independently but also in concert with nonstandard, mismatched, and precarious employment histories.

The Consequences of Nonstandard, Mismatched, and Precarious Work

Against the backdrop of a changing economic landscape, scholars have produced a large body of evidence about the subjective and material consequences of nonstandard, mismatched, and precarious employment for workers themselves. Although there is certainly variation, workers in these positions earn less and receive worse fringe benefits, on average, than their counterparts in full-time, standard jobs at their level of skill and experience.[1] Beyond the material circumstances, there are myriad challenges that workers in these positions experience, from stigmatization to exclusion and self-blame.[2] Yet, much less is known about how workers with employment experiences that diverge from "good jobs" are evaluated in the labor market. A central goal of this book has therefore been to shift our lens from examining workers' experiences—both material and subjective—when they labor in nonstandard, mismatched, and precarious positions and to focus on how these workers are perceived and treated by potential future employers. What have we learned from taking this perspective?

Three overarching patterns emerge throughout the book. First, histories of nonstandard, mismatched, and precarious work are salient markers on job applicants' resumes. Hiring professionals notice them, make meaning from them, and ultimately use them—albeit in complex ways—to decide whom to interview. Indeed, we saw compelling evidence that these distinct types of employment histories map onto key evaluative criteria that employers utilize during the hiring process, such as technical skills and knowledge, soft skills and personality, and ideal worker norms of commitment and competence. Part-time work, for example, frequently signaled to future employers that a worker was likely to have obligations and demands outside of the workplace that were important and potentially distracting. For that reason, part-time work largely violates ideal worker norm expectations of complete commitment and dedication to one's employer. Unemployment, by contrast, commonly raised concerns about workers' personality and soft skills, echoing previous scholarship that uncovered stereotypes about unemployed workers as lazy workers.

Beyond the substance of the meanings attributed to nonstandard, mismatched, and precarious work, these types of employment positions also induced in hiring professionals palpable uncertainty about candidates. Each type of employment could mean many different things. Grasping for reasons, hiring professionals wanted to understand why workers strayed from what might be considered a more conventional employment trajectory. In an attempt to resolve this ambiguity and uncertainty, employers placed the onus on workers to explain their experiences. Rather than turning to structural explanations about the challenges of navigating the new economy, they wanted workers to tell their story. Workers are effectively held responsible for weaving a compelling narrative about their employment trajectory, particularly when that trajectory deviates from seamless, continuous, full-time, standard employment. Yet as we saw in the field experiment, workers with nonstandard, mismatched, and precarious employment experiences are often screened out of the hiring process before they are able to tell their story.

The second key set of findings centers on the variation in employment opportunities afforded to workers across different types of work experiences. Indeed, skills underutilization generally results in severe penalties for workers compared to those who had maintained employment at their level of skill and experience. It was also the one type of employment experience whose consequences did not vary in a significant way for any sociodemographic group of workers. Job applicants with experiences in positions below their skill level rarely have the opportunity to tell their stories to employers. Instead, employers appear to attribute negative meanings to skills underutilization nearly across the board, perceiving these workers as lacking technical skills or having skills that may have atrophied and violating the ideal worker norm of competence.

By contrast, workers with experiences in THA employment generally avoided significant penalties; their experiences were comparable to those of workers who maintained employment in full-time, standard positions. While employers certainly expressed some negative perceptions of and concerns about THA employment experience, these concerns seemed to be outweighed by other aspects of temping. The vast majority of temp agency workers are employed full-time and may work in their occupation of choice, as they were in the field experiment analyzed in this book.[3] They also have the opportunity to move between organizations, potentially getting the chance to see new and innovative ways to conduct certain tasks. Comparing skills underutilization and THA employment experiences, we see the contingent effects of different employment experiences. Far from all employment experiences that deviate from "good jobs" penalizing workers' employment opportunities, the picture that emerges is one of heterogeneity.

Yet just as different types of employment experiences have divergent consequences, their effects are also shaped by the social group to which a worker belongs. In other words: identities matter. Among the strongest effects in the field experiment is the persistence of racial discrimination. African American workers are called back for jobs at approximately half the rate of whites, a finding that is consistent with existing scholarship in this area.[4] Race continues to play a central role in shaping employment opportunities. A core insight of this book is that the powerful stereotypes and meanings that employers attribute to workers' social group membership—such as race and gender—are intimately connected to the ways that employers make sense of different employment histories.

Part-time work has differential effects for women and men with white or neutral names. While part-time work is as penalizing as a year of unemployment for this group of men, it has no negative consequences for this group of women. Also, the effects of unemployment are not the same for white and black workers. While white workers experience significant penalties for a year of unemployment, African American workers face no additional penalties for unemployment beyond the deep levels of discrimination they already face. This pattern is driven largely by employers' treatment of African American men. We also see that THA employment has a unique and surprising effect for African American men. Indeed, black men with THA employment experiences received a higher callback rate than African American men with a full-time, standard employment trajectory.

What unifies these findings about part-time work and gender, unemployment and race, and THA employment for African American men? The interviews with hiring professionals reveal that these patterns are driven, at least in part, by the stratified stories that hiring professionals use to interpret and evaluate different employment histories. Employers want a narrative from workers explaining their employment experiences, but those narratives are generally not available, particularly at the early stages of the job applicant review process. Therefore, hiring professionals draw—consciously or unconsciously—on deep-seated cultural beliefs and stereotypes about race and gender to make sense of workers' employment experiences. With part-time work, employers' stereotypes of women as caregivers align easily with perceptions of part-time work as an indicator that a worker has competing demands and obligations outside of the workplace. Men's part-time work experience violates expectations about breadwinning, resulting in exclusion for men who move into part-time positions. At the same time, stereotypes about African American workers often have similar content to stereotypes about the unemployed. Both emphasize a lack of motivation, work ethic, and competence. The penalties for unemployment effectively remain concentrated among white workers. In both of these situations, the intertwined stereotypes about workers' employment positions and their social group memberships provide employers with compelling narratives—stratified stories—that they can draw upon for one group and that are not available for other groups.

For African American men with THA experience, a similar process appears to be at play, although it operates slightly differently. In this case, ingrained stereotypes about African American men are strong and negative, often focusing on concerns not just of competence and motivation but also related to having a criminal background. In the interviews with hiring professionals, it became clear that hiring agents are often aware that many temp agencies conduct serious screening before hiring temps. Temp workers often undergo personality tests, drug tests, and criminal background checks. This high level of screening may counteract some of hiring professionals' negative stereotypes about African American men, allaying their concerns and resulting in more positive outcomes for black men.

Theoretical Implications

Beyond their significance for understanding the patterns that emerge in the labor market, the findings presented throughout the book also make inroads into important theoretical conversations about how gatekeepers make decisions. The results have implications for understanding the processes that give rise to labor market inequality, how race and gender discrimination operate, and the ways that social categories combine.

WHEN EXPECTATIONS LAG

While the economic landscape in the United States has changed in many ways over recent decades, hiring professionals appear to hang on to outdated expectations about what an employment trajectory should look like. The complex, often challenging economic context was certainly something that the hiring professionals I spoke with are aware of. Yet they held on to a sense that workers should be able to maintain very particular types of employment trajectories. The ideal worker—the applicant whom they want to hire—has a history of continuous employment in full-time, standard jobs at his (the ideal worker is generally conceived of as a man) level of skill and education. He always has a "good" job.

This type of employment trajectory can be difficult to attain for workers in the contemporary United States. There have been many changes in the economy that have left workers in challenging positions. Occupations have become polarized, fringe benefits have become more difficult to come by, and many work protections have eroded. Millions of people find themselves working in part-time jobs, through temp agencies, in positions below their skill level, or unable to find work altogether. There is therefore a sizeable disjuncture between the lived experiences of workers and the expectations of key economic gatekeepers: hiring professionals. The result, as we have seen throughout the book, is that a complex set of inequalities emerges.

Gatekeepers' lagged expectations in producing divergent evaluations and, in turn, disparate outcomes likely extend beyond the hiring process in the labor market. Other powerful decision makers may also have lagged expectations for individuals that are at odds with the context in which individuals live: judges in the criminal justice system, for instance. Continued work mapping the ways that decision makers' expectations are misaligned with current realities will be valuable for understanding the drivers of persistent inequality.

STRATIFIED STORIES: DIVERGENT EVALUATIONS, DIVERGENT OUTCOMES

The hiring process has many phases: there is the job advertisement, the passive and active recruitment of applications, and the decisions of whom to interview, then whom to hire, and then what to offer them by way of compensation. Each of these procedural components has received attention from scholars, but this book focuses on one discrete moment: the decision about who in a large group of applicants should be interviewed. As we saw, this moment is filled with challenges. Time and information are limited. Employers thus infer information about difficult-to-observe and hard-to-measure applicant characteristics from the concrete, observable features that can be gleaned from their resumes: educational credentials, age, race, gender, and community involvement.

Much of this book has focused on how employers make sense of one component of a worker's resume: a history of nonstandard, mismatched, or precarious employment. Technical skills, personality and soft skills, and the ideal worker norms of competence and commitment were all salient signals extracted from these different employment histories. Yet histories of part-time work, temporary agency employment, skills underutilization, and long-term unemployment also induce significant uncertainty in hiring professionals. They want to understand what drove someone having a particular type of employment experience. They want to know why. As we saw, workers are put on the hook to allay gatekeepers' own concerns about a particular employment history. But in many cases workers never get to tell their story. They are often filtered out before they get a callback or an interview. But the exclusion generated by these types of employment experiences is not universal. Some types of workers get screened out, while others are given an opportunity to interview for a job. Why is this the case?

I develop the concept of stratified stories to describe the ways that hiring professionals integrate stereotypes and cultural beliefs about the social group memberships of job applicants with information about applicants' nonstandard, mismatched, and precarious work histories to arrive at an evaluation of the worker. In other words, group-based stereotypes become useful tools in weaving a narrative about job applicants when their employment trajectories deviate from common conceptions of a "good" job.

There are compelling and easy narratives that employers can tell about part-time work for women: they were taking care of young children. For men, this type of narrative is not as readily available. In fact, for men part-time work violates key ideas of them as breadwinners. The result: men experience penalties for part-time work that women evade. Likewise, unemployment experience carries with it stereotypes of laziness, low work ethic, and lack of competence. These ideas overlap heavily with stereotypical beliefs about African American workers. Hiring professionals therefore appear to draw on narratives about unemployment for African Americans that are in line with their already negative perceptions, producing limited effects of unemployment for black workers, particularly black men. For white workers, different beliefs and stereotypes exist that are at odds with long-term unemployment. Overall, African American workers experience significant discrimination when they maintain full-time, standard, seamless employment histories, but face limited additional penalties for long-term unemployment.

Stratified stories likely transcend the hiring process. In many situations, gatekeepers and decision makers have limited time but need to make important, evaluative judgments. We can think about the criminal justice context in which judges are evaluating many cases in a very short amount of time. Various fact patterns and information about the crime may very well be read through the social characteristics of the defendant. Judges may produce one narrative for a middle-aged white woman and a different one for a young African American man, even if the information in the cases is fundamentally the same. These divergent narratives likely produce divergent decisions. Similar processes may be at play in hospitals, where doctors and nurses are making complex decisions about managing patients' symptoms. When time is scarce, information is limited, and decisions need to be made, the deep-seated cultural beliefs that we hold about social groups—men and women, whites and African Americans, and so on—provide easy fodder for weaving narratives and shaping decisions.

HOW SOCIAL CATEGORIES AGGREGATE: THE CONSEQUENCES OF STRATIFIED STORIES

Researchers of social inequality are interested in how social categories aggregate to produce key social, economic, and political outcomes. In general, scholars tend to think about the ways that social categories aggregate to produce inequality in one of two primary ways. In the first case, a secondary category will have similar consequences across the different levels of the first category. We can think of this as an "additive effects" pattern. In the second case, the secondary category may exacerbate the negative effects of the first category. This can be referred to as the "amplified congruence" pattern. Research has produced empirical findings that align with both of these underlying patterns.[5]

There are two additional social category aggregation patterns, however, that are possible and that have been shown throughout the book. Yet these alternative aggregation patterns have received less attention in the existing literature. The first is what I refer to as "muted congruence." The idea here is that when two categories have heavily overlapping stereotypes, the second characteristic may have limited additional impact beyond the first characteristic. In other words, there is declining marginal impact of stereotypically consistent information from any additional social category.[6] A final aggregation pattern that can emerge is that of "offsetting effects." Here, the underlying stereotypes or meanings attributed to one's social group membership may be canceled out by membership in a second group.[7]

The stratified stories that have been documented in this book assist in illuminating the ways that these different aggregation patterns emerge. When decision makers are able to draw on social-group-based narratives that are easy to deploy in understanding a second characteristic—as in the case of gender and part-time work, or race and long-term unemployment—a muted congruence pattern may emerge because the second category provides limited additional information or meaning. In other words, when stereotypical group-based understandings are highly overlapping with the meanings attributed to an additional worker characteristic, that second characteristic may have limited influence over the ultimate evaluation of the applicant. By contrast, when some category provides counterstereotypical information—as in the case of THA employment experiences for African American men—new stories may be able to be told. In these cases, an offsetting effects pattern may emerge, resulting in a more positive evaluation of a job applicant than might have been expected.

While there is significant utility in conceptualizing the hiring evaluation process through the different types of narratives that employers create, important questions remain about the conditions under which these different narratives are drawn upon. Why might an amplified congruence pattern emerge in some cases and a muted congruence pattern emerge in others? When is the counterstereotypical information provided by a secondary characteristic adequate to overcome a set of deep-seated negative stereotypes and produce an offsetting effects pattern? And when does a simple additive effects pattern result from the aggregation of social categories? While the field experiment and interviews in this book are not able to provide answers to these questions, they lay the groundwork for these issues to be pursued.

One potential path forward in this area is to examine evaluation processes across contexts where the institutional structures vary, such as comparing evidence from different countries. In national contexts where part-time work is less heavily gendered or where disparities in unemployment are less racially and ethnically pronounced, for example, different types of stratified stories are likely to be drawn upon and produce distinct aggregation patterns. This type of comparative analysis of evaluations would be highly beneficial for theorizing why there is variation in the ways that social categories combine with one another.

Future Directions

While this book has provided a detailed look into the ways that nonstandard, mismatched, and precarious employment shape the evaluation of job applicants, it is not free from limitations. A key challenge with the type of field-experimental data presented in this book is that they are drawn from formal applications submitted through a national online job posting website. Estimates suggest, however, that roughly half of all jobs are filled through referral channels and word of mouth.[8] That slice of the labor market is not captured in the field-experimental data. And we could imagine that the ways that nonstandard, mismatched, and precarious employment affect hiring evaluations are indeed different when applications are submitted through informal networks. For example, a referrer may be able to provide a narrative to a future employer about why workers were in a position below their skill level. Similar explanations would be possible if the workers have experienced long-term unemployment, part-time work, or temporary agency employment. Finding a way to include informal job search processes in our understanding of the consequences of nonstandard, mismatched, and precarious work—potentially through data that track workers through their job search—would be an important extension of this scholarship.

The interviews with hiring professionals discussed throughout the book were vital to making sense of the findings in the field experiment and to understanding the consequences of these types of employment positions. However, the individuals I spoke with were often hesitant to discuss race. They often skirted questions about racial bias, even when these questions were posed with respect to their colleagues at other companies and not their own attitudes about race. They were more open to talking about race when presented with findings from the field experiment about racial discrimination, but even then some hiring professionals remained on guard. Interestingly though, the hiring professionals were somewhat more willing to talk about gender differences, particularly with regard to part-time employment. This distinction between race and gender—with gender being less stilting to the conversation—is intriguing.

Unlike race, age was a topic that the hiring professionals were quite open to discussing. I have not focused on these age-based discussions in the book, largely because the field experiment held the age of the worker constant. There are therefore no behavioral outcomes against which to compare the hiring professionals' discussions about age and nonstandard, mismatched, and precarious employment. However, there is important work to be done—potentially with field-experimental techniques—to compare the consequences of long-term unemployment, part-time work, temporary agency employment, and skills underutilization for workers of different ages. Some evidence suggests that unemployment is not particularly scarring for recent college graduates.[9] And it is possible that the consequences of gender and part-time work, for example, would look quite different for workers who are older and beyond their prime childbearing years. Given the willingness of hiring professionals—at least those hiring professionals in our sample—to discuss age, there would also be compelling opportunities to tie together interview-based and field-experimental work in this area.

In this book, the racial and ethnic variation that is examined is highly truncated. The field-experimental data are able to compare individuals with African American names to those with names that are likely perceived as white or that do not prime a particular race. This leaves outstanding questions about how nonstandard, mismatched, and precarious employment operates for Hispanic and Latino workers, Asian workers, and workers from other racial and ethnic backgrounds. African Americans are not the only group that is overrepresented in some of these categories, and thus there may be telling interactions between other racial and ethnic group memberships and the different types of employment experiences investigated here.

One important thing to keep in mind when thinking about and interpreting data from the field experiment is that the data were generated at one moment in time—November 2012 to June 2013—during the recovery from the Great Recession. While this does not bias the findings, it may have consequences for their generalizability. Would things look different in today's social and economic landscape? What about twenty years from now? As the business cycle and economy change, so too may the consequences of the employment histories examined here. In the longer term, if certain employment histories change in terms of their social meaning—for example, if part-time work becomes a less feminized category—the ways that each employment history intersects with a given sociodemographic category may also change. Revisiting this set of issues at a future date, with a similar research design, could provide new insights about how employment experiences intersect with race and gender to shape economic opportunities. Related to this, the field experiment was limited to five labor markets and four occupations. The consequences of different employment histories and their intersections with race and gender may differ to some extent in other geographies and occupation types.

In terms of timing, it is also relevant to remember that the interview data were collected after the field experiment and from a different sample of employers. On the positive side, this staggered timing of the two data collection efforts enabled the hiring professionals I interviewed to respond to the field-experimental findings. However, the narratives that the employers offered were not reflective of the exact same moment as the decisions that hiring professionals were making in the field experiment.

Additionally, the data in this book provide limited insights into how new technologies may impact race and gender bias in hiring as well as the evaluations of applicants with different types of employment experiences. The hiring professionals with whom we spoke discussed their use of online job posting websites and ATSs. Over time, the role of these technologies—and others—in the hiring process is likely to increase and change.[10] Yet there are some concerns about the consequences of these technologies both for the quality of matches between workers and companies as well as for broader patterns of social inequality.[11] And as employers are utilizing new technologies for hiring decision making, job seekers both are responding to these changes and have access to a range of technological tools.[12] Theoretical models of the hiring process and strategies for empirical data collection about hiring decisions will need to keep up with these changes to better understand how technological interventions and their various designs shape inequality-generating processes during the hiring process.[13] As more and more job applications are first vetted by algorithms, field-experimental approaches will be well served by considering innovative approaches to assessing discrimination in applicant screening and decomposing any detected discrimination into that which is driven by algorithms, that which is driven by human decision making, and that which is driven by the nexus of the two.

Broader Implications

While not the primary focus of this book, the results presented here may be relevant beyond the academic context. Below I present a few key areas where the findings presented in *Making the Cut* may be relevant for policy conversations.

The underlying processes that lead hiring professionals to use group-based stereotypes about race and gender are similar to those that lead them to use group-based stereotypes about the long-term unemployed, part-time workers, temporary agency employees, and workers in jobs below their skill level. Time is limited, information is scarce, and the decisions have significant consequences. Thus, stereotypes become easy and quick heuristic devices to sort workers into piles of "good" and "bad" workers and then determine whom to interview. While any single strategy to reduce bias in hiring, and employment processes more broadly, is unlikely to be a silver bullet, a growing body of scholarship points to some promising ideas. One strategy that has been shown to have some—although not universally—positive effects for reducing bias and discrimination is the formalization of practices. By making evaluative processes more detailed and structured, stereotypes and group-based heuristics are less likely to creep in, and opportunities for the best people to get hired—regardless of their race, gender, or nonstandard, mismatched, or precarious employment history—increase.[14] Related to this, formal accountability structures within organizations can be a powerful tool for reducing bias.[15] When individuals know that there are processes and structures in place to evaluate their decisions and to hold them accountable for those decisions, race and gender biases may be less likely to be deployed. While much of the scholarship in this area has focused on biases against sociodemographic groups—such as women or African Americans—their consequences may be similar for reducing biased evaluations of nonstandard, mismatched, and precarious work as well.

The field experiment also demonstrates that workers who end up in positions of skill underutilization have a hard time obtaining opportunities at their level of skill and experience in the future. Thus, economic policies designed to prevent workers from being involuntarily displaced from their jobs may prevent workers from needing to take positions below their skill level. Additionally, ensuring that unemployment insurance and other types of benefits are adequate to support individuals and their families while they try to find a job that matches their level of skill could reduce the need for workers to enter positions of skills underutilization in the first place. And, certainly, policy interventions that promote the development of "good" jobs, where workers are able to fully utilize their skills and work full-time in standard positions—when that is what they want—would be an important step toward curbing workers' exposure to nonstandard, mismatched, and precarious employment.

The findings from the field experiment also highlight the dire need for continued policy attention to reduce racial discrimination. While racial discrimination is illegal, it is still rampant. Indeed, a recent meta-analysis that

brought together evidence from experiments of racial discrimination conducted by different researchers over time demonstrated that there has been
no decline in racial discrimination in hiring in the United States since 1989.[16]
Scholars have shown that negative stereotypes about African Americans
likely play a key role in driving racial discrimination.[17] One of the surprising
findings from the field-experimental evidence presented here is that employment experience with a THA actually boosts the callback rate for African
American men, when compared to those who had a standard, seamless,
full-time employment history. This finding is suggestive for policy interventions to reduce racial discrimination against African American men. Institutional actors that can potentially counteract employers' negative stereotypes
about African American men could serve as a framework for interventions
to promote employment opportunities for this group of workers. And, more
broadly, attention and resources devoted to challenging racial discrimination and holding employers accountable for discriminatory behavior remain
important in the contemporary United States.[18]

Another arena to which the findings from this book speak is work-family
policy. Part of the penalty that accrues to men—at least men with white or
race-neutral names—for part-time work is that they are perceived as less
dedicated to their careers and are seen as not complying with masculinity
norms about breadwinning. This is in part due to women being significantly more likely than men to move into part-time positions, often to
care for young children or take care of other family responsibilities. Insofar as work-family policies—including the option at some companies to
work part-time—are increasingly appealing to and utilized by men, some
of the gendering of part-time work as well as caretaking responsibilities in
the United States may be reduced. Additionally, if the gender distribution
of part-time employment becomes more equal over time—similar to how
things changed for temporary agency employment between World War II
and the present—then the consequences of part-time work for job applicants' employment opportunities and outcomes may become less divergent
by gender. Indeed, we saw in the field experiment that there were limited
differences in the callback rates for white men and women workers with
THA employment histories. The future of part-time work could also look
this way, and creating supportive work-family policies that work well for
both men and women could assist in moving in that direction.

Making the Cut provides new insights about how hiring works in the
contemporary economy. It offers a unique lens onto how recruiters, hiring
managers, and other individuals involved in the hiring process make sense

of the employment experiences of millions of workers that deviate from our common conceptions of "good" employment trajectories: part-time work, temporary agency employment, skills underutilization, and long-term unemployment. These types of employment experiences have tangible consequences for workers' outcomes during the hiring process, sending meaningful signals to hiring professionals about a worker's technical skills, personality and soft skills, compliance with ideal worker norms of competence and commitment, and to some extent fit. While the effects of these different employment experiences are contingent on many factors—including the race and gender of the worker—they serve as an important driver of unequal outcomes among workers traversing the challenges of the contemporary economic landscape.

———

I began this book by asking you to imagine that your boss had tasked you with hiring a new employee for your company. The applications pour in and you need to make a quick decision about which candidates to interview. Who would make the cut?

Knowing what you know now, what would you think of that applicant who had been unemployed for the past year? Would you give her a call or screen her out? And what about the man with a year of part-time employment experience? Is it worth giving him a chance?

Regardless of how you answer these questions, I hope that this book has made you think in more complex ways about the hiring process and the employment histories that workers often carry with them. By better understanding the challenges workers face in the so-called new economy, we can begin to find pathways forward to promote equal opportunity for workers across the labor market.

Methodological Appendix

In this Methodological Appendix I shed additional light on the techniques used to collect the data presented throughout *Making the Cut*. While Chapter 1 introduced the basic information about the research design to enable an understanding of the data used throughout the book, here I provide more detail about both the field experiment and the interviews with hiring professionals.

The Field Experiment

A key challenge with studying employers' hiring behavior is that it can be difficult to observe. Researchers are often not present during the hiring process, and even if they were, there may be concerns that their presence would shift the dynamics and decisions about hiring. For *Making the Cut*, I was particularly interested in studying how employers treat workers who differ only on selected characteristics—employment history, race, and gender—while holding everything else constant. Thus, even if I had direct access to information about the hiring process at different companies, it would be difficult to ensure that the applicants being reviewed differed only on the key characteristics of interest and did not also differ on other factors that may drive the hiring process, such as education and other background characteristics related to productivity.

As was discussed earlier, one approach that researchers can use when they want to understand how a given characteristic, such as race, affects whether or not an employer decides to interview or hire an applicant—holding all else equal—is to utilize an experimental research design where key characteristics are randomly assigned to different application materials. To collect the field-experimental data analyzed in *Making the Cut*, I submitted 4,822 fictitious job applications to apply for 2,411 job openings in five US labor markets: Atlanta, Boston, Chicago, Los Angeles, and New York.[1] These five labor markets differed in their unemployment rates as well as their racial composition. They are also major labor markets where I was confident there would be an adequate number of job openings to apply for to complete the study. The applications were sent to openings in four broad occupational groups: administrative/clerical, sales, accounting/bookkeeping, and project management/management. The occupations vary in their gender composition and the skills required for the positions, broadening the scope of the experiment beyond any one particular slice of the labor market.[2]

MANIPULATING EMPLOYMENT HISTORIES

There were two primary axes of variation in the experiment: the employment history of the applicants and the sociodemographic characteristics of the applicants—their race and gender. In terms of the employment histories, each applicant was randomly assigned twelve months of recent employment experience in one of the following five types of positions:

- Full-time, standard employment at the worker's skill level
- Part-time employment in the worker's occupation of choice
- Temporary agency employment in the worker's occupation of choice
- Skills underutilization, where the worker was employed in a job below his or her skill level
- Long-term unemployment

Histories of nonstandard, mismatched, and precarious employment were carefully signaled on workers' resumes. Part-time work was presented on a worker's resume by including "part-time" in parentheses after the occupational title for the most recent job on the full-time, standard employment resume. Thus, the occupation in which the part-time employment occurred was identical to the occupation in which the full-time, standard employment occurred. This method of signaling part-time work experience is consistent with how workers present this information in online resume banks.

Temporary agency employment was presented on the applicant's resume as working through one of two major temporary help agencies and in the worker's chosen occupation (e.g., sales). The descriptions of the tasks and responsibilities completed as a temporary worker were very similar in content to those presented on the full-time, standard resume.

While the part-time and temporary agency employment histories were in the worker's occupation of choice, skills underutilization—for all workers— was denoted as having worked as a sales representative at a large retail store. The details of the position indicated that the individual worked with customers in the retail space. The year of employment in this position followed approximately six years of work experience in professional jobs and thus clearly indicates that the worker was employed at a level below his skill and experience.

Finally, a spell of long-term unemployment was presented on workers' resumes by indicating that their most recent job ended one year before the application date.[3] To ensure that resumes in the unemployment condition had the same number of employment experiences as resumes in the other conditions, a summer internship in college was added to resumes for the "unemployed" workers. Examples of the resumes used for each of the employment history conditions are presented in Chapter 4.

Each of the employment trajectories for the job applicants in the field experiment was local to the labor market where the application was submitted. Thus, for example, if an application was being submitted for a job opening in New York City, all of the applicants' prior employment experience would also be in New York City. Additionally, applicants' prior employment experience was all at real companies that exist in that local labor market.

MANIPULATING THE RACE AND GENDER OF THE APPLICANT

The second axis of variation in the experiment was the applicants' race and gender, which were signaled using racialized and gendered names. The first set of names included Jon Murphy and Matthew Stevens for men and Katherine Murphy and Emily Stevens for women. It is not clear whether these names actively led employers to think an applicant was white or whether these names simply did not prime a race of the applicant and thus gatekeepers defaulted to assumptions of whiteness or evaluations that were not racialized in a particular way.

To signal an African American racial background, racialized male and female names were used: Darnell Washington and Tyrone Jackson for men and Kimora Washington and Kenya Jackson for women. Using names to signal race is complicated since heavily racialized names may signal more than just the race of the applicant, such as the applicant's social class.[4] To gain some traction on this issue, I obtained data on the first names of all New York State resident births in 2008–2009 by the mother's race and educational attainment.[5] I then selected names that were highly likely to have a black mother and that were likely to have a white mother (at least 60 percent for the black-sounding names and 70 percent for the white/neutral-sounding names).[6] Next, I took this group of names and selected a set where the average level of maternal education was somewhat similar. While there were still some maternal education differences by race, this approach assists in addressing the potential confounding effects of social class.

Throughout the book I have referred to applicants with a particular demographic-sounding name as applicants from that demographic background (i.e., "African American" applicants). However, this approach is not perfect because in the real world an African American racialized name does not necessarily mean that an applicant is black. White workers can have names that are racialized as black. Additionally, I used the label "white/neutral" to represent the names Jon, Matthew, Emily, and Katherine because these names may not actually prime employers to think in racialized ways. And certainly African American workers do have names such as Emily or Jon. While there are challenges that arise when using names to signal race on job application materials, it is among the strongest approaches social scientists have found to provide traction on the ways that employers respond to applicants who are likely to be perceived as belonging to different racial groups.[7]

APPLICATION PROCEDURES

I submitted two applications to each job posting. A resume and a cover letter were included with each job application. Each cover letter was crafted with similar language, while also accurately reflecting the work history presented on the corresponding resume. The cover letter for each experimental condition remained consistent across employers, except that each letter was personalized with the employer's name and the job title for the open position.

Because two resumes were submitted for each job opening, I constructed two resume templates that were similar in content but aesthetically distinct. Each resume indicated that the applicant graduated from one of two large, public universities in the Midwest with similar rankings by *U.S. News & World Report*.[8] Each resume indicated that after graduating from college the applicant had a first job that lasted for just under two years. Each applicant then had a second job that lasted for nearly four and a half years. All applicants then transitioned to a new job, which is where the experimental manipulations were implemented, randomly assigning the applicants to the different types of employment experiences discussed above.

I drew the sample of job openings for the experiment from a leading national online job posting website.[9] To compile the job postings to apply to, a computer programmer wrote a script that could execute the necessary queries. Each search for a set of job postings was for a given occupation (e.g., administrative assistant) within a twenty-mile radius of the city in the field experiment (e.g., Boston) that was posted over the previous thirty days and that could be applied for directly through the job posting website.[10] Any duplicate postings from the same employer were removed to reduce the likelihood that employers would perceive the applications as fictitious.

After the final set of job openings was selected for a given job type in a given city, I randomly assigned each job opening to a race and gender demographic category and to receive applications with two different employment histories. However, the randomization ensured that each employer received at least one application with either the full-time or unemployment treatment. Two applications were sent to each employer, separated by one day to reduce suspicion that the applications may have been fictitious. The names at the top of the resumes, the formats of the resumes, and the order in which the resumes were sent were randomized and counterbalanced to ensure that these aspects of the job application would not be correlated with the experimental manipulations.

CODING THE OUTCOME: CALLBACKS

The primary outcome variable for the field experiment was whether the applicant received a "callback" (a positive response) from the employer via phone or email. Each applicant had email addresses and phone numbers to which employers could respond. And each of the voicemail boxes had a race- and gender-specific greeting message. Responses were coded as callbacks if the employer requested an interview with the applicant or if the employer asked the applicant to contact the employer to discuss the position in more depth. Auto-generated responses and simple requests for more information were not coded as positive responses.

The field experiment was designed to provide direct evidence of the ways that nonstandard, mismatched, and precarious employment histories affect how employers treat workers at the hiring interface and how those effects vary with the race and gender of the worker.

REGRESSION RESULTS

In this section, I present the results from regression models examining the effects of the different treatments in the field experiment. These models present many of the underlying statistical tests that are utilized throughout the book. I estimate logistic regression models with standard errors clustered at

TABLE A1. Logistic Regression Models of Callbacks, by Employment History

	Callback from Employer				
	All Applicants (1)	White/ Neutral Men (2)	African American Men (3)	White/ Neutral Women (4)	African American Women (5)
EMPLOYMENT HISTORY					
Full-time, standard (omitted)	—	—	—	—	—
	—	—	—	—	—
Part-time	−0.282†	−0.821*	−0.330	0.0484	−0.195
	(0.162)	(0.341)	(0.503)	(0.272)	(0.297)
Temporary agency	−0.0387	−0.419	0.971**	−0.251	−0.435
	(0.156)	(0.285)	(0.337)	(0.305)	(0.396)
Skills underutilization	−0.607**	−0.859*	0.0400	−0.748*	−0.682
	(0.196)	(0.397)	(0.420)	(0.348)	(0.451)
Unemployment	−0.335*	−0.960**	0.371	−0.352	−0.257
	(0.145)	(0.294)	(0.350)	(0.255)	(0.305)
DEMOGRAPHIC GROUP					
African American applicants	−0.304*	—	—	—	—
	(0.145)	—	—	—	—
Women applicants	0.161	—	—	—	—
	(0.144)	—	—	—	—
Constant	−2.377***	−2.158***	−3.085***	−2.154***	−2.589***
	(0.145)	(0.179)	(0.274)	(0.181)	(0.208)
Job postings (clusters)	2,411	599	606	611	595
Applications (observations)	4,822	1,198	1,212	1,222	1,190

Source: Field-experimental data.
Notes: Clustered standard errors in parentheses. Log-odds presented. Statistical significance (two-tailed tests): †$p < .10$. *$p < .05$. **$p < .01$. ***$p < .001$.

the level of the job posting.[11] Table A1 presents five models: one pooled with all applicants and no interactions and then four models that are subset to each demographic group. Table A2 examines the ways that race and gender interact with the different employment histories. Table A3 presents results of the ways that race, gender, and unemployment (compared to full-time, standard, seamless employment) shape callbacks in cases where job postings contain different language about motivation and work ethic.

TABLE A2. Logistic Regression Models of Callbacks, by Employment History
(with Interactions)

	Callback from Employer		
	Race Interactions (1)	Gender Interactions (2)	Race and Gender Interactions (3)
EMPLOYMENT HISTORY			
Full-time, standard (omitted)	—	—	—
	—	—	—
Part-time	−0.319	−0.647*	−0.821*
	(0.209)	(0.281)	(0.341)
Temporary agency	−0.334	0.198	−0.419
	(0.208)	(0.208)	(0.285)
Skills underutilization	−0.807**	−0.487†	−0.859*
	(0.261)	(0.277)	(0.397)
Unemployment	−0.611**	−0.366†	−0.960**
	(0.190)	(0.214)	(0.294)
DEMOGRAPHIC GROUP			
African American applicants	−0.647**	−0.311*	−0.926**
	(0.208)	(0.144)	(0.327)
Women applicants	0.173	0.170	0.00457
	(0.143)	(0.201)	(0.254)
African American applicants × Women applicants			0.491 (0.427)
INTERACTIONS			
Part-time × African American applicants	0.0854	—	0.491
	(0.332)	—	(0.607)
Temporary agency × African American applicants	0.678*	—	1.390**
	(0.318)	—	(0.441)
Skills underutilization × African American applicants	0.475	—	0.899
	(0.396)	—	(0.578)
Unemployment × African American applicants	0.644*	—	1.330**
	(0.293)	—	(0.456)
Part-time × Women applicants	—	0.597†	0.869*
	—	(0.345)	(0.436)
Temporary agency × Women applicants	—	−0.514	0.168
	—	(0.317)	(0.417)

TABLE A2. (*continued*)

	Callback from Employer		
	Race Interactions (1)	Gender Interactions (2)	Race and Gender Interactions (3)
Skills underutilization × Women applicants	—	−0.227	0.111
	—	(0.390)	(0.528)
Unemployment × Women applicants	—	0.0580	0.608
	—	(0.288)	(0.389)
Part-time × African American × Women applicants	—	—	−0.734
	—	—	(0.728)
Temporary agency × African American × Women applicants	—	—	−1.574*
	—	—	(0.666)
Skills underutilization × African American × Women applicants	—	—	−0.833
	—	—	(0.811)
Unemployment × African American × Women applicants	—	—	−1.235*
	—	—	(0.605)
Constant	−2.244***	−2.379***	−2.158***
	(0.152)	(0.168)	(0.179)
Job postings (clusters)	2,411	2,411	2,411
Applications (observations)	4,822	4,822	4,822

Source: Field-experimental data.
Notes: Clustered standard errors in parentheses. Log-odds presented. Statistical significance (two-tailed tests): $^{†}p < .10$. $^{*}p < .05$. $^{**}p < .01$. $^{***}p < .001$.

The Interviews with Hiring Professionals

While the data from the field experiment provide compelling information about employers' actual hiring behaviors, field experiments often provide less direct traction on understanding the underlying mechanisms driving the outcomes that are observed. For this task, I turn to in-depth interview data with individuals directly involved in the hiring process. These interview data provide detailed accounts of how employers, HR professionals, recruiters, and other hiring agents make sense of different employment histories and how the ways they understand nonstandard, mismatched, and precarious employment histories may be linked to workers' gender and race.

TABLE A3. Logistic Regression Models of the Effect of Race and Unemployment on Callbacks, Subset by Applicant Gender and Job Posting Characteristics

	Callback from Employer			
	Men Applicants		Women Applicants	
	Motivation/ Work Ethic Emphasis (1)	No Motivation/ Work Ethic Emphasis (2)	Motivation/ Work Ethic Emphasis (3)	No Motivation/ Work Ethic Emphasis (4)
Unemployment	−1.455**	−0.345	−0.080	−0.732*
	(0.428)	(0.492)	(0.428)	(0.364)
African American applicants	−1.325**	−0.624	−0.268	−0.630[†]
	(0.457)	(0.608)	(0.462)	(0.377)
Unemployment × African American applicants	2.265***	0.478	0.006	0.441
	(0.645)	(0.834)	(0.625)	(0.554)
Controls included	Yes	Yes	Yes	Yes
Job postings (clusters)	431	321	351	532
Applications (observations)	497	372	401	616

Source: Field-experimental data.

Notes: Clustered standard errors in parentheses. Log-odds presented. Analyses limited to full-time, standard and unemployed applications. Controls included for the occupation, labor market, and wave in which the application was submitted (there were two waves in each labor market), as well as all two- and three-way interactions between these three variables. A control is also included for the resume template that was used for the application. Some observations were dropped because a control variable perfectly predicted the outcome. Results are robust to the exclusion of the control variables. A similar table appeared in Pedulla (2018). Statistical significance (two-tailed tests): $^†p < .10.$ $^*p < .05.$ $^{**}p < .01.$ $^{***}p < .001.$

These in-depth interviews with employers serve two key roles in guiding our understanding of how nonstandard, mismatched, and precarious employment may impact workers' hiring outcomes. First, the interviews provide insights into the signals employers receive from and the meanings they attribute to different types of work histories. For example, when employers see that someone has worked part-time, what does that make them think? Is it a concern? Do their impressions of a given type of employment history—such as part-time work—vary with the gender of the worker? The interviews therefore provide detailed narratives of how employers think and talk about the core issues of the book.

Of course, as was discussed throughout the book, what employers say in the interviews does not necessarily map exactly onto how they behave when they are making hiring decisions.[12] Employers may not be aware of their own biases or of how those biases play out. But the interviews provide a sense of the potential sources that drive the outcomes seen in the field experiment and illustrate the ways that employers conceptualize various types of employment experiences. Indeed, how employers talk about different types of employment experiences is, in and of itself, interesting and useful information about the hiring process.

THE INTERVIEW SAMPLE

The interview sample for this book consists of fifty-three individuals who are directly involved in the hiring process. Background information about these individuals was presented in Chapter 1. As a quick reminder though, the interview participants represent a diverse set of companies and industries and are primarily, although not exclusively, located in the same five labor markets where the field experiment was conducted: Atlanta, Boston, Chicago, Los Angeles, and New York. The group is a convenience sample and therefore is not necessarily representative of the perspectives of hiring professionals in general. However, while generating the sample I attempted to ensure that there was significant variation in the types of companies where individuals worked as well as their background characteristics. One challenge was finding men to participate in the study: human resources and related occupations tend to have high rates of women incumbents.[13] Consequently, there are fewer men than women in our sample.

Outreach for the study was conducted through multiple channels. First, significant outreach was conducted by posting online advertisements in multiple locations, including job boards. Second, we used the same online job posting board from the field experiment to search for companies that were actively hiring in the occupations that were examined in the field experiment. We then searched for contact information for those companies and reached out to them to try to interview someone involved in the hiring process there. Third, we asked the individuals we interviewed for referrals to other people who might be interested in participating in the study. We also attempted to recruit individuals through alumni associations and student organizations at colleges, universities, and business schools. However, this approach did not result in any interview subjects.

The primary inclusion criterion for participation in the interview study was that the respondents were actively involved in the hiring process and in screening job applicants as part of their job. Recruitment focused on individuals who were directly involved in hiring for their own companies and who were currently employed. However, external staffing consultants are also an important part of the hiring landscape, so some of these individuals were included in the sample as well. There were also three individuals who had left their jobs recently—within the past three months—and who were not currently employed. For nearly all respondents, their resume or LinkedIn profile was collected before conducting the interviews to ensure that they were an appropriate match for the study and had the type of experience in hiring that would be relevant for the study. In the few cases where this information was not collected in advance of the interview, it was obtained afterward, resulting in a complete set of resumes or LinkedIn profiles for the sample.

CONDUCTING AND ANALYZING THE INTERVIEWS

The interviews were conducted primarily via videoconference (e.g., FaceTime, Skype). Video interviews provided the opportunity to see the interview subject and build rapport, which was a benefit over phone interviewing. In a few cases, however, respondents did not have access to videoconferencing or requested not to do the interview via video. In these cases the interviews were conducted over the phone. No systematic differences were detected in the data between the few interviews that were conducted over the phone and those that were conducted over videoconference.

Prior to the interviews, respondents were sent a detailed information sheet about the study, the potential risks and benefits of participation, as well as my contact information and the contact information for the Stanford University Institutional Review Board (IRB). At the beginning of the interviews respondents were provided with additional information about the study and asked for their informed consent to participate. The description of the study highlighted an interest in learning more about employer decision making and that the questions would focus on the types of things that the respondent looked for when making decisions about hiring job applicants. Each respondent was provided with a fifty-dollar gift card for participating.

The interviews were conducted either by myself or by one of two PhD students in the Department of Sociology at Stanford University: Bethany Nichols and Jeff Sheng. To ensure reliability across the interviewers, we conducted the first three interviews together and then developed norms and standards around the use of the protocol and probing. Throughout the project we met as a research team to troubleshoot issues that were arising with the interviews and to make adjustments to the protocol and probing strategies as necessary.

The interviews generally lasted between sixty and eighty minutes. All of the interviews were audio recorded and then transcribed in full by a professional. The transcripts were then uploaded into Dedoose, a qualitative analysis software package, for coding and analysis. We first assigned general codes to blocks of text where the codes corresponded to the major components of the interview protocol. The interviews were then coded for key themes using a set of codes that developed iteratively over time.[14] The coding was conducted by the same team of individuals who conducted the interviews. As with the interviews, we met as a research team throughout the coding process to develop coding norms and to troubleshoot issues that arose. In some cases additional coding of the interviews and counting of key themes was conducted in Excel. Close readings of the individual interview transcripts were conducted at multiple points in time to inform the coding, analysis, and interpretation.

When presenting the interview data throughout the book, pseudonyms are used for all of the interview participants. In line with the IRB protocol, research subjects were guaranteed confidentiality, so their real names are not used. When direct quotations from interviews are utilized, they are presented nearly verbatim. In some instances I have removed stutters or filler words, such as "um" or "like," in order to ease readability.

———

The Methodological Appendix has provided additional information about the research design and data collection for *Making the Cut*. The field-experimental data and the interview data—while distinct—complement each other in important ways and together offer a more holistic picture of how nonstandard, mismatched, and precarious employment histories shape the opportunity structure for workers in the new economy.

NOTES

Chapter 1

1. Logan (1996).
2. Rivera (2015); Fernandez and Sosa (2005); Pager and Pedulla (2015).
3. For reviews of the literature, see Bills, Di Stasio, and Gërxhani (2017) and Moss and Tilly (2001).
4. For recent scholarship on how workers find jobs in the "new economy," see Gershon (2017).
5. Correll, Benard, and Paik (2007).
6. Moss and Tilly (2001).
7. Rivera (2012, 2015). While the aforementioned criteria of evaluation may appear innocuous on the surface, they can systematically disadvantage some social groups—women and racial minorities—more than others (see Correll, Benard, and Paik 2007 and Rivera and Tilcsik 2016). This set of topics will be discussed in depth throughout the book.
8. Kalleberg (2011); Cappelli et al. (1997).
9. Morris and Western (1999).
10. Wright and Dwyer (2003).
11. Autor, Katz, and Krueger (1998); DiMaggio and Bonikowski (2008).
12. Davis-Blake and Broschak (2009).
13. Cappelli et al. (1997); DiPrete, Goux, and Maurin (2002).
14. Kalleberg (2000); Autor (2003); Leung (2014).
15. Kim and Sakamoto (2008).
16. Cooper (2014); Western et al. (2016).
17. Pugh (2015).
18. Hacker (2006); Cappelli et al. (1997); Kalleberg (2011); Barley and Kunda (2004).
19. Kalleberg (2000, 2007); Smith (1997); Bureau of Labor Statistics (2018).
20. Cunningham (2018).
21. Bernhardt (2014).
22. Kalleberg (2000); Kosanovich and Sherman (2015); Autor (2003).
23. Kalleberg, Reskin, and Hudson (2000); Kalleberg (2011); Henson (1996); Rogers (1995); Epstein et al. (1999); Smith (2002); Meiksins and Whalley (2002); Webber and Williams (2008).
24. Bertrand and Mullainathan (2004); Pager, Western, and Bonikowski (2009); Correll, Benard, and Paik (2007); Rivera and Tilcsik (2016).
25. Pager and Shepherd (2008).
26. Stainback and Tomaskovic-Devey (2012); Bertrand and Mullainathan (2004); Pager, Western, and Bonikowski (2009). Indeed, a recent meta-analysis found that racial discrimination in hiring against African Americans has not declined in the United States over the past twenty-five years (Quillian et al. 2017).

27. For discussions, see Rissing and Castilla (2014) and Correll and Benard (2006).

28. Rissing and Castilla (2014). As Rissing and Castilla (2014) note, however, these clusters of theories produce different empirical predictions in information-rich environments. "Statistical" theories predict that discrimination will decline or even disappear when there is more information available about individuals, whereas "preference-based" theories predict that discrimination will be durable as information increases.

29. See Bills, Di Stasio, and Gërxhani (2017) for a review. See also Rivera (2015).

30. See Moss and Tilly (2001); Correll, Benard, and Paik (2007); Turco (2010); Rivera (2012, 2015).

31. Rivera and Tilcsik (2016).

32. Acker (1990); Correll, Benard, and Paik (2007); Turco (2010); Williams (2001).

33. Rivera (2015); Moss and Tilly (2001); Correll, Benard, and Paik (2007).

34. The limited information available to make decisions about whom to interview separates this point in the hiring process from other consequential decision-making processes, such as deciding whom to admit to an elite college (Stevens 2007).

35. Correll, Benard, and Paik (2007); Bertrand and Mullainathan (2004).

36. Lahey (2008).

37. Bertrand and Mullainathan (2004); Gaddis (2015).

38. Rivera (2015); Rivera and Tilcsik (2016).

39. See Bertrand and Mullainathan (2004); Gaddis (2015); Rivera (2015); Rivera and Tilcsik (2016); Pager, Western, and Bonikowski (2009); Neumark, Bank, and Van Nort (1996); Correll, Benard, and Paik (2007); Tilcsik (2011); Mishel (2016); Jackson (2009); Oreopoulos (2011); Wallace, Wright, and Hyde (2014); Wright et al. (2013).

40. Ridgeway (2011); Heilman (2012); Fiske et al. (2002).

41. Moss and Tilly (2001).

42. Cuddy, Fiske, and Glick (2007); Massey (2007).

43. Correll, Benard, and Paik (2007).

44. Kalleberg (2011).

45. Kalleberg (2011).

46. Hollister (2011).

47. Bureau of Labor Statistics (2018, 2019a).

48. Kalleberg (2011, 172). The analyses are drawn from analyzing the General Social Survey. The decline in job satisfaction is robust to controlling for the unemployment rate. There also appear to be interesting cohort effects that shape changes over time in job satisfaction (Kalleberg 2011).

49. Sharone (2013); Pugh (2015); Gershon (2017).

50. Gershon (2017).

51. A significant body of recent scholarship attempting to understand employers' behaviors has drawn on similar methods. For examples, see Bertrand and Mullainathan (2004); Correll, Benard, and Paik (2007); Gaddis (2015); Rivera and Tilcsik (2016); Weisshaar (2018); Quadlin (2018). Additionally, my dissertation (Pedulla 2014a) as well as two articles (Pedulla 2016, 2018) present results from the field experiment.

52. Each job opening received two resumes from applicants of the same demographic group.

53. Similar strategies have been used in studies deploying this type of research design. For example, see Correll, Benard, and Paik (2007) as well as Rivera and Tilcsik (2016).

54. Using names to signal race is a common, albeit complex, strategy in studies of this kind. See Bertrand and Mullainathan (2004) and Gaddis (2015) for examples. For an in-depth discussion of the complexity of using names to signal race in this type of field experiment, see Gaddis (2017).

55. It is important to note that this approach loses some precision because, for example, the African American racialized names do not necessarily mean that the applicant is actually black.

And the white/neutral names do not necessarily mean that the applicant is actually white. For example, people with names that are racialized as African American could actually be white, and vice versa.

56. Rivera (2015); Gershon (2017).

57. In addition to myself, Bethany Nichols and Jeff Sheng—two PhD students in sociology at Stanford University—conducted the interviews. Bethany and Jeff were also involved with the recruitment and screening of interview subjects as well as coding the interview transcripts.

58. We were able to obtain either a resume or a LinkedIn profile for all participants in our study. In a few cases, these were obtained after the interview.

59. In 2018, more than 70 percent of human resources managers and human resources workers were women (Bureau of Labor Statistics 2019b).

60. Pager and Quillian (2005); Jerolmack and Khan (2014).

61. Moss and Tilly (2001); Rivera (2015).

Chapter 2

1. It is important to note that "good jobs" as we conceive of them today are a relatively modern construct. The type of secure, relatively safe work with solid wages and fringe benefits largely took hold in the United States in the middle of the twentieth century (Cappelli et al. 1997; Kalleberg 2009).

2. See media coverage in leading national outlets, such as the *New York Times* (Scheiber 2015; Benner 2015), CNN (Wells 2016), and National Public Radio (2016).

3. There has also been significant public concern about protecting customers and consumers who utilize services provided through online platforms, such as Uber and Lyft. See news coverage by Woodyard and Toppo (2016) for a discussion of how these issues played out in Austin, Texas.

4. Pasquale (2016) outlines the competing narratives around online platform work. Similarly, Kalleberg and Dunn (2016) offer a summary of key issues related to working in the "gig economy" (see also Dokko, Mumford, and Schanzenbach 2015; Donovan, Bradley, and Shimabukuro 2016). Ticona and Mateescu (2018) offer important insights about how online platforms outside of ride sharing—in the realm of carework—shape workers' experiences. For a discussion of measuring the prevalence of the "gig economy," see Abraham et al. (2018).

5. Katz and Krueger (2016) and JPMorgan Chase & Co. Institute (2016) report similar estimates.

6. Kalleberg (2011).

7. Morris and Western (1999).

8. Piketty and Saez (2003).

9. DiMaggio and Bonikowski (2008); Fernandez (2001). Significant scholarship—generally falling under the umbrella of skill-biased technological change—focuses on the connection between technology and income inequality.

10. Weil (2014); Cappelli et al. (1997). David Weil (2011, 2014) discusses the idea of the "fissured" workplace, which he describes as the process "where the lead firms that collectively determine the product market conditions in which wages and conditions are set have become separated from the actual employment of the workers who provide goods or services" (2011, 34). He then discusses how this process results in challenges with enforcement of employment protections, particularly for low-wage workers.

11. Western and Rosenfeld (2011).

12. Morris and Western (1999). Indeed, 21.6 percent of workers were in the manufacturing sector in 1979. By 2001, only 8.9 percent were (Mishel et al. 2012).

13. Wright and Dwyer (2003).

14. Pugh (2015).

15. Kalleberg (2009).

16. The historical time frame over which one looks is important in thinking about these issues. Scholars have pointed to the ways that the current set of economic arrangements may actually be similar to those prior to the postwar period. Thus, it may be the middle of the twentieth century that is the aberration in employment relationships, inequality, and insecurity (Kalleberg 2009). Also see Hyman (2018) for a detailed discussion of the historical changes in the US economy that have resulted in less secure and more temporary employment.

17. Best et al. (2011).

18. Stainback and Tomaskovic-Devey (2012). See Dobbin (2009) for a compelling analysis of the development and implementation of equal opportunity policies and programs in the United States and the central role that personnel managers played in this process. Scholars who work in this area also point to ways that many of the policies implemented to provide opportunities to women and workers of color were not as effective as many had hoped they would be (Kalev, Dobbin, and Kelly 2006; Dobbin, Schrage, and Kalev 2015).

19. Kalev, Dobbin, and Kelly (2006).

20. Livingston (2016).

21. Kossek et al. (2011); Waldfogel (1999).

22. Rosenfeld and Kleykamp (2012).

23. Farber (2008); Hollister (2011).

24. Hollister and Smith (2014).

25. Kalev (2014).

26. Blau and Kahn (2017).

27. Alliance for Board Diversity (2017).

28. Snipp and Cheung (2016).

29. Alliance for Board Diversity (2017).

30. Kalleberg (2007, 2011).

31. Kalleberg, Reskin, and Hudson (2000).

32. Ruhm (1991); Gangl (2006); Newman (1988); Sharone (2013).

33. Kalleberg (2007, 2009).

34. Kalleberg (2000).

35. Feldman (1990); Kalleberg (2000).

36. Bureau of Labor Statistics (2019c); Valletta, Bengali, and van der List (2018).

37. Kalleberg (2000); Valletta, Bengali, and van der List (2018).

38. Bureau of Labor Statistics (2019c).

39. Bureau of Labor Statistics (2019a).

40. The idea that gendered choices around balancing work and family life are "voluntary" is somewhat suspect, given gendered norms and expectations about caregiving and breadwinning. Nevertheless, I utilize this term since it is most common in the literature.

41. Tilly (1996).

42. Tilly (1996).

43. Pitts (1998).

44. Stratton (1996).

45. Bureau of Labor Statistics (2018).

46. Bureau of Labor Statistics (2018).

47. Kalleberg (2000).

48. Hatton (2011). Hatton (2011) argues that the temporary help agency (THA) industry used various tools, including gendered conceptions of work, to challenge the "asset" model of work.

49. Kalleberg, Reskin, and Hudson (2000).

50. Ofstead (1999); Smith and Neuwirth (2008).

51. Smith and Neuwirth (2008).

52. Autor (2003).

53. Kalleberg (2000). Specifically, temporary agency employment provides companies with numerical flexibility. This is distinct from functional flexibility, which describes the flexibility that comes with having workers who are able to perform various tasks within the organization (Cappelli and Neumark 2004).

54. Houseman (1997).

55. Autor (2003).

56. Kalleberg (2007).

57. McKee-Ryan and Harvey (2011); Vaisey (2006); Erdogan and Bauer (2011). As will be discussed below, part-time and temporary agency employment can also be considered mismatched work insofar as they are at odds with workers' preferences (Kalleberg 2007).

58. Handel (2003).

59. Rose (2017).

60. Cappelli (2015).

61. Cappelli (2015); Abraham (2015).

62. McGuinness (2006).

63. Rose (2017).

64. McGuinness (2006).

65. Kalleberg (2007); McKee-Ryan and Harvey (2011).

66. Kalleberg (2009, 2).

67. Kalleberg (2009, 6).

68. Kroft, Lange, and Notowidigdo (2013). See also Brand (2015) for a review.

69. Bureau of Labor Statistics (2019d); Kosanovich and Sherman (2015). Being unemployed for twenty-seven weeks or more is often considered long-term unemployment in the United States (Rothstein 2016). However, the Organisation for Economic Co-operation and Development defines long-term unemployment as being unemployed for twelve months or more (see https://stats.oecd.org/glossary/detail.asp?ID=3586).

70. See Figure 2.1, which presents data from the Current Population Survey (CPS), Bureau of Labor Statistics.

71. Kosanovich and Sherman (2015).

72. Bureau of Labor Statistics (2019e); Kosanovich and Sherman (2015).

73. Bureau of Labor Statistics (2019c).

74. Bureau of Labor Statistics (2019c).

75. Cajner et al. (2018).

76. Cajner et al. (2018).

77. Hatton (2011).

78. According to Bureau of Labor Statistics (2018) estimates, in 2017, 52.3 percent of THA workers were men and 47.7 percent were women.

79. Bureau of Labor Statistics (2018).

80. Vaisey (2006). However, there is some evidence that, among college-educated workers, the rate of skills underutilization was higher among women than among men in 1980. But that gender gap disappeared in estimates calculated for both 2000 and 2014 (Rose 2017).

81. Vaisey (2006).

82. Vaisey (2006).

83. Kosanovich and Sherman (2015).

84. Kosanovich and Sherman (2015).

85. Kosanovich and Sherman (2015).

86. Cunningham (2018).

87. Tilly (1996).

88. Shierholz (2014).

89. Changes to the Current Population Survey make the data from 1994 to the present not directly comparable with data from 1993 and earlier.

90. Valletta, Bengali, and van der List (2018); see also Golden (2016).

91. Valletta (2018).

92. Autor (2003).

93. Bureau of Labor Statistics (2005, 2018).

94. Unlike other data presented in this chapter, County Business Patterns (CBP) data are collected not via surveys of individual workers but through information on employment at US employers. The CBP data do not differentiate between temporary and standard employees on the payroll at temp agencies, although the proportion of standard employees on temp agency payrolls is likely quite small. These data have been used in existing scholarship examining change over time in temporary agency employment (Autor 2003) and offer a longer time series than is possible using individual-level survey data from the Current Population Survey.

95. Vaisey (2006).

96. Vaisey (2006).

97. Kalleberg (2007, 77).

98. Horowitz (2018).

99. Kalleberg (2000); Vaisey (2006).

100. Kalleberg (2009).

101. Autor (2003); Gonos (1997).

102. Clawson and Clawson (1999).

103. Kalleberg (2000); Schilling and Steensma (2001).

104. Vaisey (2006).

105. Bernhardt (2014).

106. See Brand (2015) for a review.

107. Young (2012).

108. Burgard and Lin (2013, 1112).

109. Virtanen et al. (2005); see also Quesnel-Vallée, DeHaney, and Ciampi (2010).

110. Virtanen et al. (2005). For a review of the relationship between underemployment—a broad term that overlaps with nonstandard, mismatched, and precarious work—and psychological and physical health, see Anderson and Winefield (2011).

111. Rosenthal et al. (2012).

112. Dooley and Prause (2004).

113. McKee-Ryan and Harvey (2011).

114. Killewald (2016).

115. Killewald (2016).

116. Booth and van Ours (2009).

117. Booth and van Ours (2009).

118. See Halpin (2015).

119. Maume and Sebastian (2012).

120. Strazdins et al. (2006).

121. Davis-Blake, Broschak, and George (2003); George (2003); Smith (1997); Lautsch (2002); Chen and Brudney (2009); Chattopadhyay and George (2001). See Smith (2001) for a discussion of how managers navigate integrating temporary workers.

122. Pedulla (2013).

Chapter 3

1. See Aigner and Cain (1977); Spence (1973).

2. Textio (https://textio.com), for example, is a company that provides companies with information about how to write job postings to improve the quality of the applicants that they receive.

3. Gaucher, Friesen, and Kay (2011); Askehave and Zethsen (2014).

4. See the Indeed.com "About" page, available at www.indeed.com/about.

5. Smith (2005); Fernandez, Castilla, and Moore (2000).

6. For a review of scholarship on networks and hiring, see Castilla, Lan, and Rissing (2013a, 2013b).

7. Burks et al. (2015); CareerBuilder (2012).

8. Gershon (2017).

9. See Cappelli (2019a). For a discussion of the ways that algorithms may be able to have positive consequences for the evaluation of job applicants, see Kuncel, Klieger, and Ones (2014).

10. SHRM (2017).

11. Cappelli (2019a, 2019b).

12. See Mann and O'Neil (2016).

13. Gershon (2017).

14. See Sharone (2017).

15. Beyond the organization, the context of the local labor market may also shape hiring outcomes, as queuing theories of the labor market would suggest. From a queuing theory perspective, job seekers and employers both rank their job preferences, and the ways that these queues overlap with one another can explain job outcomes (Reskin and Roos 2009; Fernandez and Mors 2008; Weisshaar 2018). In competitive labor market contexts, a negative signal—such as unemployment—may result in workers being further back in the queue than they would have been in a less competitive labor market. This is the case because there are simply more applicants in the queue and thus more applicants who are unlikely to have that negative signal on their resume and therefore be ahead of unemployed workers in the queue. For a compelling and intuitive example of drawing on labor market queueing theories to make predictions about employment outcomes in field experiments, see Weisshaar (2018). For a more in-depth explanation of labor market queueing theories, see Reskin and Roos (2009).

16. Dobbin (2009); Stainback and Tomaskovic-Devey (2012).

17. Dobbin, Schrage, and Kalev (2015); Kalev, Dobbin, and Kelly (2006).

18. Dobbin, Schrage, and Kalev (2015); Kalev, Dobbin, and Kelly (2006); Stainback and Tomaskovic-Devey (2012).

19. Kalev, Dobbin, and Kelly (2006).

20. Dobbin, Schrage, and Kalev (2015).

21. The data used in this book are not able to directly examine how hiring decisions about workers with nonstandard, mismatched, and precarious employment histories may vary across organizations with different policies and practices. This task would require having detailed measures of organizational policies and practices for the companies in the field experiment. Yet future work would be well served to collect this type of data.

22. See Kroft, Lange, and Notowidigdo (2013). The duration of unemployment also came up frequently in the interviews with hiring professionals as a marker of concern.

23. Moss and Tilly (2001).

24. Moss and Tilly (2001).

25. Shih (2002). As Shih (2002) explores in more depth, these perceptions of personality and how they map on to manageability and pliability are related to race, gender, and nativity status.

26. Goffman (1963).

27. Letkermann (2002); Karren and Sherman (2012); Blau, Petrucci, and McClendon (2013).

28. Acker (1990); Turco (2010).

29. Correll, Benard, and Paik (2007).

30. Fiske et al. (2002); Correll, Benard, and Paik (2007); Cuddy, Fiske, and Glick (2007).

31. Bielby and Bielby (2002); Correll and Benard (2006); Turco (2010).

32. Scholars of gender inequality often pay close attention to ideal worker norms, including commitment, because of the disproportionate amount of unpaid household and caretaking labor that women perform. Given the nonwork responsibilities that women disproportionately hold and the often lacking policy support for women, employers may perceive women as being more likely to violate ideal worker norms. Thus, the dual wings of the ideal worker norm, competence and commitment, are likely at play during the hiring and evaluation process and may differentially impact evaluations of men and women. We will return to the gender-differentiated effects of the ideal worker norm in Chapter 5, which examines the varied effects of part-time work experiences.

33. Cha (2010); Cha and Weeden (2014).

34. Rivera (2012, 2015).

35. In their meta-analysis of gender bias in hiring evaluations, Koch, D'Mello, and Sackett (2013, 131) write, "Numerous studies have shown that when individuating information is ambiguous regarding a trait or role in question, decision makers rely heavily on stereotypes." See also Kunda and Thagard (1996) and Dovidio and Gaertner (2000).

36. Sharone (2013).

37. Pugh (2015).

38. Gershon (2017).

39. Gershon (2017). It is important to note here that much of this scholarship focuses on the experiences of professional and white-collar work. There are myriad, although somewhat distinct, challenges faced by lower skilled and manual workers.

40. See Tversky and Kahneman (1974). For a recent review of the decision-making literature, see Bruch and Feinberg (2017).

41. Weisshaar (2018).

42. See Weick (1995) for an in-depth discussion of sensemaking in organizations.

Chapter 4

1. As I discussed in Chapter 1, I use the language of "white (or neutral)" here to note that hiring professionals in the field experiment may not have racialized these names as white.

2. Kroft, Lange, and Notowidigdo (2013) find that a worker's likelihood of receiving a "callback" from an employer decreases with the length of unemployment that was randomly assigned to the worker's application. This phenomenon is referred to as "duration dependence." Importantly, though, the majority of this decrease in "callbacks" happens in the first eight months of unemployment and then levels out. Additionally, they find that the effects of unemployment duration are not consistent across locations. In places where the labor market is tighter (e.g., the unemployment rate is lower), "duration dependence" is stronger (Kroft, Lange, and Notowidigdo 2013). In another US-based study using field-experimental techniques, Ghayad (2013) finds that unemployment duration is negatively associated with the likelihood of getting an interview and that this effect is particularly strong after six months of unemployment. Additionally, Ghayad (2013) finds that, among the long-term unemployed, having concrete job experience related to the job to which one is applying does *not* protect one against the penalizing effects of unemployment. There is also evidence from Sweden that long-term unemployment at the time of one's application can have negative consequences on callbacks (Eriksson and Rooth 2014). There are also two other US-based field-experimental studies that do *not* find negative effects of unemployment on

callbacks (Nunley et al. 2017; Farber, Silverman, and von Wachter 2017). While it is not entirely clear why the divergent findings emerge in the Farber, Silverman, and von Wachter (2017) study, the Nunley et al. (2017) study focuses on recent college graduates for whom employers may have different expectations about continuous employment experience. Thus, different, more negative effects of unemployment may emerge for workers who are further past their college graduation.

3. The statistical significance tests for these differences, as well as those in the rest of this chapter, are drawn from a logistic regression model with standard errors clustered at the level of the job posting. The full set of regression results is presented in the Methodological Appendix.

4. Statistical significance tests comparing part-time work, temporary agency employment, and skills underutilization to unemployment were conducted with post-estimation tests after implementing the relevant regression model presented in the Methodological Appendix.

5. See Mandel and Semyonov (2014); Blau and Kahn (2017); Smith (2002); Elliott and Smith (2004).

6. Catalyst (2018); Alliance for Board Diversity (2017); Center for American Women and Politics (2018).

7. Davies and Frink (2014).

8. There are some interesting parallels between the pattern identified here for white men and McDermott's (2006) findings regarding the perceptions of and treatment of whites in different contexts. Whiteness is generally a privileged status that conveys social and economic advantages. Yet McDermott (2006, 40) finds that whiteness can work differently for poor or working-class whites who live in a geographic location with a significant population of working-class blacks. In this context, she writes, "whiteness becomes a badge of inferiority." Thus, characteristics that generally convey privilege and status may have different consequences depending on the broader social context and the additional characteristics of the individual.

9. For examples, see Rudman and Mescher (2013); Heilman and Wallen (2010). For a review, see Vandello and Bosson (2013).

10. Kimmel (2006); Vandello et al. (2008).

11. Vandello et el. (2008); Willer et al. (2013).

12. Mize and Manago (2018).

13. Bertrand and Mullainathan (2004); Pager (2003); Pager, Western, and Bonikowski (2009); Gaddis (2015).

14. The callback rate for black men who have experienced unemployment is not statistically significantly different from the callback rate for black men with part-time work or skills underutilization.

15. Neumark, Bank, and Van Nort (1996); Kalev (2009); Cha and Weeden (2014); Srivastava and Sherman (2015); Castilla (2008).

16. Correll, Benard, and Paik (2007); Rivera and Tilcsik (2016).

17. While the callback rates for black women and white/neutral women are not statistically significantly different in each employment history category, the callback rate for black women is statistically significantly lower than it is for white/neutral women ($p < .05$), after controlling for the different types of employment histories.

18. Crenshaw (1989); Collins ([1990] 2000).

19. Ridgeway and Kricheli-Katz (2013); Purdie-Vaughns and Eibach (2008).

20. I am conceptualizing the distinct effects of nonstandard, mismatched, and precarious work as some employment experiences having discernable penalties compared to full-time, standard employment, while other types of employment experiences do not have these discernable penalties. This is distinct from testing whether the callback rates for each type of employment experiences differ from one another.

While there is a statistically significant penalty only for white/neutral men and white/neutral women, the callback rate for skills underutilization is lower than full-time employment for African American men and women as well. And there is no statistically significant variation of skills underutilization across sociodemographic groups.

21. This claim is made based on a logistic regression where receiving a callback is the dependent variable and each employment history is interacted with race and gender (see Model 3 in Table A2 in the Methodological Appendix).

22. Vaisey (2006).

23. At least two other groups of scholars have used field-experimental techniques to examine how skills underutilization or overqualification impacts workers' future hiring outcomes (Nunley et al. 2017; Baert and Verhaest 2014). Importantly, though, these studies examine recent college graduates (Nunley et al. 2017), rather than workers with significant experience, or are conducted in another country, Belgium (Baert and Verhaest 2014), where the underlying evaluation processes may be distinct due to unique institutional processes. The Nunley et al. (2017) study finds strong, negative effects of working in a job below the applicant's skills level on callbacks for recent college graduates. The Baert and Verhaest (2014) field experiment, which was conducted in Belgium, finds that there is a limited penalty for workers who are in positions for which they are overqualified. Given that their study was implemented in a different national context, the divergent findings may emerge due to the different institutional and policy landscapes in the two countries. An important area for future research on this topic will be to systematically compare the effects of skills underutilization across a wide range of institutional and policy regimes to identify key macro-level forces that may be implicated in the treatment of workers who are downwardly mobile into jobs beneath their skill or education level.

24. As will be discussed in future chapters, many of the key findings from the field experiment were presented to hiring professionals during the interviews.

25. Hiring agents' general agreement that the field-experimental finding about skills underutilization made sense, however, was not likely a result of them simply going along with the findings presented to them because the findings came from academic scholarship. In certain cases, the hiring professionals we spoke with indicated that they did not entirely agree with the findings from the field experiment.

26. Some existing observational research examines the consequences of temporary employment for workers as they move through the labor market (Addison, Cotti, and Surfield 2009; Addison and Surfield 2009). And there is one US-based study that has attempted to deal with endogeneity concerns related to unobserved selection into temporary work by using a quasi-experimental research design. Autor and Houseman (2010) address the problem of selection bias by exploiting the random assignment of people in Detroit's welfare-to-work program to different types of job placements (i.e., a temporary help agency placement vs. no job placement). Importantly, they find quite different results depending on whether or not they correct for unobserved selection processes. Specifically, after correcting for selection, they find that temporary agency employment is actually no better for workers than remaining unemployed. While the generalizability of the Autor and Houseman (2010) study is unknown, their findings clearly suggest that selection bias makes identifying the causal effects of temporary employment difficult using observational data.

27. There were nine respondents who either were not asked this question—as it was added after the first few interviews—or did not provide an answer that was able to be coded.

28. In general, the hiring professionals I interviewed indicated that they would be least likely to recommend that someone remain unemployed.

29. There were a few other reasons that respondents mentioned about why THA employment would be the best option for those who recently lost their job. Some respondents mentioned the financial benefits, the ability to leave whenever they want, and the ability to be able to explore new areas of the economy as positives of taking a temporary agency position.

Chapter 5

1. Bureau of Labor Statistics (2019c); Kalleberg (2000); Valletta, Bengali, and van der List (2018).

2. Acker (1990); Correll, Benard, and Paik (2007); Turco (2010).

3. Correll, Benard, and Paik (2007).

4. Williams (2001); Kelly et al. (2010).

5. See Bianchi et al. (2000); Grigoryeva (2017).

6. Acker (1990).

7. Williams (2001); Davies and Frink (2014).

8. Allen and Russell (1999); Wayne and Cordeiro (2003).

9. Thébaud (2010).

10. Rudman and Mescher (2013).

11. Bureau of Labor Statistics (2019c).

12. The quotation from Marie comes from her response to the findings from the field experiment. This line of questioning, which came toward the end of the interview, will be discussed in more detail later in the chapter.

13. Eagly and Steffen (1986).

14. Discussions of caretaking were less common, although still prevalent, when hiring agents discussed unemployment.

15. Example resumes are presented in Chapter 4. More details about the design and implementation of the field experiment are available in Chapter 1 and the Methodological Appendix.

16. The pooled callback rate for all men, including African American men, with part-time histories is 4.1 percent, compared to 8.2 percent for all women, including African American women.

17. This finding comes from a test for differences in proportions between these groups ($p < .10$).

18. Approximately 2 percent of job postings applied to were for part-time positions. The findings presented here hold whether or not these job postings are included in the analysis.

19. A test for the difference in proportions of callbacks between men and women with white/neutral names indicates that this difference is statistically significant ($p < .05$). Additionally, using a logistic regression model, the interaction between working part-time (compared to full-time work) and being female (compared to male) is also positive and statistically significant ($p < .05$) among the white or race-neutral applicants.

20. Hirsch (2005).

21. Ferber and Waldfogel (1998).

22. Aaronson and French (2004).

23. Aaronson and French (2004).

24. Bureau of Labor Statistics (2019b).

25. Breaking the findings down by occupation results in a large reduction in sample size for each occupational category. The differences in the callback rates for men and women in the part-time condition generally do not reach statistical significance in these occupationally disaggregated findings, likely due to reduced statistical power.

26. Weick (1995).

27. Ridgeway (2011).

28. Thébaud (2010).

29. Eagly and Karau (2002); Rudman (1998); Rudman and Glick (1999). Researchers have also focused on how race and ethnicity intersect with evaluations of criminal activity or how race and age jointly shape perceptions of a target's facial expressions, among other areas (Bodenhausen and Wyer 1985; Kang and Chasteen 2009; Correll et al. 2002). The role of racial stereotypes in shaping the evaluations of different employment histories will be addressed in the following chapter.

30. This question about the findings from the field experiment was asked after asking employers more general questions about part-time work in order to avoid biasing their initial responses.

31. Eagly and Karau (2002) provide a thorough and synthetic review of role congruity theory, which focuses on the ways that congruence and incongruence between particular social roles can produce prejudice. They write, for example, "When a stereotyped group member and an incongruent social role become joined in the mind of the perceiver, this inconsistency lowers the evaluation of the group member as an actual or potential occupant of the role" (Eagly and Karau 2002, 574).

32. See Heilman (2012) for a discussion of descriptive and prescriptive gender stereotypes.

33. Williams (2001); Blair-Loy (2003); Feldman (1990).

34. There is some empirical evidence that part-time employment can assist with facilitating work-life balance and reducing work-life conflict in the United States (Hill et al. 2004) and around the world (Higgins, Duxbury, and Johnson 2000; van Rijswijk et al. 2004). In practice, of course, part-time work does not always provide the types of flexibility and balance that enable individuals—often women—to balance their careers and family responsibilities.

35. Kimmel (2006); Thébaud (2010).

36. Albiston (2007, 2010).

37. Coltrane et al. (2013); Munsch (2016); Rudman and Mescher (2013).

38. I conducted a separate survey experiment with hiring professionals where they reviewed applicant profiles similar to those in the field experiment presented here and then evaluated the candidate on a set of survey items (for additional details, see Pedulla 2016). I found that male applicants with part-time work histories were less likely to be highly recommended for interviews than male applicants with full-time work histories and that a significant portion of this penalty could be attributed to hiring professionals perceiving part-time male applicants as less committed. Female applicants with part-time employment experience, by contrast, were not penalized compared to female applicants with full-time employment experience, which is consistent with the field-experimental evidence. Importantly, though, a statistically significant difference between men and women with part-time experience did not emerge in the survey experiment, limiting the ability to explore the mechanisms that account for gender-differentiated evaluations of part-time employment histories (Pedulla 2016).

39. See Benard and Correll (2010) for a discussion of how the gender of the evaluator can shape the ways that targets are evaluated.

40. See Correll, Benard, and Paik (2007) and England et al. (2016). Research on the "motherhood penalty" is complicated, in part because the penalty that accrues to mothers may be due to both supply-side and demand-side factors. On the supply side, becoming a mother can be associated with changes in one's employment status or occupation or taking time out of the labor force. On the demand side, employers may discriminate against mothers.

41. In a few cases, hiring professionals noted that they thought part-time work would have negative consequences for women at the hiring interface. For example, Jennifer—who is a call center operations supervisor—said, "I guess where it's male or female in the part-time, I guess I would be concerned, does the female have a family? Does she have kids? Is that going to interfere with work? Is it going to interfere with what schedule she can work? Will she be able to work weekends? That would be my concern there." This take on gender and part-time work is different from that of many other respondents but is one way that gender and part-time work could be expected to interact.

42. Stevens (2007); Posselt (2016); Lamont (2009); Moss and Tilly (2001); Kiviat (2017). For a recent discussion of the ways that cognitive psychology could benefit from insights offered by cultural sociology, see Lamont et al. (2017). Additionally, Vaisey and Valentino (2018) offer a compelling argument about the overlapping insights offered by cultural sociology and judgment and decision-making scholars (see also the review by Bruch and Feinberg 2017).

43. Kiviat (2017, 14).

44. Correll, Benard, and Paik (2007); Ridgeway (2011).

Chapter 6

1. For example, Ruhm (1991) finds that there are lasting negative consequences of job displacements for workers' future wages. Relatedly, Gregg (2001) draws on data from the United Kingdom to show that men who experience unemployment when they are young are also more likely to experience unemployment when they are prime working-age adults. Also there is some previous field-experimental work that shows a negative effect of unemployment on callbacks (Kroft, Lange, and Notowidigdo 2013; Ghayad 2013; Eriksson and Rooth 2014; but see Nunley et al. 2017 and Farber, Silverman, and von Wachter 2017).

2. For examples, see Kroft, Lange, and Notowidigdo (2013); Ghayad (2013); Eriksson and Rooth (2014); Nunley et al. (2017); Farber, Silverman, and von Wachter (2017).

3. Nunley et al. (2015) uses the same field-experimental data as Nunley et al. (2017) to examine racial variation in the consequences of unemployment. They do not find variation in the effects of unemployment by race. However, the fictitious applicants in their study are recent college graduates, for whom the effects of unemployment may be distinct. Additionally, they do not find negative effects of unemployment (see Nunley et al. 2017).

4. Kroft, Lange, and Notowidigdo (2013, 1135). See also Ghayad (2013).

5. Bureau of Labor Statistics (2015). See also Figure 2.1 in Chapter 2.

6. This difference is statistically significant ($p < .01$) using a test for differences in proportions.

7. This difference is statistically significant ($p < .01$). See Model 2 in Table A1 in the Methodological Appendix.

8. These results are presented in Model 1 in Table A2 in the Methodological Appendix. I estimated a logistic regression model where the dependent variable was whether or not an applicant received a callback for the job and the independent variables were whether the applicant was black, the applicant's employment history, and an interaction between the two. The interaction term between being black and being unemployed was positive and statistically significant. The findings were consistent when using other estimation strategies, such as a linear probability model.

9. These types of additive effects have been found, for example, in field-experimental research examining the consequences of race and the selectivity of educational credentials in the United States (Gaddis 2015) and ethnicity and unemployment in Norway (Birkelund, Heggebo, and Rogstad 2017).

10. Beale (1970); King (1988).

11. Karren and Sherman (2012).

12. For discussions of this literature, see DiMaggio (1997); Lamont (2012); Lamont et al. (2017); and Bruch and Feinberg (2017).

13. Correll and Ridgeway (2003, 34). See also Berger et al. (1992).

14. Fiske and Neuberg (1990).

15. Fiske and Neuberg (1990, 6–7).

16. Moss and Tilly (2001); Kirschenman and Neckerman (1991); Waldinger and Lichter (2003); Pager and Karafin (2009); Karren and Sherman (2012).

17. For a review of the literature on expectation states theory, see Correll and Ridgeway (2003).

18. Complementing the overlapping stereotypes set of stories, some hiring professionals pointed to population-level differences in the experiences of unemployment for whites and African Americans. This type of narrative is reflected in Angela's response to the field experiment findings. Angela, a former talent manager at a manufacturing company who recently became unemployed, reported, "I would think that the unemployment rate would somehow reflect that

statistic in some way. . . . Well I would want to know overall what the unemployment rate looks like for white people and for minorities because I think that there's probably a difference there. I would imagine there's more unemployment with the minority group than the white group. I don't know for a fact but I would think that. So, if an employer has that assumption, like I do without having the research in front of me, it could be more understandable just very generally speaking why that minority may have an unemployment history versus their counterpart."

19. There was one other explanation that was brought up by hiring professionals for the field-experimental finding regarding race and unemployment. I refer to it as employer sympathy. For example, Jennifer, a call center operations supervisor, stated, "With black workers, you feel like it might just be their skin color that's holding them back so much. And it has nothing to do with their skill set or their experience of their personality or anything like that. They're just kind of getting pushed to the side based off of their race. Which is really unfair, but I feel like people are more sympathetic to that." This sympathetic view of hiring professionals is unlikely to drive the findings in the field experiment given the deep-seated racial discrimination that was observed among applicants with seamless employment histories. However, it may be interesting for future research to explore this potential additional pathway.

20. Pager and Karafin (2009); Moss and Tilly (2001).

21. Kennelly (1999); Moss and Tilly (2001); Hall and Farkas (2011).

22. Research has also documented a "welfare mother" stereotype about African American women (Gilens 1996). However, given that the job applicant profiles in the field experiment had significant employment experience before becoming unemployed, welfare stereotypes are unlikely to be particularly salient in this context.

23. Moss and Tilly (2001, 127).

24. At the same time, given gendered expectations around caregiving and breadwinning, employers may be more forgiving of unemployment or employment gaps for women than for men. Thus, both black and white women may face weaker penalties for unemployment than white men.

25. The three-way interaction between being unemployed, being African American, and being a woman is statistically significant in a logistic regression model. See Model 3 in Table A2 in the Methodological Appendix.

26. Here I follow Tilcsik (2011), who employed a similar approach to understand the role of stereotypes in driving discrimination against gay men in the labor market.

27. I thank Emily Paine for research assistance with coding the job postings. I independently coded a random subset of fifty job postings for a motivation and work ethic emphasis. My coding for motivation and work ethic matched the initial coding in forty-seven out of the fifty job postings, 94 percent of the time.

28. Variants of these terms, such as "reliability" and "passion," were also coded as desiring motivation.

29. The results from this analysis are presented in Table A3 in the Methodological Appendix (see also Pedulla 2018).

30. Correll and Ridgeway (2003); Fiske and Neuberg (1990).

Chapter 7

1. Interpreting "null" effects of this sort is challenging, given that our standard statistical procedures provide evidence about whether we can reject a null hypothesis, not whether we can support a null hypothesis. The null effect in this case may emerge due to a limitation in statistical power. Yet it is still interesting that for all other employment histories there was at least one sociodemographic group for whom the employment history was statistically significantly penalizing. That is not the case for THA employment.

2. Granovetter (1973); Smith (2005). For reviews of social networks and employment outcomes, see Castilla, Lan, and Rissing (2013a, 2013b).

3. Examples of the resumes used for the field experiment are presented in Chapter 4. Additional details about the design and implementation of the field experiment are available in the introductory chapter as well as the Methodological Appendix.

4. See Model 3 in Table A1 in the Methodological Appendix for this statistical test ($p < .01$).

5. This finding is derived from a post-estimation test after estimating Model 3 in Table A1 in the Methodological Appendix ($p < .05$).

6. To test for this possibility, I implemented a logistic regression model with standard errors clustered by job posting. The outcome variable was whether the application resulted in a callback or not. The predictors were all of the employment history categories in the field experiment (with full-time, standard employment excluded), the race and gender of the applicants, and interactions between the employment experiences and demographic categories. See Model 3 in Table A2 in the Methodological Appendix.

7. Likely due to the reduction in sample size when examining occupation-specific and city-specific callback rates by employment history condition, statistical significance is lost in some cases.

8. Smith and Neuwirth (2008).

9. Smith and Neuwirth (2008, 200).

10. Smith and Neuwirth (2008, 151).

11. Bussey and Trasviña (2003).

12. For existing scholarship on the ways the temporary help industry actively worked to promote the image of its workers as "good temps," see Smith and Neuwirth (2008).

13. Moss and Tilly (2001); Waldinger and Lichter (2003); Pager (2007).

14. Moss and Tilly (2001); Pager (2007).

15. See Blair (2002) for a discussion of literature in this area.

16. Kaas and Manger (2011).

17. Kaas and Manger (2011) interpret their finding as evidence of statistical discrimination in the German labor market. Their finding is also consistent with the idea that individuating information can reduce prejudicial attitudes (Peffley, Hurwitz, and Sniderman 1997).

18. Similar empirical patterns—where black gay men are perceived more positively than straight black men—have been found in other experimental studies as well. See, for example, Remedios et al. (2011) as well as Wilson, Remedios, and Rule (2017).

Chapter 8

1. Kalleberg, Reskin, and Hudson (2000).

2. See Epstein et al. (1999); Smith (1998); Sharone (2013).

3. Bureau of Labor Statistics (2018).

4. Bertrand and Mullainathan (2004); Pager, Western, and Bonikowski (2009); Gaddis (2015).

5. Gaddis (2015); Pager, Western, and Bonikowski (2009). I have used these terms—"additive effects" and "amplified congruence"—to describe different aggregation patterns in previously published research (see Pedulla 2018).

6. Correll and Ridgeway (2003); see also Berger et al. (1992).

7. Pedulla (2014b); Remedios et al. (2011).

8. Mouw (2003).

9. Nunley et al. (2017).

10. See Gershon (2017) for an in-depth discussion of the use of technology in the job matching process.

11. Cappelli (2019a, 2019b); Mann and O'Neil (2016). But see Kuncel, Klieger, and Ones (2014) for an argument about the benefits of algorithmic hiring.

12. Gershon (2017).

13. For an analysis of designing online markets to mitigate against discrimination, see Levy and Barocas (2018).

14. Reskin and McBrier (2000). For a discussion of the promises and limitations of formalization, see Correll (2017) and Tomaskovic-Devey and Avent-Holt (2019).

15. Kalev, Dobbin, and Kelly (2006); Castilla (2015).

16. Quillian et al. (2017).

17. Moss and Tilly (2001).

18. Beyond policy changes, one important aspect of advancing our understanding of non-standard, mismatched, and precarious work will be to improve the ways that data are collected about workers and their experiences in the labor market. The Bureau of Labor Statistics at the US Department of Labor recently restarted collecting the Contingent and Alternative Employment Arrangements Supplement to the Current Population Survey after more than a decade hiatus. This data collection effort provides important insights about the prevalence of various types of nonstandard and contingent employment. Continued collection of these data will be vital to our understanding of workers who experience nonstandard work. Beyond the Contingent Worker Supplement, there is a real and pressing need to collect more fine-grained data about workers who are laboring in nonstandard, mismatched, and precarious employment, tracking these workers over time, and having better ways of situating these workers in their broader contexts: their households, communities, and workplace organizations. Investments in collecting these types of data will be incredibly valuable in assisting researchers and policy makers to obtain a detailed picture of the day-to-day experiences of nonstandard, mismatched, and precarious workers as they traverse the labor market.

Notes to Methodological Appendix

1. The methods that were used to collect the field-experimental data have been discussed in prior articles (Pedulla 2016, 2018) as well as in my dissertation (Pedulla 2014a).

2. The field-experimental study presented here was approved by the Princeton University Institutional Review Board (IRB).

3. Unemployment was signaled through dates that the applicant did not have a job. The formal definition of unemployment is that an individual does not have a job *and* is looking for work. Details about the second component of the definition—searching for work—are not present in the unemployment condition. This method of signaling unemployment, however, is consistent with previous field experiments in this area (see Kroft, Lange, and Notowidigdo 2013). In the continuous employment condition, the applicant transitioned to a new job for the twelve months prior to the application being submitted. Thus, there is no signaling of a promotion in the continuous employment condition.

4. Barlow and Lahey (2018). For a discussion, see also Fryer and Levitt (2004).

5. I thank S. Michael Gaddis for connecting me with these data.

6. While the proportion of white/neutral names with a white mother was similar to the proportion of whites in the population, the proportion of African American racialized names with an African American mother was more than five times the proportion of African Americans in the population (US Census Bureau 2011).

7. There are some national contexts where photos are commonly submitted with job application materials (Weichselbaumer 2003). This opens additional ways of signaling race in audit studies but is not possible in the US context.

8. Thus, an important scope condition of the findings is that they are limited to college-educated workers.

9. Although I do not have information about the size of the companies to which applications were submitted, larger companies may be somewhat overrepresented in the sample given the method through which job openings were obtained. Evidence from a nonprobability sample of HR professionals at US companies suggests that 54 percent of companies with between one and ninety-nine full-time employees utilized paid job boards for recruiting new employees, compared to between 71 percent and 79 percent for larger companies (SHRM 2016).

10. The search was limited to jobs posted within fewer than thirty days in a few cases. In these instances, the computer script would not run for the full thirty-day search period, but worked for these shorter amounts of time. The level of education included in the search criteria was also different across occupations. For accounting and sales jobs, the education level was limited to jobs requiring an associate's or bachelor's degree. For the project manager / manager openings, the search was limited to jobs requiring a bachelor's degree. Finally, I did not limit the administrative assistant searches by education because many employers did not specify any education level requirement for this job type.

11. The findings are similar when alternative modeling strategies, such a linear probability models, are deployed.

12. Pager and Quillian (2005); Jerolmack and Khan (2014).

13. Bureau of Labor Statistics (2019b).

14. Our coding of the interviews was similar in many ways to the approach discussed in Deterding and Waters (2018).

REFERENCES

Aaronson, Daniel, and Eric French. 2004. "The Effect of Part-Time Work on Wages: Evidence from the Social Security Rules." *Journal of Labor Economics* 22(2):329–352.

Abraham, Katharine G. 2015. "Is Skill Mismatch Impeding U.S. Economic Recovery?" *ILR Review* 68(2):291–313.

Abraham, Katharine G., John C. Haltiwanger, Kristin Sandusky, and James R. Spletzer. 2018. "Measuring the Gig Economy: Current Knowledge and Open Issues." National Bureau of Economic Research Working Paper 24950.

Acker, Joan. 1990. "Hierarchies, Jobs, Bodies: A Theory of Gendered Organizations." *Gender & Society* 4(2):139–158.

Addison, John T., Chad Cotti, and Christopher J. Surfield. 2009. "Atypical Work: Who Gets It, and Where Does It Lead? Some U.S. Evidence Using the NLSY79." IZA Discussion Paper 4444.

Addison, John T., and Christopher J. Surfield. 2009. "Does Atypical Work Help the Jobless? Evidence from a CAEAS/CPS Cohort Analysis." *Applied Economics* 41:1077–1087.

Aigner, Dennis J., and Glen G. Cain. 1977. "Statistical Theories of Discrimination in Labor Markets." *Industrial and Labor Relations Review* 30:749–776.

Albiston, Catherine. 2007. "Institutional Perspectives on Law, Work, and Family." *Annual Review of Law and Social Science* 3:397–426.

———. 2010. *Institutional Inequality and the Mobilization of the Family and Medical Leave Act: Rights on Leave.* Cambridge: Cambridge University Press.

Allen, Tammy D., and Joyce E. A. Russell. 1999. "Parental Leave of Absence: Some Not So Family-Friendly Implications." *Journal of Applied Social Psychology* 29(1):166–191.

Alliance for Board Diversity. 2017. "Missing Pieces Report." Deloitte. www2.deloitte.com/us/en/pages/center-for-board-effectiveness/articles/board-diversity-census-missing-pieces.html.

Anderson, Sarah, and Anthony H. Winefield. 2011. "The Impact of Underemployment on Psychological Health, Physical Health, and Work Attitudes." Pp. 165–185 in *Underemployment*, edited by Doug Maynard and Daniel C. Feldman. New York: Springer.

Askehave, Inger, and Karen Korning Zethsen. 2014. "Gendered Constructions of Leadership in Danish Job Advertisements." *Gender, Work and Organization* 21(6):531–545.

Autor, David H. 2003. "Outsourcing at Will: The Contribution of Unjust Dismissal Doctrine to the Growth of Employment Outsourcing." *Journal of Labor Economics* 21:1–42.

Autor, David H., and Susan Houseman. 2010. "Do Temporary-Help Jobs Improve Labor Market Outcomes for Low-Skilled Workers? Evidence from 'Work First.'" *Applied Economics* 2:96–128.

Autor, David H., Lawrence F. Katz, and Alan B. Krueger. 1998. "Computing Inequality: Have Computers Changed the Labor Market?" *Quarterly Journal of Economics* 113(4):1169–1213.

Baert, Stijn, and Dieter Verhaest. 2014. "Unemployment or Overeducation: Which Is a Worse Signal to Employers?" IZA Discussion Paper 8312.

Barley, Stephen R., and Gideon Kunda. 2004. *Gurus, Hired Guns, and Warm Bodies: Itinerant Experts in a Knowledge Economy.* Princeton, NJ: Princeton University Press.

Barlow, M. Rose, and Joanna N. Lahey. 2018. "What Race Is Lacey? Intersecting Perceptions of Racial Minority Status and Social Class." *Social Science Quarterly* 99(5):1680–1698.

Beale, Frances M. 1970. "Double Jeopardy: To Be Black and Female." Pp. 90–100 in *The Black Woman,* edited by Toni Cade. New York: Signet.

Becker, Gary S. 1964. *Human Capital.* New York: Columbia University Press.

Benard, Stephen, and Shelley J. Correll. 2010. "Normative Discrimination and the Motherhood Penalty." *Gender & Society* 24(5):616–646.

Benner, Katie. 2015. "Politicians Turn to Start-Ups for Grasp of 'Gig Economy.'" *New York Times,* October 4.

Berger, Joseph, Robert Z. Norman, James W. Balkwell, and Roy F. Smith. 1992. "Status Inconsistency in Task Situations: A Test of Four Status Processing Principles." *American Sociological Review* 57(6):843–855.

Bernhardt, Annette. 2014. "Labor Standard and the Reorganization of Work: Gaps in Data and Research." Institute for Research on Labor and Employment Working Paper 100-14.

Bertrand, Marianne, and Sendhil Mullainathan. 2004. "Are Emily and Greg More Employable Than Lakisha and Jamal? A Field Experiment on Labor Market Discrimination." *American Economic Review* 94:991–1013.

Best, Rachel Kahn, Lauren B. Edelman, Linda Hamilton Krieger, and Scott R. Eliason. 2011. "Multiple Disadvantages: An Empirical Test of Intersectionality Theory in EEO Litigation." *Law & Society Review* 45(4):991–1025.

Bianchi, Susan M., Melissa A. Milkie, Liana C. Sayer, and John P. Robinson. 2010. "Is Anyone Doing the Housework? Trends in the Gender Division of Household Labor." *Social Forces* 79(1):191–228.

Bielby, William T., and Denise D. Bielby. 2002. "Telling Stories about Gender and Effort: Social Science Narratives about Who Works Hard for the Money." Pp. 193–217 in *The New Economic Sociology: Developments in an Emerging Field,* edited by Mauro F. Guillen, Randall Collins, Paula England, and Marshall Meyer. New York: Russell Sage Foundation.

Bills, David B., Valentina Di Stasio, and Klarita Gërxhani. 2017. "The Demand Side of Hiring: Employers in the Labor Market." *Annual Review of Sociology* 43:291–310.

Birkelund, Elisabeth Gunn, Kristian Heggebo, and Jon Rogstad. 2017. "Additive of Multiplicative Disadvantage? The Scarring Effects of Unemployment for Ethnic Minorities." *European Sociological Review* 1(33):17–29.

Blair, Irene V. 2002. "The Malleability of Automatic Stereotypes and Prejudice." *Personality and Social Psychology Review* 6(3):242–261.

Blair-Loy, Mary. 2003. *Competing Devotions: Career and Family among Women Executives.* Cambridge, MA: Harvard University Press.

Blau, Francine D., and Lawrence M. Kahn. 2017. "The Gender Wage Gap: Extent, Trends, and Explanations." *Journal of Economic Literature* 55(3):789–865.

Blau, Gary, Tony Petrucci, and John McClendon. 2013. "Correlates of Life Satisfaction and Unemployment Stigma and the Impact of Length of Unemployment on a Unique Unemployed Sample." *Career Development International* 18(3):257–280.

Bodenhausen, Galen V., and Robert S. Wyer, Jr. 1985. "Effects of Stereotypes on Decision Making and Information-Processing Strategies." *Journal of Personality and Social Psychology* 48(2):267–282.

Booth, Alison L., and Jan C. van Ours. 2009. "Hours of Work and Gender Identity: Does Part-Time Work Make the Family Happier?" *Economica* 76:176–196.

Brand, Jennie E. 2015. "The Far-Reaching Impact of Job Loss and Unemployment." *Annual Review of Sociology* 41:359–375.

Briscoe, Forrest, and Katherine C. Kellogg. 2011. "The Initial Assignment Effect: Local Employer Practices and Positive Career Outcomes for Work-Family Program Users." *American Sociological Review* 76:291–319.

Browne, Irene, and Joya Misra. 2003. "The Intersection of Gender and Race in the Labor Market." *Annual Review of Sociology* 29:487–513.

Bruch, Elizabeth, and Fred Feinberg. 2017. "Decision-Making Processes in Social Contexts." *Annual Review of Sociology* 43:207–227.

Bureau of Labor Statistics. 2005. "Contingent and Alternative Employment Arrangements, February 2005." www.bls.gov/news.release/History/conemp.txt.

———. 2015. "Table A-2. Employment Status of the Civilian Population by Race, Sex, and Age." www.bls.gov/webapps/legacy/cpsatab2.htm.

———. 2018. "Contingent and Alternative Employment Arrangements—May 2017." www.bls.gov /news.release/conemp.nr0.htm.

———. 2019a. "Household Data Annual Averages. 21. Persons at Work in Nonagricultural Industries by Class of Worker and Usual Full- or Part-Time Status." www.bls.gov/cps/cpsaat21.htm.

———. 2019b. "Employed Persons by Detailed Occupations, Sex, Race, and Hispanic or Latino Ethnicity." www.bls.gov/cps/cpsaat11.htm.

———. 2019c. "Household Data Annual Average. 8. Employed and Unemployed Full- and Part-Time Workers by Age, Sex, Race, and Hispanic or Latino Ethnicity." www.bls.gov/cps /cpsaat08.htm.

———. 2019d. "Unemployment Rates for States, 2014 Annual Averages." www.bls.gov/lau/lastrk14 .htm.

———. 2019e. "Household Data Seasonally Adjusted. A-10. Unemployment Rates by Age, Sex, and Marital Status, Seasonally Adjusted." www.bls.gov/web/empsit/cpseea10.htm.

Burgard, Sarah A., and Katherine Y. Lin. 2013. "Bad Jobs, Bad Health? How Work and Working Conditions Contribute to Health Disparities." *American Behavioral Scientist* 57(8):1105–1127.

Burks, Stephen V., Bo Cowgill, Mitchell Hoffman, and Michael Housman. 2015. "The Value of Hiring through Employee Referrals." *Quarterly Journal of Economics* 130(2):805–839.

Bussey, Jenny, and John Trasviña. 2003. "Racial Preferences: The Treatment of White and African American Job Applicants by Temporary Employment Agencies in California." Berkeley, CA: Discrimination Research Center.

Cajner, Tomaz, Tyler Radler, David Ratner, and Ivan Vidangos. 2018. "Racial Gaps in Labor Market Outcomes in the Last Four Decades and over the Business Cycle." Federal Reserve Bank of Minneapolis System Working Paper 18-07.

Cappelli, Peter H. 2015. "Skill Gaps, Skill Shortages, and Skill Mismatched: Evidence and Arguments for the United States." *ILR Review* 68(2):251–290.

———. 2019a. "Your Approach to Hiring Is All Wrong." *Harvard Business Review*, May/June. https://hbr.org/2019/05/recruiting?ab=hero-main-text.

———. 2019b. "Data Science Can't Fix Hiring (Yet)." *Harvard Business Review*, May/June. https:// hbr.org/2019/05/recruiting#data-science-cant-fix-hiring-yet.

Cappelli, Peter, Laurie Bassi, Harry Katz, David Knoke, Paul Osterman, and Michael Useem. 1997. *Change at Work: How American Industry and Workers Are Coping with Corporate Restructuring and What Workers Must Do to Take Charge of Their Own Careers*. New York: Oxford University Press.

Cappelli, Peter, and David Neumark. 2004. "External Churning and Internal Flexibility: Evidence on the Functional Flexibility and Core-Periphery Hypotheses." *Industrial Relations* 43(1):148–182.

CareerBuilder. 2012. *Referral Madness: How Employee Referral Programs Turn Good Employees into Great Recruiters and Grow Your Bottom Line*. CareerBuilder E-Book.

Castilla, Emilio J. 2008. "Gender, Race, and Meritocracy in Organizational Careers." *American Journal of Sociology* 113(6):1479–1526.

———. 2015. "Accounting for the Gap: A Firm Study Manipulating Organizational Accountability and Transparency in Pay Decisions." *Organization Science* 26(2):311–333.

Castilla, Emilio J., George J. Lan, and Ben A. Rissing. 2013a. "Social Networks and Employment: Mechanisms (Part 1)." *Sociology Compass* 7(12):999–1012.

———. 2013b. "Social Networks and Employment: Outcomes (Part 2)." *Sociology Compass* 7(12):1013–1026.

Catalyst. 2018. "Pyramid: Women in S&P 500 Companies."

Center for American Women and Politics. 2018. "Women in the U.S. Congress 2018." https://cawp.rutgers.edu/women-us-congress-2018.

Cha, Youngjoo. 2010. "Reinforcing Separate Spheres: The Effect of Spousal Overwork on the Employment of Men and Women in Dual-Earner Households." *American Sociological Review* 75(2):303–329.

Cha, Youngjoo, and Kim A. Weeden. 2014. "Overwork and the Slow Convergence in the Gender Gap in Wages." *American Sociological Review* 79(3):457–484.

Charles, Maria. 2011. "A World of Difference: International Trends in Women's Economic Status." *Annual Review of Sociology* 37:355–371.

Chattopadhyay, Prithviraj, and Elizabeth George. 2001. "Examining the Effects of Work Externalization through the Lens of Social Identity Theory." *Journal of Applied Psychology* 86:781–788.

Chen, Chung-An, and Jeffrey L. Brudney. 2009. "A Cross-Sector Comparison of Using Nonstandard Workers: Explaining Use and Impacts on the Employment Relationship." *Administration and Society* 41:313–339.

Clawson, Dan, and Mary Ann Clawson. 1999. "What Has Happened to the U.S. Labor Movement? Union Decline and Renewal." *Annual Review of Sociology* 25:95–119.

Collins, Patricia Hill. [1990] 2000. *Black Feminist Thought: Knowledge, Consciousness, and the Politics of Empowerment*. New York: Routledge.

Coltrane, Scott, Elizabeth C. Miller, Tracy DeHaan, and Lauren Stewart. 2013. "Father and the Flexibility Stigma." *Journal of Social Issues* 69(2):279–302.

Cooper, Marianne. 2014. *Cut Adrift: Families in Insecure Times*. Berkeley: University of California Press.

Correll, Joshua, Bernadette Park, Charles M. Judd, and Bernd Wittenbrink. 2002. "The Police Officer's Dilemma: Using Ethnicity to Disambiguate Potentially Threatening Individuals." *Journal of Personality and Social Psychology* 83(6):1314–1329.

Correll, Shelley J. 2017. "Reducing Gender Biases in Modern Workplaces: A Small Wins Approach to Organizational Change." *Gender & Society* 31(6):725–750.

Correll, Shelley J., and Stephen Benard. 2006. "Biased Estimators? Comparing Status and Statistical Theories of Gender Discrimination." *Social Psychology of the Workplace* 23:89–116.

Correll, Shelley J., Stephen Benard, and In Paik. 2007. "Getting a Job: Is There a Motherhood Penalty?" *American Journal of Sociology* 112:1297–1338.

Correll, Shelley J., and Cecilia L. Ridgeway. 2003. "Expectations States Theory." Pp. 29–51 in *Handbook of Social Psychology*, edited by John DeLamater. New York: Kluwer.

Crenshaw, Kimberlé. 1989. "Demarginalizing the Intersection of Race and Sex: A Black Feminist Critique of Antidiscrimination Doctrine, Feminist Theory and Antiracist Politics." *University of Chicago Legal Forum* 1989(1):139–167.

Cuddy, Amy J. C., Susan T. Fiske, and Peter Glick. 2007. "The BIAS Map: Behaviors from Intergroup Affect and Stereotypes." *Journal of Personality and Social Psychology* 92(4):631–648.

Cunningham, Evan. 2018. "Great Recession, Great Recovery? Trends from the Current Population Survey." *Monthly Labor Review*, April.

Davies, Andrea Rees, and Brenda D. Frink. 2014. "The Origins of the Ideal Worker: The Separation of Work and Home in the United States from the Market Revolution to 1950." *Work and Occupations* 41(1):18–39.

Davis-Blake, Alison, and Joseph P. Broschak. 2009. "Outsourcing and the Changing Nature of Work." *Annual Review of Sociology* 35:321–340.

Davis-Blake, Alison, Joseph P. Broschak, and Elizabeth George. 2003. "Happy Together? How Using Nonstandard Workers Affects Exit, Voice, and Loyalty among Standard Employees." *Academy of Management Journal* 46:475–485.

Deterding, Nicole M., and Mary C. Waters. 2018. "Flexible Coding of In-Depth Interviews: A Twenty-First-Century Approach." *Sociological Methods & Research*. Online first. doi:10.1177/0049124118799377.

DiMaggio, Paul. 1997. "Culture and Cognition." *Annual Review of Sociology* 23:263–287.

DiMaggio, Paul, and Bart Bonikowski. 2008. "Make Money Surfing the Web? The Impact of Internet Use on the Earnings of U.S. Workers." *American Sociological Review* 73(2):227–250.

DiPrete, Thomas A., Dominique Goux, and Eric Maurin. 2002. "Internal Labor Markets and Earnings Trajectories in the Post-Fordist Economy." *Social Science Research* 31(2):175–196.

Dobbin, Frank. 2009. *Inventing Equal Opportunity*. Princeton, NJ: Princeton University Press.

Dobbin, Frank, and Alexandra Kalev. 2016. "Why Diversity Programs Fail." *Harvard Business Review*, July/August. https://hbr.org/2016/07/why-diversity-programs-fail.

Dobbin, Frank, Daniel Schrage, and Alexandra Kalev. 2015. "Rage Against the Iron Cage: The Varied Effects of Bureaucratic Personnel Reforms on Diversity." *American Sociological Review* 80(5):1014–1044.

Dokko, Jane, Megan Mumford, and Diane Whitmore Schanzenbach. 2015. "Workers and the Online Gig Economy." Hamilton Project.

Donovan, Sarah A., David H. Bradley, and Jon O. Shimabukuru. 2016. "What Does the Gig Economy Mean for Workers?" Congressional Research Service Report 7-570, R44365.

Dooley, David, and Joann Prause. 2004. *The Social Costs of Underemployment: Inadequate Employment as Disguised Unemployment*. New York: Cambridge University Press.

Dovidio, John F., and Samuel L. Gaertner. 2000. "Aversive Racism and Selection Decisions: 1989 and 1999." *Psychological Science* 11(4):315–319.

Eagly, Alice H., and Steven J. Karau. 2002. "Role Congruity Theory of Prejudice toward Female Leaders." *Psychological Review* 109(3):573–598.

Eagly, Alice H., and Valerie J. Steffen. 1986. "Gender Stereotypes, Occupational Roles, and Beliefs about Part-Time Employees." *Psychology of Women Quarterly* 10:252–262.

Elliott, James R., and Ryan A. Smith. 2004. "Race, Gender, and Workplace Power." *American Sociological Review* 69(3):365–386.

England, Paula, Jonathan Bearak, Michelle J. Budig, and Melissa J. Hodges. 2016. "Do Highly Paid, Highly Skilled Women Experience the Largest Motherhood Penalty?" *American Sociological Review* 81(6):1161–1189.

Epstein, Cynthia Fuchs, Carroll Seron, Bonnie Oglensky, and Robert Sauté. 1999. *The Part-Time Paradox: Time Norms, Professional Life, Family and Gender*. New York: Routledge.

Erdogan, Berrin, and Talya N. Bauer. 2011. "The Impact of Underemployment on Turnover and Career Trajectories." Pp. 215–232 in *Underemployment*, edited by Doug Maynard and Daniel C. Feldman. New York: Springer.

Eriksson, Stefan, and Dan-Olof Rooth. 2014. "Do Employers Use Unemployment as a Sorting Criterion When Hiring? Evidence from a Field Experiment." *American Economic Review* 104(3):1014–1039.

Farber, Henry S. 2008. "Short(er) Shrift: The Decline in Worker-Firm Attachment in the United States." Pp. 10–37 in *Laid Off, Laid Low: Political and Economic Consequences of Employment Insecurity*, edited by Katherine S. Newman. New York: Columbia University Press.

Farber, Henry S., Dan Silverman, and Till M. von Wachter. 2017. "Factors Determining Callback to Job Applications by the Unemployed: An Audit Study." *RSF: Journal of the Social Sciences* 3(3):168–201.

Feldman, Daniel C. 1990. "Reconceptualizing the Nature and Consequences of Part-Time Work." *Academy of Management Review* 15(1):103–112.

Ferber, Marianne A., and Jane Waldfogel. 1998. "The Long-Term Consequences of Nontraditional Employment." *Monthly Labor Review* 121:3–12.

Fernandez, Roberto M. "Skill-Biased Technological Change and Wage Inequality: Evidence from a Plant Retooling." *American Journal of Sociology* 107(2):273–320.

Fernandez, Roberto M., Emilio J. Castilla, and Paul Moore. 2000. "Social Capital at Work: Networks and Employment at a Phone Center." *American Journal of Sociology* 105(5):1288–1356.

Fernandez, Roberto M., and Marie Louise Mors. 2008. "Competing for Jobs: Labor Queues and Gender Sorting in the Hiring Process." *Social Science Research* 37(4):1061–1080.

Fernandez, Roberto M., and M. Lourdes Sosa. 2005. "Gendering the Job: Networks and Recruitment at a Call Center." *American Journal of Sociology* 111(3):859–904.

Fiske, Susan T. 1998. "Stereotyping, Prejudice, and Discrimination." Pp. 357–411 in *The Handbook of Social Psychology*, edited by Daniel Gilbert, Susan Fiske, and Gardner Lindzey. Boston: McGraw-Hill.

Fiske, Susan T., Amy J. C. Cuddy, Peter Glick, and Jun Xu. 2002. "A Model of (Often Mixed) Stereotype Content: Competence and Warmth Respectively Follow from Perceived Status and Competition." *Journal of Personality and Social Psychology* 82(6):878–902.

Fiske, Susan T., and Steven L. Neuberg. 1990. "A Continuum of Impression Formation, from Category-Based to Individuating Processes: Influences of Information and Motivation on Attention and Interpretation." *Advances in Experimental Social Psychology* 23:1–74.

Fryer, Roland G., and Steven D. Levitt. 2004. "The Cause and Consequences of Distinctively Black Names." *Quarterly Journal of Economics* 119(3):767–805.

Gaddis, S. Michael. 2015. "Discrimination in a Credential Society: An Audit Study of Race and College Selectivity in the Labor Market." *Social Forces* 93(4):1451–1479.

———. 2017. "How Black Are Lakisha and Jamal? Racial Perceptions from Names Used in Correspondence Audit Studies." *Sociological Science* 4:469–489.

Gangl, Markus. 2006. "Scar Effects of Unemployment: An Assessment of Institutional Complementarities." *American Sociological Review* 71:986–1013.

Gaucher, Danielle, Justin Friesen, and Aaron C. Kay. 2011. "Evidence the Gendered Wording in Job Advertisements Exists and Sustains Gender Inequality." *Journal of Personality and Social Psychology* 101(1):109–128.

George, Elizabeth. 2003. "External Solutions and Internal Problems: The Effects of Employment Externalization on Internal Workers' Attitudes." *Organizational Science* 14:368–402.

Gershon, Ilana. 2017. *Down and Out in the New Economy: How People Find (or Don't Find) Work Today*. Chicago: University of Chicago Press.

Ghayad, Rand. 2013. "The Jobless Trap." Working Paper, Northeastern University.

Gilens, Martin. 1996. "'Race Coding' and White Opposition to Welfare." *American Political Science Review* 90(3):593–604.

Goffman, Erving. 1963. *Stigma: Notes on the Management of Spoiled Identity*. New York: Touchstone.

Golden, Lonnie. 2016. "Still Falling Short on Hours and Pay: Part-Time Work Becoming New Normal." Economic Policy Institute.

Gonos, George. 1997. "The Contest over 'Employer' Status in the Post-war United States: The Case of Temporary Help Firms." *Law & Society Review* 31:81–110.

Granovetter, Mark S. 1973. "The Strength of Weak Ties." *American Journal of Sociology* 78(6):1360–1380.

Greenman, Emily, and Yu Xie. 2008. "'Double Jeopardy?' The Interaction of Gender and Race on Earnings in the United States." *Social Forces* 86(3):1217–1244.

Gregg, Paul. 2001. "The Impact of Youth Unemployment on Adult Unemployment in the NCDS." *Economic Journal* 111(475):F626–F653.

Grigoryeva, Angelina. 2017. "Own Gender, Sibling's Gender, Parent's Gender: The Division of Elderly Parent Care among Adult Children." *American Sociological Review* 82(1):116–146.

Hacker, Jacob S. 2006. *The Great Risk Shift: The New Economic Insecurity and the Decline of the American Dream*. New York: Oxford University Press.

Hall, Matthew, and George Farkas. 2011. "Adolescent Cognitive Skills, Attitudinal/Behavioral Traits and Career Wages." *Social Forces* 89(4):1261–1285.

Halpin, Brian W. 2015. "Subject to Change without Notice: Mock Schedules and Flexible Employment in the United States." *Social Problems* 62:419–438.

Handel, Michael J. 2003. "Skills Mismatch in the Labor Market." *Annual Review of Sociology* 29:135–165.

Hatton, Erin. 2011. *The Temp Economy: From Kelly Girls to Permatemps in Postwar America*. Philadelphia: Temple University Press.

Heilman, Madeline E. 2012. "Gender Stereotypes and Workplace Bias." *Research in Organizational Behavior* 32:113–135.

Heilman, Madeline E., and Aaron S. Wallen. 2010. "Wimpy and Undeserving of Respect: Penalties for Men's Gender-Inconsistent Success." *Journal of Experimental Social Psychology* 46:664–667.

Henson, Kevin Daniel. 1996. *Just a Temp*. Philadelphia: Temple University Press.

Higgins, Christopher, Linda Duxbury, and Karen Lea Johnson. 2000. "Part-Time Work for Women: Does It Really Help Balance Work and Family?" *Human Resource Management* 39(1):17–32.

Hill, E. Jeffrey, Vjollca K. Martinson, Maria Ferris, and Robin Zenger Baker. 2004. "Beyond the Mommy Track: The Influence of New-Concept Part-Time Work for Professional Women on Work and Family." *Journal of Family and Economic Issues* 25(1):121–136.

Hirsch, Barry T. 2005. "Why Do Part-Time Workers Earn Less? The Role of Worker and Job Skills." *ILR Review* 58(4):525–551.

Hollister, Matissa N. 2011. "Employment Stability in the U.S. Labor Market: Rhetoric versus Reality." *Annual Review of Sociology* 37:305–324.

Hollister, Matissa N., and Kristin E. Smith. 2014. "Unmasking the Conflicting Trends in Job Tenure by Gender in the United States, 1983–2008." *American Sociological Review* 79(1):159–181.

Horowitz, Jonathan. 2018. "Relative Education and the Advantage of a College Degree." *American Sociological Review* 83(4):771–801.

Houseman, Susan N. 1997. "Why Employers Use Flexibility Staffing Arrangements: Evidence from an Establishment Survey." *Industrial and Labor Relations Review* 55(1):149–170.

Hyman, Louis. 2018. *Temp: How American Work, American Business, and the American Dream Became Temporary*. New York: Viking.

Jackson, Michelle. 2009. "Disadvantaged through Discrimination? The Role of Employer in Social Stratification." *British Journal of Sociology* 60(4):669–692.

Jerolmack, Colin, and Shamus Khan. 2014. "Talk Is Cheap: Ethnography and the Attitudinal Fallacy." *Sociological Methods and Research* 43(2):178–209.

JPMorgan Chase & Co. Institute. 2016. "The Online Platform Economy: Has Growth Peaked?" www.jpmorganchase.com/corporate/institute/document/jpmc-institute-online-platform-econ-brief.pdf.

Kaas, Leo, and Christian Manger. 2011. "Ethnic Discrimination in Germany's Labour Market: A Field Experiment." *German Economic Review* 13(1):1–20.

Kalev, Alexandra. 2009. "Cracking the Glass Cages? Restructuring and Ascriptive Inequality at Work." *American Journal of Sociology* 114(6):1591–1643.

———. 2014. "How You Downsize Is Who You Downsize: Biased Formalization, Accountability, and Managerial Diversity." *American Sociological Review* 79(1):109–135.

Kalev, Alexandra, Frank Dobbin, and Erin Kelly. 2006. "Best Practices or Best Guesses? Assessing the Efficacy of Corporate Affirmative Action and Diversity Policies." *American Sociological Review* 71:589–617.

Kalleberg, Arne L. 2000. "Nonstandard Employment Relations: Part-Time, Temporary and Contract Work." *Annual Review of Sociology* 26:341–365.

———. 2007. *The Mismatched Worker*. New York: Norton.

———. 2009. "Precarious Work, Insecure Workers: Employment Relations in Transition." *American Sociological Review* 74(1):1–22.

———. 2011. *Good Jobs, Bad Jobs: The Rise of Polarized and Precarious Employment Systems in the United States, 1970s to 2000s*. New York: Russell Sage Foundation.

Kalleberg, Arne L., and Michael Dunn. 2016. "Good Jobs, Bad Jobs in the Gig Economy." *Perspectives of Work*. http://michael-dunn.org/wp-content/uploads/2017/05/ALK-MD.-JQ-in-Gig -Economy.pdf.

Kalleberg, Arne L., Barbara F. Reskin, and Kenneth Hudson. 2000. "Bad Jobs in America: Standard and Nonstandard Employment Relations and Job Quality in the United States." *American Sociological Review* 65:256–278.

Kang, Sonia K., and Alison L. Chasteen. 2009. "Beyond the Double-Jeopardy Hypothesis: Assessing Emotion on the Faces of Multiply-Categorizable Targets of Prejudice." *Journal of Experimental Social Psychology* 45:1281–1285.

Karren, Ronald, and Kim Sherman. 2012. "Layoffs and Unemployment Discrimination: A New Stigma." *Journal of Managerial Psychology* 27(8):848–863.

Katz, Lawrence F., and Alan B. Krueger. 2016. "The Rise and Nature of Alternative Work Arrangements in the United States, 1995–2015." National Bureau of Economic Research Working Paper 22667.

Kelly, Erin L., Samantha K. Ammons, Kelly Chermack, and Phyllis Moen. 2010. "Gendered Challenge, Gendered Response: Confronting the Ideal Worker Norm in a White-Collar Organization." *Gender & Society* 24(3):281–303.

Kennelly, Ivy. 1999. "'That Single-Mother Element': How White Employers Typify Black Women." *Gender & Society* 13(2):168–192.

Killewald, Alexandra. 2016. "Money, Work, and Marital Stability: Assessing Change in the Gendered Determinants of Divorce." *American Sociological Review* 81(4):696–719.

Kim, ChangHwan, and Arthur Sakamoto. 2008. "The Rise of Intra-occupational Wage Inequality in the United States, 1983 to 2002." *American Sociological Review* 73(1):129–157.

Kimmel, Michael. 2006. *Manhood in America: A Cultural History*. 2nd ed. New York: Oxford University Press.

King, Deborah K. 1988. "Multiple Jeopardy, Multiple Consciousness: The Context of a Black Feminist Ideology." *Signs: Journal of Women in Culture and Society* 14:42–72.

Kirschenman, Joleen, and Katherine M. Neckerman. 1991. "We'd Love to Hire Them, But . . . : The Meaning of Race for Employers." Pp. 203–234 in *The Urban Underclass*, edited by Christopher Jencks and P. E. Peterson. Washington, DC: Brookings Institution.

Kiviat, Barbara. 2017. "The Art of Deciding with Data: Evidence from How Employer Translate Credit Reports into Hiring Decisions." *Socio-Economic Review*. Online first. doi:10.1093/ser /mwx030/4098110.

Koch, Amanda J., Susan D. D'Mello, and Paul R. Sackett. 2015. "A Meta-analysis of Gender Stereotypes and Bias in Experimental Simulations of Employment Decision Making." *Journal of Applied Psychology* 110(1):128–161.

Kosanovich, Karen, and Eleni Theodossiou Sherman. 2015. "Trends in Long-Term Unemployment." Spotlight on Statistics. US Bureau of Labor Statistics.

Kossek, Ellen Ernst, Shaun Pichler, Todd Bodner, and Leslie B. Hammer. 2011. "Workplace Social Support and Work-Family Conflict: A Meta-analysis Clarifying the Influence of General and Work-Family-Specific Supervisor and Organizational Support." *Personnel Psychology* 64:289–313.

Kroft, Kory, Fabian Lange, and Matthew J. Notowidigdo. 2013. "Duration Dependence and Labor Market Conditions: Evidence from a Field Experiment." *Quarterly Journal of Economics* 128(3):1123–1167.

Krueger, Alan B., and Andreas Mueller. 2011. "Job Search, Emotional Well-Being and Job Finding in a Period of Mass Unemployment: Evidence from High-Frequency Longitudinal Data." *Brookings Papers on Economic Activity* 1:1–57.

Kuncel, Nathan R., David M. Klieger, and Deniz S. Ones. 2014. "In Hiring, Algorithms Beat Instinct." *Harvard Business Review*, May.

Kunda, Ziva, and Paul Thagard. 1996. "Forming Impressions from Stereotypes, Traits, and Behaviors: A Parallel-Constraint-Satisfaction Theory." *Psychological Review* 103(2):284–308.

Lahey, Joanna N. 2008. "Age, Women, and Hiring: An Experimental Study." *Journal of Human Resources* 43(1):30–56.

Lamont, Michèle. 2009. *How Professors Think: Inside the Curious World of Academic Judgement.* Cambridge, MA: Harvard University Press.

———. 2012. "Toward a Comparative Sociology of Valuation and Evaluation." *Annual Review of Sociology* 38:201–221.

Lamont, Michèle, Laura Adler, Bo Yun Park, and Xin Xiang. 2017. "Bridging Cultural Sociology and Cognitive Psychology in Three Contemporary Research Programmes." *Nature Human Behaviour* 1:866–872.

Lautsch, Brenda A. 2002. "Uncovering and Explaining Variance in the Features and Outcomes of Contingent Work." *Industrial and Labor Relations Review* 56:23–43.

Letkermann, Paul. 2002. "Unemployed Professionals, Stigma Management and Derivative Stigmata." *Work, Employment, and Society* 16(3):511–522.

Leung, Ming D. 2014. "Dilettante or Renaissance Person? How the Order of Job Experiences Affects Hiring in an External Labor Market." *American Sociological Review* 79(1):136–158.

———. 2018. "Learning to Hire? Hiring as a Dynamic Experiential Learning Process in an Online Market for Contract Labor." *Management Science* 64:5461–5959.

Levy, Karen, and Solon Barocas. 2018. "Designing Against Discrimination in Online Markets." *Berkeley Technology Law Journal* 32(3):1183–1237.

Livingston, Gretchen. 2016. "Among 41 Nations, U.S. Is the Outlier When It Comes to Paid Parental Leave." Pew Research Center.

Logan, John Allen. 1996. "Opportunity and Choice in Socially Structured Labor Markets." *American Journal of Sociology* 102(1):114–160.

Mandel, Hadas, and Moshe Semyonov. 2014. "Gender Pay Gap and Employment Sector: Sources of Earnings Disparities in the United States, 1970–2010." *Demography* 51:1597–1618.

Mann, Gideon, and Cathy O'Neil. 2016. "Hiring Algorithms Are Not Neutral." *Harvard Business Review*, December.

Margalit, Yotam. 2013. "Explaining Social Policy Preferences: Evidence from the Great Recession." *American Political Science Review* 107(1):80–103.

Marler, Janet H., Melissa Woodard Barringer, and George T. Milkovich. 2002. "Boundaryless and Traditional Contingent Employees: Worlds Apart." *Journal of Organizational Behavior* 23:425–453.

Massey, Douglas S. 2007. *Categorically Unequal: The American Stratification System.* New York: Russell Sage Foundation.

Maume, David J., and Rachel A. Sebastian. 2012. "Gender, Nonstandard Work Schedules, and Marital Quality." *Journal of Family and Economic Issues* 33(4):477–490.

McCall, Leslie. 2005. "The Complexity of Intersectionality." *Signs: Journal of Women in Culture and Society* 30(3):1771–1800.

McDermott, Monica. 2006. *Working-Class White: The Making and Unmaking of Race Relations.* Berkeley: University of California Press.

McGuinness, Séamus. 2006. "Overeducation in the Labour Market." *Journal of Economic Surveys* 20(3):387–418.

McKee-Ryan, Frances M., and Jaron Harvey. 2011. "'I Have a Job But . . .': A Review of Underemployment." *Journal of Management* 37:962–996.

Meiksins, Peter, and Peter Whalley. 2002. *Putting Work in Its Place: A Quiet Revolution.* Ithaca, NY: Cornell University Press.

Mishel, Emma. 2016. "Discrimination Against Queer Women in the U.S. Workforce: A Resume Audit Study." *Socius: Sociological Research for a Dynamic World.* https://journals.sagepub .com/doi/pdf/10.1177/2378023115621316.

Mishel, Lawrence, Josh Bivens, Elise Gould, and Heidi Shierholz. 2012. *The State of Working America.* 12th ed. Ithaca, NY: ILR Press/Cornell University Press.

Mize, Trenton D., and Bianca Manago. 2018. "Precarious Sexuality: How Men and Women Are Differentially Categorized for Similar Sexual Behavior." *American Sociological Review* 83(2):305–330.

Morris, Martina, and Bruce Western. 1999. "Inequality in Earnings at the Close of the Twentieth Century." *Annual Review of Sociology* 25:623–657.

Moss, Philip I., and Chris Tilly. 2001. *Stories Employers Tell: Race, Skill, and Hiring in America.* New York: Russell Sage Foundation.

Mouw, Ted. 2003. "Social Capital and Finding a Job: Do Contacts Matter?" *American Sociological Review* 68(6):868–898.

Munsch, Christin L. 2016. "Flexible Work, Flexible Penalties: The Effect of Gender, Childcare, and Type of Request on the Flexibility Bias." *Social Forces* 94(4):1567–1591.

National Public Radio. 2016. "How Gig Economy Workers Make a Living." *Weekend Edition,* August 14.

Neumark, David, Roy J. Bank, and Kyle D. Van Nort. 1996. "Sex Discrimination in Restaurant Hiring: An Audit Study." *Quarterly Journal of Economics* 111(3):915–941.

Newman, Katherine S. 1988. *Falling from Grace: Downward Mobility in the Age of Affluence.* Berkeley: University of California Press.

Nunley, John M., Adam Pugh, Nicholas Romero, and R. Alan Seals. 2015. "Racial Discrimination in the Labor Market for Recent College Graduates: Evidence from a Field Experiment." *BE Journal of Economic Analysis & Policy* 15(3):1093–1125.

———. 2017. "The Effects of Unemployment and Underemployment on Employment Opportunities: Results from a Correspondence Audit of the Labor Market for College Graduates." *ILR Review* 70(3):642–669.

Ofstead, Cynthia M. 1999. "Temporary Help Firms as Entrepreneurial Actors." *Sociological Forum* 14(2):272–294.

Oreopoulos, Philip. 2011. "Why Do Skilled Immigrants Struggle in the Labor Market? A Field Experiment with Thirteen Thousand Resumes." *American Economic Journal: Economic Policy* 3(4):148–171.

Owens, Lindsay A., and David S. Pedulla. 2014. "Material Welfare and Changing Political Preferences: The Case of Support for Redistributive Social Policies." *Social Forces* 92(3):1087–1113.

Pager, Devah. 2003. "The Mark of a Criminal Record." *American Journal of Sociology* 108(5):937–975.

————. 2007. *Marked: Race, Crime, and Finding Work in an Era of Mass Incarceration*. Chicago: University of Chicago Press.

Pager, Devah, and Diana Karafin. 2009. "Bayesian Bigot? Statistical Discrimination, Stereotypes, and Employer Decision Making." *Annals of the American Academy of Political and Social Science* 621(1):70–93.

Pager, Devah, and David S. Pedulla. 2015. "Race, Self-Selection, and the Job Search Process." *American Journal of Sociology* 120(4):1005–1054.

Pager, Devah, and Lincoln Quillian. 2005. "Walking the Talk? What Employers Say versus What They Do." *American Sociological Review* 70(3):355–380.

Pager, Devah, and Hana Shepherd. 2008. "The Sociology of Discrimination: Racial Discrimination in Employment, Housing, Credit, and Consumer Markets." *Annual Review of Sociology* 34:181–209.

Pager, Devah, Bruce Western, and Bart Bonikowski. 2009. "Discrimination in a Low-Wage Labor Market: A Field Experiment." *American Sociological Review* 74:777–799.

Pasquale, Frank. 2016. "Two Narratives of Platform Capitalism." *Yale Law & Policy Review* 35(1):309–319.

Pedulla, David S. 2013. "The Hidden Costs of Contingency: Employers' Use of Contingent Workers and Standard Employees' Outcomes." *Social Forces* 92(2):691–722.

————. 2014a. "Non-standard, Contingent, and Precarious Work in the 'New Economy.'" Doctoral dissertation, Princeton University.

————. 2014b. "The Positive Consequences of Negative Stereotypes: Race, Sexual Orientation, and the Job Application Process." *Social Psychology Quarterly* 77(1):75–94.

————. 2016. "Penalized or Protected? Gender and Consequences of Nonstandard and Mismatched Employment Histories." *American Sociological Review* 81(2):262–289.

————. 2018. "How Race and Unemployment Shape Labor Market Opportunities: Additive, Amplified, or Muted Effects?" *Social Forces* 96(4):1477–1506.

Peffley, Mark, Jon Hurwitz, and Paul M. Sniderman. 1997. "Racial Stereotypes and Whites' Political Views of Blacks in the Context of Welfare and Crime." *American Journal of Political Science* 41(1):30–60.

Piketty, Thomas, and Emmanuel Saez. 2003. "Income Inequality in the United States, 1913–1998." *Quarterly Journal of Economics* 118(1):1–41.

Pitts, Melinda K. 1998. "Demand for Part-Time Workers in the U.S. Economy: Why Is the Distribution across Industries Uneven?" *Social Science Research* 27:87–108.

Posselt, Julie R. 2016. *Inside Graduate Admissions: Merit, Diversity, and Faculty Gatekeeping*. Cambridge, MA: Harvard University Press.

Pugh, Allison J. 2015. *The Tumbleweed Society: Working and Caring in and Age of Insecurity*. New York: Oxford University Press.

Purdie-Vaughns, Valerie, and Richard P. Eibach. "Intersectional Invisibility: The Distinctive Advantages and Disadvantages of Multiple Subordinate-Group Identities." *Sex Roles* 59:377–391.

Quadlin, Natasha. 2018. "The Mark of a Woman's Record: Gender and Academic Performance in Hiring." *American Sociological Review* 83(2):331–360.

Quesnel-Vallée, Amélie, Suzanne DeHaney, and Antonio Ciampi. 2010. "Temporary Work and Depressive Symptoms: A Propensity Score Analysis." *Social Science & Medicine* 70:1982–1987.

Quillian, Lincoln, Devah Pager, Ole Hexel, and Arnfinn H. Midtbøen. 2017. "Meta-analysis of Field Experiments Shows No Change in Racial Discrimination in Hiring over Time." *Proceedings of the National Academy of Sciences* 114(41):10870–10875.

Ransford, Edward. 1980. "The Prediction of Social Behavior and Attitudes: The Correlates Tradition." Pp. 265–303 in *Social Stratification: A Multiple Hierarchy Approach*, edited by Vincent Jeffries and H. Edward Ransford. Boston: Allyn & Bacon.

Remedios, Jessica D., Alison L. Chasteen, Nicholas O. Rule, and Jason E. Plaks. 2011. "Impressions at the Intersection of Ambiguous and Obvious Social Categories: Does Gay + Black = Likable?" *Journal of Experimental Social Psychology* 47(6):1312–1315.

Reskin, Barbara F., and Debra Branch McBrier. 2000. "Why Not Ascription? Organizations' Employment of Male and Female Managers." *American Sociological Review* 65(2):210–233.

Reskin, Barbara F., and Patricia A. Roos. 2009. *Job Queues, Gender Queues: Explaining Women's Inroads into Male Occupations.* Philadelphia: Temple University Press.

Ridgeway, Cecilia L. 2011. *Framed by Gender: How Gender Inequality Persists in the Modern World.* New York: Oxford University Press.

Ridgeway, Cecilia L., and Tamar Kricheli-Katz. 2013. "Intersecting Cultural Beliefs in Social Relations: Gender, Race, and Class Binds and Freedoms." *Gender & Society* 27(3):294–318.

Rissing, Ben A., and Emilio J. Castilla. 2014. "House of Green Cards: Statistical or Preference-Based Inequality in the Employment of Foreign Nationals." *American Sociological Review* 79(6):1226–1255.

Rivera, Lauren A. 2012. "Hiring as Cultural Matching: The Case of Elite Professional Service Firms." *American Sociological Review* 77(6):999–1022.

———. 2015. "Go with Your Guy: Emotion and Evaluation in Job Interviews." *American Journal of Sociology* 120(5):1339–1389.

———. 2016. *Pedigree: How Elite Students Get Elite Jobs.* Princeton, NJ: Princeton University Press.

Rivera, Lauren A., and András Tilcsik. 2016. "Class Advantage, Commitment Penalty: The Gendered Effect of Social Class Signals." *American Sociological Review* 81(6):1097–1131.

Rogers, Jackie Krasas. 1995. "Just a Temp: Experience and Structure of Alienation in Temporary Clerical Employment." *Work and Occupations* 22(2):137–166.

Rose, Stephen. 2017. "Mismatch: How Many Workers with a Bachelor's Degree Are Overqualified for Their Jobs?" Washington, DC: Urban Institute.

Rosenfeld, Jake, and Meredith Kleykamp. 2012. "Organized Labor and Racial Inequality in the United States." *American Journal of Sociology* 117(5):1460–1502.

Rosenthal, Lisa, Amy Carroll-Scott, Valerie A. Earnshaw, Alycia Santilli, and Jeannette R. Ickovics. 2012. "The Importance of Full-Time Work for Urban Adults' Mental and Physical Health." *Social Science & Medicine* 75:1692–1696.

Rothstein, Donna. 2016. "An Analysis of Long-Term Unemployment." *Monthly Labor Review*, July.

Rudman, Laurie A. 1998. "Self-Promotion as a Risk Factor for Women: The Costs and Benefits of Counterstereotypical Impression Management." *Journal of Personality and Social Psychology* 74(3):629–645.

Rudman, Laurie A., and Peter Glick. 1999. "Feminized Management and Backlash toward Agentic Women: The Hidden Costs to Women of a Kinder, Gentler Image of Middle Managers." *Journal of Personality and Social Psychology* 77(5):1004–1010.

Rudman, Laurie A., and Kris Mescher. 2013. "Penalizing Men Who Request a Family Leave: Is Flexibility Stigma and Femininity Stigma?" *Journal of Social Issues* 69(2):322–340.

Ruhm, Christopher J. 1991. "Are Workers Permanently Scarred by Job Displacements?" *American Economic Review* 81:319–324.

Scheiber, Noam. 2015. "Growth in the 'Gig Economy' Fuels Work Force Anxieties." *New York Times*, July 12.

Schilling, Melissa A., and H. Kevin Steensma. 2001. "The Use of Modular Organizational Forms: An Industry-Level Analysis." *Academy of Management Journal* 44(6):1149–1168.

Schlozman, Kay Kehman, and Sidney Verba. 1981. *Injury to Insult: Unemployment, Class, and Political Response.* Cambridge, MA: Harvard University Press.

Sharone, Ofer. 2013. *Flawed System/Flawed Self: Job Searching and Unemployment Experiences.* Chicago: University of Chicago Press.

———. 2017. "LinkedIn or LinkedOut? How Social Networking Sites Are Reshaping the Labor Market." *Research in the Sociology of Work* 30:1–33.

Shierholz, Heidi. 2014. "Involuntary Part-Time Work Is Falling, Voluntary Part-Time Work Is Rising." Economic Snapshot. Economic Policy Institute.

Shih, Johanna. 2002. "'. . . Yeah, I Could Hire This One, But I know It's Gonna Be a Problem': How Race, Nativity and Gender Affect Employers' Perceptions of the Manageability of Job Seekers." *Ethnic and Racial Studies* 25:99–119.

Smith, Ryan A. 2002. "Race, Gender, and Authority in the Workplace: Theory and Research." *Annual Review of Sociology* 28:509–542.

Smith, Sandra Susan. 2005. "'Don't Put My Name on It': Social Capital Activation and Job-Finding Assistance among the Black Urban Poor." *American Journal of Sociology* 111(1):1–57.

Smith, Vicki. 1997. "New Forms of Work Organization." *Annual Review of Sociology* 23:315–339.

———. 1998. "The Fractured World of the Temporary Worker: Power, Participation, and Fragmentation in the Workplace." *Social Problems* 45(4):411–430.

———. 2001. "Teamwork vs. Tempwork: Managers and the Dualism of Workplace Restructuring." Pp. 7–28 in *Working in Restructured Workplaces: New Directions for the Sociology of Work*, edited by Karen Campbell, Daniel Cornfield, and Holly McCammon. Thousand Oaks, CA: Sage.

Smith, Vicki, and Esther B. Neuwirth. 2008. *The Good Temp*. Ithaca, NY: Cornell University Press.

Snipp, C. Matthew, and Sin Yi Cheung. 2016. "Changes in Racial and Gender Inequality since 1970." *Annals of the American Academy of Political and Social Sciences* 663(1):80–98.

Society for Human Resource Management (SHRM). 2016. "Talent Acquisition: Recruitment." PowerPoint presentation.

———. 2017. "2017 Talent Acquisition Benchmarking Report." PowerPoint presentation.

Spence, Michael. 1973. "Job Market Signaling." *Quarterly Journal of Economics* 87(3):355–374.

Srivastava, Sameer B., and Eliot L. Sherman. 2015. "Agents of Change or Cogs in the Machine? Reexamining the Influence of Female Managers on the Gender Wage Gap." *American Journal of Sociology* 120(6):1778–1808.

Stainback, Kevin, and Donald Tomaskovic-Devey. 2012. *Documenting Desegregation: Racial and Gender Segregation in Private-Sector Employment since the Civil Rights Act*. New York: Russell Sage Foundation.

Stevens, Mitchell L. 2007. *Creating a Class: College Admissions and the Education of Elites*. Cambridge, MA: Harvard University Press.

Stratton, Leslie S. 1996. "Are 'Involuntary' Part-Time Workers Indeed Involuntary?" *Industrial and Labor Relations Review* 49(3):522–536.

Strazdins, Lyndall, Mark S. Clements, Rosemary J. Korda, Dorothy H. Broom, and Rennue M. D'Souza. 2006. "Unsociable Work? Nonstandard Work Schedules, Family Relationships, and Children's Well-Being." *Journal of Marriage and Family* 68:394–410.

Thébaud, Sarah. 2010. "Masculinity, Bargaining, and Breadwinning: Understanding Men's Housework in the Cultural Context of Paid Work." *Gender & Society* 24(3):330–354.

Ticona, Julia, and Alexandra Mateescu. 2018. "Trusted Strangers: Carework Platforms' Cultural Entrepreneurship in the On-Demand Economy." *New Media & Society* 20:4384–4404.

Tilcsik, András. 2011. "Pride and Prejudice: Employment Discrimination Against Openly Gay Men in the United States." *American Journal of Sociology* 117(2):586–626.

Tilly, Chris. 1992. "Dualism in Part-Time Employment." *Industrial Relations* 31(2):330–347.

———. 1996. *Half a Job: Bad and Good Part-Time Jobs in a Changing Labor Market*. Philadelphia: Temple University Press.

Tomaskovic-Devey, Donald, and Dustin Avent-Holt. 2019. *Relational Inequalities: An Organizational Approach*. New York: Oxford University Press.

Turco, Catherine J. 2010. "Cultural Foundations of Tokenism: Evidence from the Leveraged Buyout Industry." *American Sociological Review* 75(6):894–913.

Tversky, Amos, and Daniel Kahneman. 1974. "Judgement under Uncertainty: Heuristics and Biases." *Science* 185(4157):1123–1131.

US Census Bureau. 2011. "2010 Census Shows American's Diversity." www.census.gov/newsroom/releases/archives/2010_census/cb11-cn125.html.

Vaisey, Stephen. 2006. "Education and Its Discontents: Overqualification in America, 1972–2002." *Social Forces* 85(2):834–864.

Vaisey, Stephen, and Lauren Valentino. 2018. "Culture and Choice: Toward Integrating Cultural Sociology with the Judgment and Decision-Making Sciences." *Poetics* 68:131–143.

Valletta, Robert. 2018. "Involuntary Part-Time Work: Yes, It's Here to Stay." *SF Fed Blog*. www.frbsf.org/our-district/about/sf-fed-blog/involuntary-part-time-work-here-to-stay/.

Valletta, Robert G., Leila Bengali, and Catherine van der List. 2018. "Cyclical and Market Determinants of Involuntary Part-Time Employment." Federal Reserve Bank of San Francisco Working Paper 2015-19.

Vandello, Joseph A., and Jennifer K. Bosson. 2013. "Hard Won and Easily Lost: A Review and Synthesis of Theory and Research on Precarious Manhood." *Psychology of Men & Masculinity* 14(2):101–113.

Vandello, Joseph A., Jennifer K. Bosson, Dov Cohen, Rochelle M. Burnaford, and Jonathan R Weaver. 2008. "Precarious Manhood." *Journal of Personality and Social Psychology* 95(6):1325–1339.

van Rijswijk, Karen, Marrie H. J. Becker, Christel G. Rutte, and Marcel A. Croon. 2004. "The Relationships among Part-Time Work, Work-Family Interference, and Well-Being." *Journal of Occupational Health Psychology* 9(4):286–295.

Virtanen, Marianna, Mika Kivimaki, Matti Joensuu, Pekka Virtanen, Marko Elovainio, and Jussi Vahtera. 2005. "Temporary Employment and Health: A Review." *International Journal of Epidemiology* 34:610–622.

Waldfogel, Jane. 1999. "The Impact of the Family and Medical Leave Act." *Journal of Policy Analysis and Management* 18(2):281–302.

Waldinger, Roger David, and Michael Ira Lichter. 2003. *How the Other Half Works: Immigration and the Social Organization of Labor*. Berkeley: University of California Press.

Wallace, Michael, Bradley R. E. Wright, and Allen Hyde. 2014. "Religious Affiliation and Hiring Discrimination in the American South: A Field Experiment." *Social Currents* 1(2):189–207.

Wayne, Julie Holliday, and Bryanne L. Cordeiro. 2003. "Who Is a Good Organizational Citizen? Social Perception of Male and Female Employees Who Use Family Leave." *Sex Roles* 49(5/6):233–246.

Webber, Gretchen, and Christine Williams. 2008. "Part-Time Work and the Gender Division of Labor." *Qualitative Sociology* 31:15–36.

Weichselbaumer, Doris. 2003. "Sexual Orientation Discrimination in Hiring." *Labour Economics* 10:629–642.

Weick, Karl E. 1995. *Sensemaking in Organizations*. Thousand Oaks, CA: Sage.

Weil, David. 2011. "Enforcing Labour Standards in Fissured Workplaces: The US Experience." *Economic and Labour Relations Review* 22(2):33–54.

———. 2014. *The Fissured Workplace: Why Work Became So Bad for So Many and What Can Be Done to Improve It*. Cambridge, MA: Harvard University Press.

Weisshaar, Katherine. 2018. "From Opt Out to Blocked Out: The Challenges for Labor Market Reentry after Family-Related Employment Lapses." *American Sociological Review* 83(1):34–60.

Wells, Nick. 2016. "The 'Gig Economy' Is Growing—And Now We Know by How Much." *CNN*, October 13.

Western, Bruce, Deirdre Bloome, Benjamin Sosnaud, and Laura M. Tach. 2016. "Trends in Income Insecurity among U.S. Children, 1984–2010." *Demography* 53:419–447.

Western, Bruce, and Jake Rosenfeld. 2011. "Unions, Norms, and the Rise in U.S. Wage Inequality." *American Sociological Review* 76(4):513–537.

Willer, Robb, Christabel L. Rogalin, Bridget Conlon, and Michael T. Wojnowicz. 2013. "Overdoing Gender: A Test of the Masculine Overcompensation Thesis." *American Journal of Sociology* 118(4):980–1022.

Williams, Joan C. 2001. *Unbending Gender: Why Family and Work Conflict and What to Do about It.* New York: Oxford University Press.

Wilson, John Paul, Jessica D. Remedios, and Nicholas O. Rule. 2017. "Interactive Effects of Obvious and Ambiguous Social Categories on Perceptions of Leadership: When Double-Minority Status May Be Beneficial." *Personality and Social Psychology Bulletin* 43(6):888–900.

Woodyard, Chris, and Greg Toppo. 2016. "Uber, Lyft Halt Austin Service after Losing Vote." *USA Today*, May 8.

Wright, Bradley R. E., Michael Wallace, John Bailey, and Allen Hyde. 2013. "Religious Affiliation and Hiring Discrimination in New England: A Field Experiment." *Research in Social Stratification and Mobility* 34:111–126.

Wright, Erik Olin, and Rachel E. Dwyer. 2003. "The Patterns of Job Expansions in the USA: A Comparison of the 1960s and 1990s." *Socio-Economic Review* 1:289–325.

Young, Cristobal. 2012. "Losing a Job: The Nonpecuniary Cost of Unemployment in the United States." *Social Forces* 91(2):609–634.

INDEX

A NOTE ON THE TYPE

This book has been composed in Adobe Text and Gotham. Adobe Text, designed by Robert Slimbach for Adobe, bridges the gap between fifteenth- and sixteenth-century calligraphic and eighteenth-century Modern styles. Gotham, inspired by New York street signs, was designed by Tobias Frere-Jones for Hoefler & Co.